European Union

Vasileios Vlachos · Aristidis Bitzenis
Editors

European Union

Post Crisis Challenges and Prospects for Growth

palgrave
macmillan

Editors
Vasileios Vlachos
Department of International
and European Studies
University of Macedonia
Thessaloniki, Greece

Aristidis Bitzenis
Department of International
and European Studies
University of Macedonia
Thessaloniki, Greece

ISBN 978-3-030-18102-4 ISBN 978-3-030-18103-1 (eBook)
https://doi.org/10.1007/978-3-030-18103-1

This Palgrave Macmillan imprint is published by the registered company Springer Nature Switzerland AG
The registered company address is: Gewerbestrasse 11, 6330 Cham, Switzerland

To my wife for the years that she took care 24/7 our son who passed away
—Aristidis Bitzenis

To Anastasis, getting a glimpse of the past may bring hope to the future
—Vasileios Vlachos

Preface

A discussion about the economic aspects of the ongoing challenges that the European integration project currently faces led to the development of this book. A fitting prologue to these challenges would be to consider the benefits of European integration from a historical perspective (throughout its evolution). A great distance has been covered from the development of the European Communities as mean to secure long-term peace and stability in Europe in the aftermath of the Second World War and to create a favorable environment for economic growth and recovery, to the establishment of the European Union (EU) as a mean for European stability and prosperity. These benefits are secured through several binding treaties that give the EU the features of both a supranational entity, where the sovereignty of the member states is shared with EU institutions, and an intergovernmental organization based on consensus. The only objections to the course of European integration may be the decision of some EU member states to opt out of certain aspects, such as the use of a single currency. Nevertheless, historically the EU has been enlarging and integrating further as the member states' governments have aimed to increase their economic and political power through the union, and European citizens have valued the freedom to move, work, and live throughout Europe.

The unprecedented impact of the financial and economic crisis on member states' government finances, performance of their economies, and prosperity of their citizens has led to EU contraction for the first time in history. Ultimately, the European Commission worked on scenarios for the future course of European integration, where further EU deepening may be just one out of five alternatives. The leaders of 27 EU member states may have renewed their commitment to the European integration project during the 60th anniversary of the Treaties of Rome, but still the negative stance of governments toward European institutions and the support for populist, nationalist, and anti-establishment political parties are in favor of developing a multispeed EU.

The failure to reach pre-crisis levels of prosperity and economic performance across all member states and the simultaneous challenges from the refugee/migrant crisis management and security concerns from terrorist attacks have altogether shattered the belief on solidarity between member states as a founding principle of European unity and ultimately, on the ability of the union to promote prosperity. The history of European integration indicates that its future will be based much on the belief that it will be able to promote economic prosperity. Within this perspective, we have assembled reflections from various experts on issues challenging the economic prosperity of EU citizens: convergence, enlargement, employment, informal economic activity, institutional quality, and monetary policy to name but a few. Some chapters focus on the case Greece, which has been the greatest challenge faced by EU institutions in the context of the sovereign debt crisis. Bearing in mind the depression and the severe cost of economic adjustment on the Greek economy, it is reasonable to assume that a united Europe may rise to all other challenges if it overcomes successfully the Greek challenge. Finally, one of the chapters discusses the flaws of the analysis about the costs of Brexit on the UK. If the cost of exiting the EU is lesser than believed, can the sum of EU exit be positive? Although the chapter does not attempt to answer this question, it may be useful for starting a debate. The reader should note that in the time of writing this book, there were many discussions about extending the scheduled March 29 exit date for the UK to avoid a no deal Brexit.

We would like to thank all the authors for entrusting us with their work. We believe that this book will be a stimulating and thought-provoking step toward an open debate on the future course of European integration.

Thessaloniki, Greece — Vasileios Vlachos
Thessaloniki, Greece — Aristidis Bitzenis

Contents

Contributors

Karl Aiginger Policy Crossover Center: Vienna-Europe, Vienna, Austria; Vienna University of Economics, Vienna, Austria

Achilleas Anagnostopoulos University of Thessaly, Larissa, Greece

Mazzocchetti Andrea University of Genova, Genova, Italy

Themis Anthrakidis University of Macedonia, Thessaloniki, Greece

Aristidis Bitzenis Department of International and European Studies, University of Macedonia, Thessaloniki, Greece

Jordan Buchanan Ulster University Economic Policy Centre, Newtownabbey, Northern Ireland, UK

Mark Clough QC Dentons Europe, Brussels, Belgium

Ken Coutts University of Cambridge, Cambridge, UK

Lamperti Francesco Sant'Anna School of Advanced Studies, Pisa, Italy; European Institute of Economics and the Environment, Milan, Italy

Daniel Gros Centre for European Policy Studies, Brussels, Belgium

Graham Gudgin University of Cambridge, Cambridge, UK

Konstantinos J. Hazakis Democritus University of Thrace, Komotini, Greece

Adrian V. Horodnic "Grigore T. Popa" University of Medicine and Pharmacy, Iasi, Romania

Dimitris Manolopoulos Athens University of Economics and Business, Athens, Greece

John Marangos University of Macedonia, Thessaloniki, Greece; Hellenic Open University, Patras, Greece

Guerini Mattia Université Côte d'Azur – GREDEG, Valbonne, France; OFCE – SciencesPo, Paris, France;
Sant'Anna School of Advanced Studies, Pisa, Italy

Tania Pantazi Hellenic Civil Aviation Authority, Thessaloniki, Greece; Aristotle University, Thessaloniki, Greece

Pyrros Papadimitriou University of Peloponnese, Korinthos, Greece

Friedrich Schneider Johannes Kepler University, Linz, Austria

Eirini Triarchi University of Macedonia, Thessaloniki, Greece; University of Ioannina, Ioannina, Greece

Vasileios Vlachos Department of International and European Studies, University of Macedonia, Thessaloniki, Greece

Colin C. Williams University of Sheffield, Sheffield, UK

List of Figures

Convergence Is Alive and Well in Europe

Unconventional Monetary Policy in the USA and in Europe

European Union Transport Policy

Size of the Shadow Economies of 28 European Union Countries from 2003 to 2018

Political Economy, Inward Foreign Direct Investment and EU Accession of the Western Balkans

The Third Hellenic Economic Adjustment Program

How the Economics Profession Got It Wrong on Brexit

List of Tables

Political Economy, Inward Foreign Direct Investment and EU Accession of the Western Balkans

Greece as a Bridge to the Most Vibrant Region of the Next Decades

The Third Hellenic Economic Adjustment Program

The Quality of Domestic Institutions as a Driver for the Initiation of Firms' Exporting in the EU Post-crisis Period

Labour Market Duality Under the Insider-Outsider Theory, Labour Division, Rent-Seeking, and Clientelism

How the Economics Profession Got It Wrong on Brexit

Post-crisis Growth Prospects in the European Union

Vasileios Vlachos and Aristidis Bitzenis

The global crisis, which emerged as a credit crunch and subprime mortgage crisis that was triggered in 2007 and gradually developed into a financial, sovereign debt and eventually, an economic crisis without precedent in postwar economic history, has admittedly ended (see for example Buti 2017). In the aftermath, recovery in the European Union (EU) has been slower than in the USA and overall incomplete, the financial sector has weakened and the fiscal space has been limited.

The experience of jobless recovery (or sluggish recovery of employment rates) 10 years after the crisis has raised the concerns of EU citizens about the current direction of the Union on economic matters and has contributed to the rise of Euroscepticism. Of course, the lack of enthusiasm toward the European integration project is not only due to the economic impact of the crisis, but also due to several other different reasons: the management of the refugee and migrant flows, the issue of the suppressed national identities of member states, good-neighborhood issues between peripheral member states and extra-EU, and the stance toward the military conflicts in Ukraine and Syria (to name a few). These

V. Vlachos (✉) · A. Bitzenis
Department of International and European Studies,
University of Macedonia, Thessaloniki, Greece

V. Vlachos and A. Bitzenis (eds.), *European Union*,
https://doi.org/10.1007/978-3-030-18103-1_1

problems have resulted altogether to EU contraction (Brexit), caused upheaval in several member states and the rise of populist, nationalist, antiestablishment political parties, and have inevitably led to a fierce challenge of the current course of European integration.

And what may that course be 10 years after the crisis spread in Europe? According to EU officials the efforts should concentrate on deepening the Union by (Buti 2017):

- Strengthening the macroeconomic stability of the euro area (continuing reforms for further structural convergence and the formation of stabilization factions to reduce the impact of shocks).
- The introduction of EU public goods.
- Further EU involvement in (noneconomic) matters that affect the future of the Union, such as security and migration.

The accomplishment of all the above requires to bridge several different views through trust. The latter has decreased significantly ten years after the crisis, as approximately 4 in 10 EU citizens trusted the EU in March 2018 in contrast to 57% in early 2007. The issue of trust is even more complicated on a national level as it ranged in March 2018 from a minimum of 27% in Greece to a maximum of 66% in Lithuania, and was at a low of 34% in founding member states such as France (European Commission 2018, pp. 12–13).

Although noneconomic issues (immigration and terrorism) have taken the lead as the main concerns of EU citizens, the level of unemployment and health and social security have on a national level been the primary concerns in 15 member states (European Commission 2018, pp. 4–11). Both issues reflect the agony of EU citizens over the current and future state of their economic condition. This is also obvious by the concerns of EU citizens about the performance of their national economy. Although 49% of EU citizens think that the current situation of their national economy is good, the differences between member states are spectacular: from 2% in Greece (lowest), and the low of 32% in founding member states such as France to 93% in Luxembourg and the Netherlands, which is the highest in the EU (European Commission 2018, pp. 22–23).

The indicators of economic growth that shape these different perspectives and expectations among EU citizens regarding the economic situation of their country (vis-à-vis other member states) are briefly discussed in the next pages of this chapter. An overview of the recovery pace and a brief discussion about whether some member states benefit more than others from the EU economic policy response to the crisis of the late 2000s introduce the main economic challenges that the European integration project currently faces.

Has Europe Been Divided After the Crisis? Are There Winners and Losers from Integration?

The economic recession (depression for Greece) that followed the spread of the sovereign debt crisis across Europe raised concerns over the policy mix adopted to contain it. Despite the consideration that the origins of the crisis were different across member states (Bitzenis et al. 2013), there was a one-size-fits-all response/solution through structural reforms aiming to strengthen integration. Demand-side policies were not an option (either as an EU or euro area institutional initiative or due to the limited fiscal space of national governments) and national policy-makers were required to undertake structural reforms (including the liberalization of labor and product markets) to lessen the impact of asymmetric shocks (Gibson et al. 2014). Although structural reforms are unavoidable in indebted countries to improve productivity and increase competitiveness, their results become visible in the long term (Moro 2014). The lack of results in the short term has raised severe criticism of the one-size-fits-all response/solution and concerns about who actually benefits from it, and in particular about the presence of German hegemony in the euro area. For example, studies about Germany's benefit from the crisis (Dany et al. 2015) have spread the concerns about a German hegemony versus a genuine EU solution to the crisis. Currie and Teague (2017) state that German hegemony leads to a dualistic (core versus periphery and creditor versus debtor member states) and more asymmetric euro area, where the systematic deregulation of labor markets has compromised the integrity of industrial relations systems as a whole. Within this framework, the political support for further EU deepening is constantly decreasing and the European integration based on economic performance and social inclusion is shattered (Currie and Teague 2017, p. 170).

Following the preceding discussion, the aim of this introductory chapter is not to debate on Germany's hegemonic role. The aim is to pinpoint whether there has been a financial gain for Germany throughout the crisis and whether the policy mix adopted seems to support this gain. The points made here may serve as a basis that could stimulate further discussion on what has gone wrong with the European integration project.

A starting point based on facts may well be the very interesting findings of Dany et al. (2015) about Germany's gains from "flight to safety" (seek of safe investments) during the 2010–2015 period. The authors calculate that the reduced cost of finance for the German government (as a result of the German government bond yields reduction) led to savings of 100 billion euros (ranging between 93 and 126 billion euros depending on different scenarios). Under the consideration that the sovereign debt crisis concerned mainly Greece and as such Greece would only be affected from a default, and since Germany's contribution to Greek economic adjustment programs was 90 billion euros, Dany et al. (2015) claim that Germany would still benefit from the crisis even if Greece would default on all its debt.

However, one could argue that a Greek default would not only impact Greece, and as such the cost would have been much greater. In addition, there were benefits for other member states as well and not only for Germany. Firstly, the 2010–2015 European flight to safety was not exclusively the outcome of the financial tremors caused by the Greek sovereign and banking crises. Altogether 8 EU member states received financial assistance from European financial assistance mechanisms (4 being members of the euro area at the time of receiving assistance), namely Cyprus, Greece, Hungary, Ireland, Latvia, Portugal, Romania, and Spain. These member states (and possibly others as well) would require for further financial assistance if a member state defaulted. Secondly, the preference for German government bonds indicates that investors lacked confidence in other government bonds from euro area core member states (seemingly) not affected by the crisis. As such, the savings of 100 billion euros from flight to safety may well have been the outcome of a more serious and more general problem of the euro area (than the Greek sovereign debt crisis exclusively). Thirdly, the purchases of public sector bonds made by the European Central Bank (2013, 2019) either through the Securities Markets Programme or the Public Sector Purchase Programme have benefited all euro area member states. The purchase of public sector bonds issued by the governments of member states preserves their macroeconomic stability by lowering the term premium of their long-term securities and leads to an additional interest income that benefits their public budgets.

These three points indicate that Germany's financial gain cannot be determined against the cost of managing the impact of the crisis on a member state alone. In addition, the crisis has affected all member states as much as all member states have benefited from the way the crisis has been managed. In our opinion, the starting for a discussion about Germany's gain should be the outcome of the way it contributed to the EU management of the crisis. The crisis management (some key points are mentioned in the beginning of this section) is not discussed here.[1] What follows is a brief overview of its outcomes.

Tables 1, 2, and 3 indicate that not only all EU member states were affected by the crisis, but they also experienced a serious setback on key macroeconomic indicators. The tables present the GDP, gross fixed capital formation (GFCF), and employment performance of EU member states in 2017 (most recent data available from Eurostat), the pre- and post-crisis growth rates of these indicators, and whether the size of any of these indicators has been greater than its respective size in the year before its downturn (the year of full recovery in terms of performance is indicated). The tables indicate that although most EU member states have recovered the loss caused by the crisis in terms of GDP, they have not reached the pre-crisis levels of investment and employment.

Table 1 indicates that 4 member states of the euro area (Finland, Greece, Italy, and Portugal) and Croatia (member state of the EU) did not fully recover from the crisis until 2017 in terms of GDP. Table 1 also indicates that only 5 member states of the euro area (Belgium, Germany, Ireland, Luxemburg, and Malta) had greater post-crisis than pre-crisis GDP growth rates. In addition, Denmark, Hungary, and Sweden (only member states of the EU) also had greater post-crisis GDP growth rates (Poland also had a positive GDP growth rate).

Tables 2 and 3 present a much gloomier picture. Table 2 indicates that only 14 EU member states (9 of the euro area) recovered until 2017 the impact of the crisis in terms of GFCF performance. Table 2 also indicates that only Austria, Germany, Ireland, Luxembourg, Malta,

[1]The reader may refer to the European financial assistance mechanisms (European Financial Stabilisation Mechanism, European Stability Mechanism, and balance of payments assistance) and the asset purchase programmes of the European Central Bank. The reader may also refer to Bitzenis et al. (2013) and Gibson et al. (2014).

Table 1 GDP chain-linked volumes (2010=100)

GEO/Time	*2017*	*Pre-*	*Post-*	*Recovered*
Euro area	108.6	10.6	10.6	2015
Ireland	161.4	23.8	58.1	2014
Malta	147.3	14.4	50.7	2010
Lithuania	128.3	41.2	29.9	2014
Slovakia	120.8	33.8	25.6	2011
Luxembourg	119.4	19.4	19.7	2011
Germany	113.7	8.8	17.6	2011
Estonia	130.2	39.5	15.5	2016
Austria	110.4	13.6	12.2	2011
Slovenia	110.3	24.9	11.5	2017
Belgium	108.7	12.2	11.4	2010
France	108.8	9.9	10.7	2011
Netherlands	109.1	12.8	10.4	2015
Finland	105.7	17.7	8.6	–
Spain	105.5	17.8	5.5	2017
Latvia	127.0	47.3	5.4	2017
Cyprus	101.0	22.6	2.3	2017
Portugal	100.3	5.7	2.2	–
Italy	99.7	6.2	−4.3	–
Greece	82.8	20.0	−27.8	–
Poland	125.4	n.a.	n.a.	n.a.
Romania	129.8	36.8	25.7	2014
Czechia	116.2	26.1	18.4	2014
Hungary	117.3	17.6	18.0	2014
Bulgaria	116.5	32.2	17.8	2013
Sweden	116.5	15.9	17.0	2011
Denmark	111.6	9.4	13.4	2014
UK	114.9	13.2	12.2	2012
Croatia	105.6	24.4	4.1	–

Source Eurostat

Notes

1. pre- is an indicator of pre-crisis growth: GDP growth for the period 2002–2007/2008 (GDP of 4 member states declined in 2008 and of 24 in 2009)
2. post- is an indicator of post-crisis growth: GDP growth for the period 2008/2009–2017 (GDP of 4 member states declined in 2008 and of 24 in 2009)
3. Recovered is about the year that the indicator is larger in size than that of the year before the member state was hit by the crisis
4. n.a. indicates the situation where the above three conditions are not applicable. Poland's GDP has been increasing on an annual basis for the period 2002–2017
5. Member states are ordered according to their post-crisis growth (first the euro area group and then the remaining EU member states)

Table 2 GFCF chain-linked volumes (2010=100)

GEO/Time	*2017*	*Pre-*	*Post-*	*Recovered*
Euro area	108.8	17.6	−3.8	–
Ireland	209.1	52.3	67.4	2015
Malta	131.8	40.2	42.1	2016
Luxembourg	138.4	30.1	41.8	2011
Slovakia	119.6	34.2	26.4	2015
Germany	118.2	12.1	23.3	2014
Austria	120.7	12.7	18.0	2016
Belgium	118.1	23.3	17.3	2014
France	110.2	17.7	12.2	2017
Finland	107.8	22.0	8.9	–
Netherlands	119.7	24.1	2.4	2016
Estonia	160.3	90.7	−2.0	–
Cyprus	96.9	45.5	−6.0	–
Lithuania	151.9	90.0	−9.4	–
Portugal	83.8	−5.4	−17.1	–
Slovenia	94.7	50.8	−20.6	–
Italy	89.4	9.0	−22.2	–
Spain	98.9	34.4	−27.5	–
Latvia	137.6	120.4	−49.3	–
Greece	61.1	47.8	−83.0	–
Sweden	131.7	28.3	37.4	2014
Hungary	129.0	19.8	18.5	2017
Poland	117.8	44.0	17.8	2011
UK	127.0	18.4	15.8	2014
Romania	118.4	103.5	15.6	–
Czechia	109.7	30.6	11.0	–
Denmark	131.0	27.0	9.1	2016
Croatia	106.5	58.7	−11.4	–
Bulgaria	99.8	89.3	−21.7	–

Source Eurostat

Notes

1. pre- is an indicator of pre-crisis growth: GFCF growth for the period 2002–2007/2008 (GFCF of 11 member states declined in 2008 and of 17 in 2009)
2. post- is an indicator of post-crisis growth: GFCF growth for the period 2008/2009–2017 (GFCF of 11 member states declined in 2008 and of 17 in 2009)
3. Recovered is about the year that the indicator is larger in size than that of the year before the member state was hit by the crisis
4. Member states are ordered according to their post-crisis growth (first the euro area group and then the remaining EU member states)

Table 3 Employment 15–64 years old (thousand persons)

GEO/Time	*2017*	*Pre-*	*Post-*	*Recovered*
Euro area	144,484	11,012	2805	–
Cyprus	370	n.a.	n.a.	n.a.
Malta	217	n.a.	n.a.	n.a.
Germany	40,482	2137	2674	2011
France	25,940	1594	396	2017
Austria	4185	166	276	2010
Belgium	4587	367	198	2016
Slovakia	2502	269	145	2016
Italy	22,444	1221	120	–
Luxembourg	270	17	68	2009
Estonia	626	62	53	–
Slovenia	943	96	−12	–
Finland	2403	152	−20	–
Ireland	2125	362	−27	–
Netherlands	8376	426	−67	–
Lithuania	1306	43	−91	–
Portugal	4515	21	−130	–
Latvia	862	86	−147	–
Sp ain	18,649	3630	−308	–
Greece	3683	348	−786	–
UK	30,783	1239	2464	2013
Poland	16,079	2159	846	–
Hungary	4373	22	555	2014
Sweden	4834	252	443	2011
Czechia	5094	257	237	2016
Denmark	2734	123	10	–
Croatia	1603	238	−105	–
Bulgaria	3073	598	−132	–
Romania	8363	280	−442	–

Source Eurostat

Notes

1. pre- is an indicator of pre-crisis growth: Employment growth for the period 2002–2006/2007/2008/2009 (employment in Hungary decreased in 2007, in 5 member states decreased in 2008, in 20 member states decreased in 2009 and in Poland decreased in 2010). For Croatia the period starts in 2003
2. post- is an indicator of post-crisis growth: Employment growth for the period 2007/2008/2009/2010–2017 (employment in Hungary decreased in 2007, in 5 member states decreased in 2008, in 20 member states decreased in 2009 and in Poland decreased in 2010)
3. Recovered is about the year that the indicator is larger in size than that of the year before the member state was hit by the crisis
4. n.a. indicates the situation where the above three conditions are not applicable. Malta's employment rate has been increasing on an annual basis for the period 2002–2017. The decrease of employment in Cyprus occurred in 2012 and was caused by the country's financial/banking crisis
5. Member states are ordered according to their post-crisis growth (first the euro area group and then the remaining EU member states)

and Sweden had greater post-crisis than pre-crisis GFCF growth rates. Table 3 indicates that only 10 EU member states (6 of the euro area) recovered until 2017 the impact of the crisis in terms of employment performance. In addition, Austria, Germany, Hungary, Luxembourg, Sweden, and the UK had greater post-crisis than pre-crisis employment growth rates (Malta also had a positive employment growth rate, and Cyprus only from 2016 onwards).

The obvious conclusion regarding the macroeconomic performance of member states as depicted in Tables 1, 2, and 3 is that it took almost a decade for all EU member states economies to grow bigger in size than they were before the crisis. Investment shortfalls, however, have impacted on the post-crisis rate of economic growth, and the number of jobs available, and thus the economic growth achieved has led to greater inequalities of income distribution. The EU member states government finances, by contrast, have improved significantly. All OECD countries but Finland and Hungary improved their structural balances in 2016 (OECD 2017, pp. 60–61), leaving thus positive signs that they will meet their medium-term budgetary objectives. Eurostat data reveal that all EU member states respect the deficit limit of 3% of GDP (only Spain had a deficit of 3.1% of GDP in 2017). Eurostat data also reveal that only in the cases of Greece, Italy, and Portugal, the general governments' consolidated gross debt was above the limit of 120% of GDP in 2017, and that the government debt of 18 EU member states has been following a steadily declining trend.

In our opinion, it is the performance of government finances that sums up Germany's gain. The financial gain occurring from the way that the crisis has been managed does not appear to be a reason for adopting a policy mix on the EU level, which focuses on the condition of EU member state government finances (and possibly may have not been predicted beforehand). Even the impact of "quantitative easing" through the asset purchase programs of the European Central Bank is more visible on the performance of government finances than on the performance of the economies of member states. Securing the health of government finances through informal debt reliefs occurring from the asset purchase programs and/or the financial assistance through the economic adjustment programs, cost less than the introduction of Stability Bonds (European Commission 2011). In addition, except from increasing the costs, the introduction of Stability Bonds would have threatened the leading role of Germany in managing the crisis (and in the direction of EU integration project).

Therefore, are there winners and losers from integration (post-crisis)? Tables 1, 2, and 3 indicate that there are for sure. Germany (who has secured a leading role in the integration project for the reasons discussed above) is one of the winners, as much as Ireland and Malta are. Of course, a question which remains to be answered is what will the large EU economies of France, Italy, and Spain that underperform in the post-crisis era do? The expansion of informal debt relief has ended with the conclusion of the asset purchase programs of the European Central Bank (although it will be sustained for as long as the Bank reinvests principal payments from maturing securities). Will EU economies adapt to the required fiscal discipline and structural reforms on a national level to sustain their macroeconomic stability? The difficulty to answer to these questions gives rise to notions that "the only common ground that appears to tie the core and periphery together is the idea that unraveling the eurozone would be an even greater calamity than its continuation" (Currie and Teague 2017, p. 170).

Purpose and Content of This Book

A decade after the deep economic crisis, the efforts to stabilize the European economy continue as much as the attempts for further economic and political integration. Although the united Europe endured the crisis, there are several issues which question the current course and outcomes of the European integration project. The most important at the time of writing these words are those of Brexit, the negative stance of the Italian government toward European institutions, the rise of far right/left political movements (populist, nationalist, antiestablishment political parties) and (social discomfort and) civil unrest as a reaction to economic policies/reforms, and the management of the migration/ refugee crisis.

The European Commission (2017) has also expressed its concern by issuing a white paper on the future of Europe. As "insecurity… given rise to a growing disaffection with mainstream politics and institutions at all levels," the "support for the European project… is no longer unconditional" (European Commission 2017, p. 12). Under the assumption that the 27 member states will move forward together as a union, the European Commission (2017) makes five scenarios for how this union will evolve. Maybe in the future, the key to understanding the debacle of

European integration will lie in the fact that further integration of EU27 has been considered as one of several options.

The purpose of this book is not to provide scenarios about the future of Europe. The discussion begins on the fact that the economic growth and prosperity calamity caused by the crisis (according to Tables 1, 2, and 3) is the major economic challenge that the EU faces. The book brings together contributions from leading and distinguished scholars and experts on the most relevant and pressing economic aspects of the issues that will shape the future of the union: economic convergence, monetary policy, anti-competitive behavior, transport policy, institutional quality, shadow economy, self-employment, labor market duality, EU accession, Brexit, and the success of exits from bailouts (with a focus on Greece). The content can be divided into two parts with Chapters 2 to 7 focusing on the union as a whole, and Chapters 8 to 13 focusing on regions or member states. In the first part, (i) the issue of catching-up, (ii) the role of quantitative easing, (iii) the classification of concerted practices, (iv) transport in the EU (both iii and iv are critical to the functioning of the internal market), and aspects of the informal economy in terms of (v) size and (vi) employment (both very important to meeting 2020 targets for inclusive growth) are discussed. In the second part, (i) EU enlargement in the prospect of Western Balkan accession countries and (ii) a revision of the economic impact of Brexit on the UK are two of the issues discussed. Other issues are the effects of (iii) labor market deregulation, (iv) institutional quality and (v) economic adjustment on economic recovery and performance, and (vi) the requirement for developing a strategic vision which is shared and supported by EU institutions. These issues are discussed in the case of Greece, whose economy has suffered the most by the crisis. If Greece will manage to overcome successfully the challenge of recovering its economy within the EU terms, then the EU will rise to all other challenges.

In the chapter following this brief introduction, Daniel Gros discusses economic convergence in the EU. Gross indicates that convergence in the EU is happening as newer member states are catching up. The author also observes a North–South divergence within the euro area since the start of the crisis, which has roots in causes other than the single currency. Although the distance between newer member states and the EU15 in terms of achieving the Europe 2020 indicators is narrowing, it is still considerable. Further catching-up would require from newer member states to succeed in reorienting their growth models toward more domestic innovation.

Mattia Guerini, Francesco Lamperti, and Andrea Mazzocchetti discuss how the central banks have reacted to the crisis through unconventional monetary policy measures and in particular, the phenomena and the objectives that have characterized the balance sheet policies in the USA and the euro area. The authors' interpretation of the available empirical evidence is that quantitative easing lowered long-term yields and eased the credit conditions, and had only mild effects on growth, inflation, and unemployment. However, these balance sheet policies may also have negative consequences through portfolio reallocations toward riskier stocks and the decrease of central bank's independence.

Mark Clough looks into competition issues of the EU regarding concerted practices, which are a form of collusion between firms. The author indicates the principles applicable to establishing when an information exchange between competitors constitutes an object restriction of competition under Article 101 TFEU, and where the information exchange takes the form of a concerted practice. The main cause of uncertainty is the complexity of the concepts involved in establishing the conditions for the application of Article 101 TFEU to an object infringement consisting of the exchange of commercially sensitive information in the form of a concerted practice. New guidelines should be adopted by the European Commission to restore legal certainty, and to reconcile the apparent conflict between recent case law and past guidelines.

Tania Pantazi and Vasileios Vlachos focus on European transport, which is a key sector of the EU economy and indispensable for the functioning of the internal market. The current major challenges for European transport can be briefly summed into the costs of congestion, the reduction of oil dependency and greenhouse gas emissions, infrastructure quality, and internal and external competition. The authors discuss how the global financial and economic crisis of the late 2000s has affected the economic activity of European transport, how the European legal order has responded to the new challenges, and the orientations and developments of EU transport policy.

Friedrich Schneider estimates the size of the shadow (unofficial) economies in the EU. The successful transfer of unregistered economic activities to the official economy is part of Europe 2020 strategy which stresses the need to move from informal or undeclared work to regular employment. The author finds that the average size of the shadow economy of the EU28 member states decreased from 22.6% (of GDP) in 2003 to 16.8% in 2018. The development of the shadow economy has not been uniform across the EU28 throughout this period. The author estimates that in 5 member states the shadow economy will increase, and that it will continue to decrease in the rest of the EU.

Colin Williams and Adrian Horodnic evaluate the prevalence and the working conditions of dependent self-employment in the EU and put under the spotlight the dominant depiction of dependent self-employment as a precarious form of work, that is conducted by marginalized groups of workers with poorer working conditions than the rest of the employed population. Dependent self-employment also has negative implications for governments, such as the loss of tax revenue, and for the economy from firms that disguise their employees under the status of self-employed to decrease their labor costs. The authors analyze the European Working Conditions Survey and afford insights into the working conditions of dependent self-employment and how it can be tackled.

John Marangos, Eirini Triarchi, and Themis Anthrakidis explore the impact of inward foreign direct investment to the EU accession of the Western Balkans, the major obstacles encountered by EU candidate countries in the region, and the vital reforms that must be implemented to complete their political and economic transformation for becoming EU members. The six transition economies of the Western Balkans on hold for the 2025 EU membership face economic, political, and social challenges that inhibit the achievement of the EU's admission criteria. Major improvements in political institutions and creating an environment conducive to FDI will help to meet the 2025 target and catch up with Eastern EU member states.

Karl Aiginger discusses how Greece could use its unique geographical position to become the bridge between Europe and Asia. The author argues that Greece will recover if a united Europe performs better. The EU institutions should strive to make Europe the region with the highest and fastest growing standards of living, with lower inequality and more ambitious environmental standards than any other region in the world. At the same time, a strategic vision is needed for a dynamic Greece in the globalizing world with new power structures and future technologies that would facilitate the country to take advantage of its unique geographical position and to grasp the chances to lead in its vibrant neighborhood.

Konstantinos Hazakis assesses the outcome of the third economic adjustment program for Greece. Fiscal consolidation through Greece's economic adjustment led to primary surpluses, viable government finances, and macroeconomic stabilization in nominal terms to the detriment of growth drivers and social welfare involving asymmetrical social and welfare cost. The terms of the economic adjustment program in Greece do not favor structural and real convergence to euro area average but mainly target nominal convergence with Eurozone economies. Excessive direct and indirect taxation, internal devaluation of incomes, institutional inertia on critical growth issues, and public expenditure contraction have undermined real economic adjustment.

Dimitris Manolopoulos investigates the role of institutional quality on firms' exporting performance. Exports are a viable strategic response to economic downturns, since drops in domestic demand drive firms to focus on foreign sales. Exports also make firms more competitive and as such they accelerate the pace of recovery of countries experiencing an economic downturn, by having a positive impact on economic growth and employment. The author frames the study of the relationship between domestic institutional quality and firms' decision to export in Greece. The author deploys perceptual, multi-item measures of three governance constructs that may challenge institutional isomorphism, and indicates that home institutional weaknesses make firms reluctant to initiate internationalization activity.

Achilleas Anagnostopoulos and Pyrros Papadimitriou explore labor market duality under the insider-outsider theory in Greece. The authors indicate how the institutions of the Greek labor market are linked with the context of insider-outsider theory, where workers with permanent contracts and high job security use their insider market power and political influence to underbid the outsiders. The authors discuss the impact of reforms during the crisis on the duality of the Greek labor market, and how the deregulation plan of the Greek labor market may provide an exit from the crisis, by reducing the size of precarious employment and creating more full-time jobs.

Ken Coutts, Graham Gudgin, and Jordan Buchanan review economists' assessments of the economic performance of the UK within the EU, and the short-term and long-term economic effects of the referendum decision to leave the EU. The authors conclude their revision by indicating that much of this work contains flaws of analysis, and a treatment of evidence that leads to exaggerated costs of Brexit. The consequences of these shortcomings may go well beyond Brexit itself, and with the flaws that they identify, the authors aim to increase skepticism about the pessimism on Brexit, and the direction that most academics and economists tend to lean ideologically.

References

Bitzenis, A., Papadopoulos, I., & Vlachos, V. A. (2013). The Euro-Area Sovereign Debt Crisis and the Neglected Factor of the Shadow Economy. In A. Bitzenis, I. Papadopoulos, & V. A. Vlachos (Eds.), *Reflections on the Greek Sovereign Debt Crisis*. Newcastle upon Tyne: Cambridge Scholars Publishing.

Buti, M. (2017, October 10). *Europe 10 Years After the Crisis: Out of the Tunnel?* Public event organized by the European Institute at Columbia University. Available at https://ec.europa.eu/info/sites/info/files/2017.10.10_columbia_the_response_to_the_crisis_marco_buti.pdf. Accessed December 18, 2018.

Currie, D., & Teague, P. (2017). The Eurozone Crisis, German Hegemony and Labour Market Reform in the GIPS Countries. *Industrial Relations Journal, 48*(2), 154–173.

Dany, G., Gropp, R. E., Littke, H., & von Schweinitz, G. (2015). *Germany's Benefit from the Greek Crisis* (IWH Online 7/2015). Halle (Saale): Leibniz-Institut für Wirtschaftsforschung Halle (IWH). Available at https://www.iwh-halle.de/fileadmin/user_upload/publications/iwh_online/io_2015-07.pdf. Accessed December 18, 2018.

European Central Bank. (2013). *Details on Securities Holdings Acquired Under the Securities Markets Programme*. Available at https://www.ecb.europa.eu/press/pr/date/2013/html/pr130221_1.en.html. Accessed January 9, 2019.

European Central Bank. (2019). *Breakdown of Debt Securities Under the PSPP*. Available at https://www.ecb.europa.eu/mopo/implement/omt/html/index.en.html. Accessed January 9, 2019.

European Commission. (2011). *European Commission Green Paper on the Feasibility of Introducing Stability Bonds* (MEMO/11/820). Available at http://europa.eu/rapid/press-release_MEMO-11-820_en.htm. Accessed January 20, 2019.

European Commission. (2017). *White Paper on the Future of Europe: Reflections and Scenarios for the EU27 by 2025*. Brussels: European Commission.

European Commission, Directorate-General for Communication. (2018). *Standard Eurobarometer 89 (Spring 2018): Public Opinion in the European Union, First Results*. Brussels: European Commission.

Eurostat. (n.d.). *Eurostat Database*. Available at https://ec.europa.eu/eurostat/data/database. Accessed December 18, 2018.

Gibson, H. D., Palivos, T., & Tavlas, G. S. (2014). The Crisis in the: An Analytic Overview. *Journal of Macroeconomics, 39*(Part B), 233–239.

Moro, B. (2014). Lessons from the European Economic and Financial Great Crisis: A Survey. *European Journal of Political Economy, 34*(Supplement), S9–S24.

OECD. (2017). *Government at a Glance 2017*. Paris: OECD.

Convergence Is Alive and Well in Europe

Inside and Outside the Euro Area

Daniel Gros

Introduction and Motivation

One of the key promises made by the European Union to its member states was, and remains, shared prosperity. The combination of the internal market (for goods, services, people and capital) with EU cohesion policies was supposed to drive convergence by allowing the poorer member states to grow faster and catch up with the richer ones. Similarly, it was thought that the common currency would accelerate the process through lower interest rates for the peripheral countries and through capital flows towards lower-income member states exhibiting lower capital-to-output ratios.

These expectations, however, have been met only partially or temporarily. Among the original 12 member states of the euro area (EA12),[1]

[1] Joining the eurozone in 1999 (with the exception of Greece, which joined two years later), the original EA12 were Austria, Belgium, Finland, France, Germany, Greece, Ireland, Italy, Luxembourg, the Netherlands, Portugal and Spain. For the purposes of this

D. Gros (✉)
Centre for European Policy Studies, Brussels, Belgium
e-mail: danielg@ceps.eu

V. Vlachos and A. Bitzenis (eds.), *European Union*,
https://doi.org/10.1007/978-3-030-18103-1_2

the poorest are the ones that are struggling with the aftermath of a devastating financial crisis. The distance between the richest and the poorest EA12 member states is higher today than when the euro was introduced, even taking into account the high-growth period before the crisis.

By contrast, the new member states (NMSs) (both euro area 'ins' and 'outs') from Central and Eastern Europe seem to have performed better.[2] Almost all of them have diminished the distance to the EU average, if one averages out the boom-bust episodes by considering the change in their position today relative to the beginning of the century. Moreover, even the countries hit the hardest by the financial crisis have resumed catch-up growth after very deep, relatively short recessions, indicating greater resilience.

These developments raise some key questions. First, does the euro hinder convergence? The link between euro area membership and convergence has been extensively analysed. The most recent contributions are major studies from the ECB (Diaz del Hoyo et al. 2017) and the IMF (Franks et al. 2018), which also emphasise the distinction between nominal and real convergence. The European Commission publishes a regular quarterly report on the euro area, the latest version of which analyses convergence in considerable detail (European Commission 2018a, b).

The key argument why euro area membership might endanger convergence is that this could induce excessive capital inflows, which lead to boom-bust cycles and a misallocation of resources. The experience of some of the Southern European economies illustrates the pattern as illustrated by both the ECB and the IMF studies. The key argument why euro area membership might foster convergence is that it should facilitate capital mobility and market integration.

Here, the experience of the NMSs is instructive. Those that have joined the euro (the Baltics, Slovenia and Slovakia) are continuing to catch up, suggesting that it is not euro area membership per se does present an obstacle to catching up. On the contrary, there is some

paper, however, the designated EA12 excludes Ireland and Luxembourg, owing to their very large offshore financial centres, which distort their GDP numbers.

[2] For the same reason that Ireland and Luxembourg are excluded from the discussions in this paper concerning the original EA12, so too are Malta and Cyprus excluded in aggregates of the NMSs.

evidence that these countries are catching up somewhat more quickly than the others. We show below that these countries are no different from the other NMSs in terms of investment rates, education and other indicators. The only evidence we could find for the idea that euro area membership leads to more instability is that the growth rates of the euro area members among the NMSs are somewhat more variable. However, given that their average growth rates are also higher, it turns out that the variability relative to the average growth rate is about the same for all NMSs, across both groups: euro and non-euro area members.

The available growth projections suggest that the asymmetry from the past is likely to persist, albeit in a more moderate form: convergence seems set to remain stronger East–West than North–South. This study offers a more in-depth investigation of this phenomenon by analysing the role of such factors as education, foreign direct investment (FDI), the size of manufacturing and the initial level of income.

Background: Major Trends in Convergence

The trends in real convergence in the EU have been investigated by the EU institutions and a large number of academic studies.[3] If there is one general conclusion, it is that convergence has been spotty and at times has gone into reverse. Given that the last ten years have been marked by the euro crisis, we start by providing some longer-term background using the standard key indicators of convergence.

Figure 1 gives the longer-term view by showing the dispersion of income per capita at purchasing power standards (PPS) across the EU15 and the original euro area 12 countries since the 1960s. This figure shows a statistical measure called the 'coefficient of variation'[4] of GDP per capita measured in PPS. A lower value means a lower degree of dispersion.

It is apparent that there was a long-term trend in convergence in Europe until about the turn of the century. Convergence among this group of countries stopped during the first years of the common currency, and the financial crisis then brought divergence, i.e. a sharp

[3] See for instance Goecke and Hüther (2016), ECB (2015), EEAG (2018), and Merler (2016).

[4] This is defined as the standard deviation divided by the average.

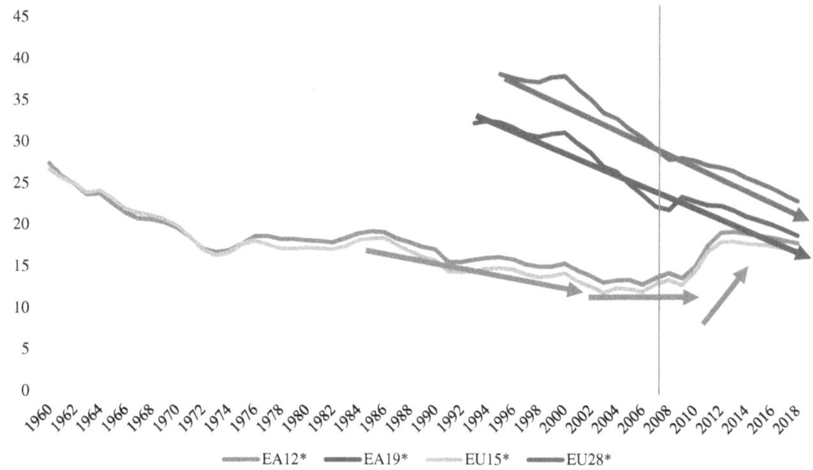

Fig. 1 Coefficient of variation of GDP per capita at PPA (*Note* All averages exclude Cyprus, Ireland, Luxembourg and Malta. *Source* Author's own elaboration based on AMECO data)

increase in the dispersion, but convergence seems to have resumed more recently, albeit at rather slow pace.

The two lines, for the EA12 and the EU15 (=old member states), move very closely together. This is not surprising since there is a great degree of overlap between the two groups. The main difference is that the UK, Sweden and Denmark are part of the EU15, but are not part of the EA12. The fact that the difference between these two figures remains roughly constant over a long period of time (and since before the start of the euro) suggests that the interruption of the convergence process around the turn of the century may have had little to do with the introduction of the euro.

However, if one considers the wider group of euro area member states, the EA19 (which comprises 5 new member states from CEE), convergence seems to have been little affected by the financial crisis, as the catching-up process of the NMSs from Central and Eastern Europe has continued after a short interruption. Moreover, the trend of declining variability among the EU28 seems to run parallel to that of the EU19, again suggesting that the euro cannot be held responsible for a lack of convergence.

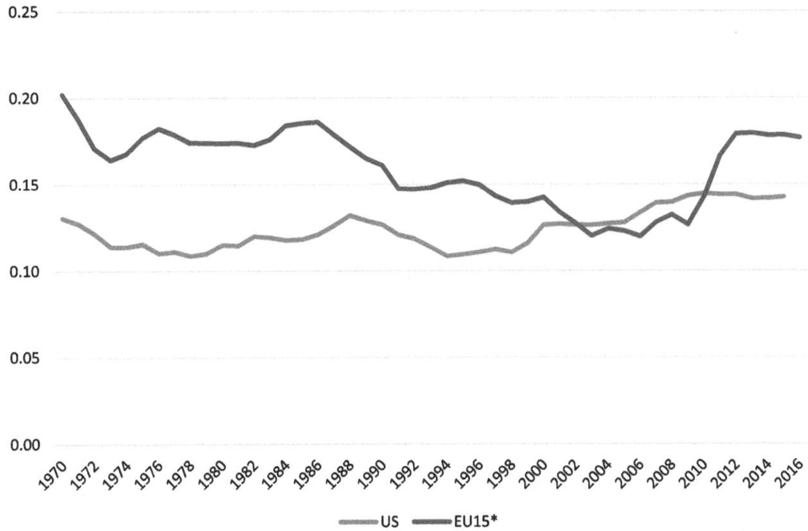

Fig. 2 Comparison of income per capita convergence/divergence on both sides of the Atlantic, 1970–2016 (*Notes* EU15 excludes Ireland and Luxembourg. US data are based on a FRED sample of 24 selected US states. The variables pictured are the [unweighted] standard deviations of the income per capita, across states relative to the average of the EU for both samples. If one were to weigh each country/state by its GDP, the picture would not change for the USA, but the EU would show a markedly stronger increase in variability [mainly because of Italy]. *Data sources* AMECO [Annual Macro-economic database of the European Commission] and FRED [Federal Reserve Economic Database])

Longer-Term Trends in Convergence: An EU–US Comparison

Since the USA always represents an interesting benchmark, we compare Europe to the USA. Figure 2 shows the variability of income per capita across US states and the variability across the 15 'old' member states, which can be considered mature market economies over the entire period.

If there were an ongoing convergence process, one would expect the cross-state variability to fall over time in the USA. But the line for the USA is relatively flat, which suggests that convergence has not progressed much there in recent decades. Today's value of the indicator (coefficient of variation) is somewhat higher than in either the 1970s or the early 1990s, but convergence seems to have stopped, and even reversed, since the turn of this century.

As shown in Fig. 2, for most of this period, the USA exhibited a lower degree of cross-state income variability than Europe. Europe started out in the 1970s with much larger differences in income per capita, but the convergence process brought the EU15 for a few years (2002–2006) to the point where income dispersion was even lower than in the USA. Much of this convergence, however, was then undone in the EU by the financial crisis (which did not have as severe an impact in the USA).

The comparison with the USA shows that convergence has its limits even in a monetary union that is generally regarded as functioning well. Some cross-state differences in income seem physiological in any large and diverse economic area. If one were to take the USA as the model for the EU or for the euro area, one should only expect some degree of further narrowing in income differentials. Expectations of full convergence might be too ambitious. A recent IMF study (Franks et al. 2018) concurs with this point of view.

Moreover, the US experience from earlier last century holds another lesson. Figure 3 provides a very long-term perspective by showing the degree of dispersion of personal income across US states since 1929. At that time, the dispersion indicator was more than two times higher than it is today, and much higher than it is in Europe today.[5] It is difficult to explain why, in 1929, roughly 150 years after the formation of the USA, there should have been such a large degree of dispersion of income in an otherwise unified area. Labour mobility had been high in the USA for a long time and the country has had a single currency at least since the end of the civil war, i.e. 60 years earlier.

The one element that was still missing for the USA in 1929 was the Banking Union. Key federal institutions, like the FDIC (Federal Deposit Insurance Corporation, which is responsible for both bank restructuring and deposit insurance) and the system of Federal agencies to insure mortgage securitisation, were created only in the wake of the devastating banking and financial crisis of 1933. One explanation for the strong decline in the dispersion of income per capita across US states, after 1933, might thus have been the financial stability achieved through the

[5] See also a FRED blog on this issue (https://fredblog.stlouisfed.org/2016/11/the-convergence-of-income-across-u-s-states/).

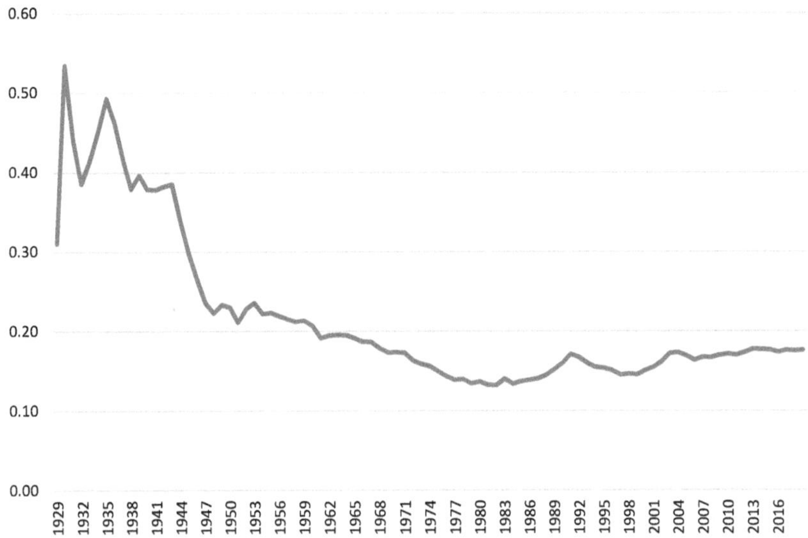

Fig. 3 Income per capita convergence in the USA (*Note* The graph excludes Alaska, Hawaii and Washington, DC. *Data source* BEA regional statistics, US Department of Commerce)

completion of the US Banking Union.[6] This would support the idea that the proposals regarding the deepening of the EMU are key not only to ensure financial stability, but would foster also convergence. See the Commission's proposal on the completion of the Banking Union, Capital Markets Union and the European Stability Mechanism.

Figure 1 showed the strong reduction in dispersion across the EU28, which now, as shown in Fig. 2, is similar to the degree of convergence achieved in the USA. These figures employ the concept of the coefficient of variation, which shows that on average the differences across member countries are around 20%. Another measure would be that of the ratio of the richest to the poorest member state (or state in the USA). For the EU, this ratio has fallen by almost one-half since 1998, when the richest member state had a GDP per capita about five times higher than

[6]The completion of the US Banking Union was of course not the only factor in the rapid decline of the income disparities. The war effort, which led to a shift in industrial production from the coast towards the heartland, also contributed.

the poorest one, to a ratio of about 2.6 in 2017. In the USA, by comparison, this ratio has hovered around 2 for the last few decades. But in the 1930s, one also finds that income per capita in the richest US state was over five times higher than that of the poorest. In this sense, one could argue that the EU has fostered a similar degree of convergence over the last two decades as that achieved in the USA during the 40 years of growth following the Great Depression.

Upwards Convergence for the Initially Poorer?

The indicators are shown so far only measure the degree of dispersion of income per capita within a group of economies. This variability could also fall if the share of the population that is better off stagnates. This is of course less desirable than 'upwards convergence', under which the better off grow, but the poorer economies also grow more strongly. This can be measured better by the concept of 'beta convergence', which puts the initial income per capita in relation to subsequent growth.

Figure 4 illustrates the pattern of this 'beta convergence' by comparing growth rates in the EU15 and the NMSs since 1999 to the initial GDP per capita of the country concerned. The horizontal axis of this figure shows the GDP per capita at PPS as a percentage of the (then) EU average. The vertical axis shows the difference between the average growth rate of the country concerned between 1999 and 2016 and the average growth rate of the EU.[7]

Convergence requires a negative relationship between initial income and subsequent growth. There is some tendency in that direction: the poorest MSs clearly grew faster (an average growth rate of 6% resulting in a cumulative increase in real income per capita in some cases of more than 200% between 1999 and 2016), versus only about 2% for the richer MSs (resulting in an increase of only 50% over these years).

But it is also apparent that there are two groups: the old EU15 and the new member states from Central and Eastern Europe (NMS11). One sees strong convergence among the latter. The (initially) poorer countries grew faster than the others. Among the group of EU15 (in the blue circles), however, one finds the opposite: there seems to be a (rather weak) positive relationship between the initial level of GDP

[7]Technically the average growth rate is measured at a continuously compounded rate.

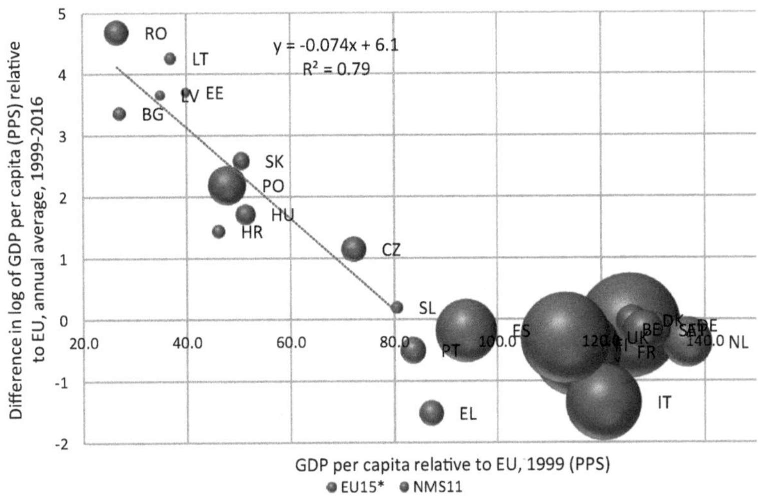

Fig. 4 GDP growth per capita relative to GDP per capita in the NMS11 and the EU15, 1999 (*Notes* EU15 excludes Ireland and Luxembourg. NMS11: Bulgaria, Croatia, Czech Republic, Estonia, Hungary, Latvia, Lithuania, Poland, Romania, Slovak Republic and Slovenia. The statistical relationship between the initial income level and subsequent growth [both relative to the EU average] intersects the horizontal line at 80%. This suggests that catch-up growth might stop at this level for the NMS11, i.e. well before they reach the EU average. *Source* Own elaboration based on AMECO data)

per capita and growth between 1999 and 2016. This indicates that there has been divergence as the lower-income countries (Greece and Portugal) grew less than the richer ones (e.g. Germany). Italy, an initially high-income country, recorded the worst growth performance (along with Greece), hence suggesting a substantial divergence from the member states in the North. In these two cases, the euro crisis clearly played a role, but for other countries, which were also affected by the crisis, there is no evidence of underperformance (Portugal, Spain and Ireland, the latter of which however is 'off the charts'). Moreover, there is also no clear link between the starting income and growth for countries not in the euro area. This is another indication that the euro cannot have been the main reason for the lack of convergence among the EU15.

The Outlook for Convergence?

The past is not always a reliable guide for the future, especially if one considers the last ten years, which were dominated by exceptional circumstances. One should thus ask what the outlook is for (renewed) convergence, now that the financial crisis has ended. For this purpose, we use the growth forecasts of the IMF, which go until 2022. The IMF seems to be the only institution to provide such medium-run forecasts on a comparable basis.

Figure 5 (right panel) shows that some further convergence can be expected as the IMF predictions imply that the poorer member states will on average grow more than the richer ones. At first glance, the convergence speed between the member states is still high, but some dynamics have shifted. The new member states no longer experience convergence within the group as they did over the past 15 years (see Fig. 4)—exemplified by the substantial growth gap between Latvia and Slovenia despite a similar level of GDP per capita in 2017. At the same time, the old member states show tentative signs of (re)-convergence with the southern peripheral countries, which are generating higher growth than their Northern peers (with the notable exception of Italy). This catch-up process is largely a rebounding of the contraction suffered

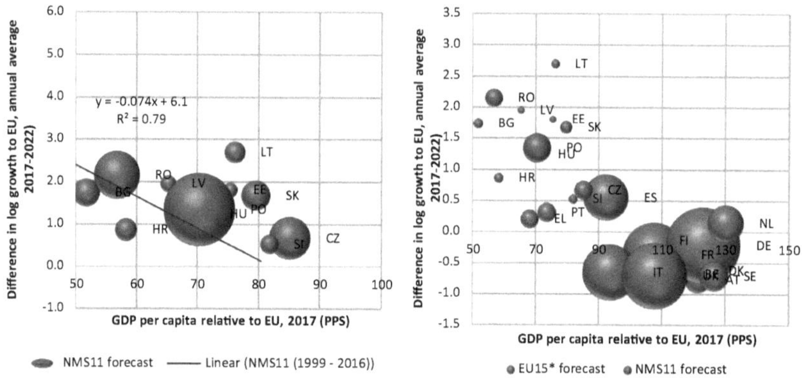

Fig. 5 GDP per capita (PPS) growth forecast (*Note* EU15 excluding Ireland and Luxembourg. *Source* Own calculations based on data from Eurostat and AMECO)

by these economies during the crisis years. Nevertheless, overall convergence within the EU15 remains weak.

Looking at the entire EU, convergence is still pronounced and significant, with the continued pattern of new member states catching up to the old ones. In 2017, however, half of the new member states overtook the poorest two 'old' euro area members, Portugal and Greece, in terms of GDP per capita (PPS). Nevertheless, these NMSs continue to show stronger growth than these two countries. Spain is the notable exception among the EU15, which is forecasted to grow at the same pace as the slowest-growing new member state Slovenia.

Figure 5 (left panel) shows more in detail the orange bubbles appearing in the right panel, referring to the NMS11, and compares them to the beta-convergence regression line based on the observations from the past period, 1999–2016, for the same group of countries. Most new points (referring to the growth between 2017 and 2022) are to the right of this line. This implies that most of the NMS11 will actually grow somewhat faster than one would expect given the past relationship between starting GDP per capita and a country's growth rate. Moreover, the intercept of the old convergence line crossed at 82% of the EU average. The data from the past thus suggest that once a member state of this group reaches the threshold of 82% of the EU average, its growth rate will no longer exceed the EU average and convergence would come to a halt. The good news, however, is that, according to the forecasts, the NMS11 will do better.[8] The ratio of the income per capita (at PPS) of the richest to the poorest MS is forecast to fall further, from the current 2.6 to 2.3 (by 2022), which is very similar to the value for the USA mentioned above.

Convergence Beyond Income

Output Convergence

Income per capita is not the only indicator of convergence. Consumption (per capita), productivity, employment and real wages constitute other important measures of good economic performance.

[8]Technically speaking, the growth forecasts imply full convergence since the intercept for the regression line for all EU member states (see Fig. 5 right panel) has shifted to around 100%, implying that the convergence process should continue beyond the previous implied threshold until the EU average is reached.

We perform a convergence test for all four of these output indicators below and find very similar patterns, which fit with the general results found for income per capita:

1. Looking at all EU member states, a catching-up process is clearly visible.
2. This convergence, however, rests solely on the NMS11.
3. The euro area members among the NMS11 tend to do slightly better than expected.
4. Most of the old member states show little growth with no clear tendency for the poorer ones to catch up.
5. The convergence process among the NMS11 has not yet allowed them to reach the EU average.

The convergence process has thus been strong for the NMS11 not only in terms of GDP per capita or productivity, but also in concrete terms of jobs, consumption and wages. This is not surprising since, in the long run, GDP, productivity, jobs and wages all tend to evolve together.

Input Convergence

Convergence should not be measured only in terms of the results or output of the economy, but also in terms of the inputs. Two key indicators used to measure a country's progress in creating the foundations for economic growth are performance of the educational system and investment in R&D.

There has been much discussion about the importance of the manufacturing sector for growth (see Fig. 6), although there is little evidence of a direct link. In the NMS11, manufacturing is a larger part of the economy and employment than in the old member states. But within these groups, there is little evidence that those countries with more important manufacturing sectors also have stronger growth.

Moreover, there is no convergence trend in terms of the share of manufacturing in employment. This is largely due to the continued dominance of manufacturing in Germany and Austria in the case of the old member states, and the services-sector orientation of Hungary and Slovenia in the case of the new member states. Thus, there remain large differences in the importance of manufacturing across MSs, but they are not systematically related to economic performance.

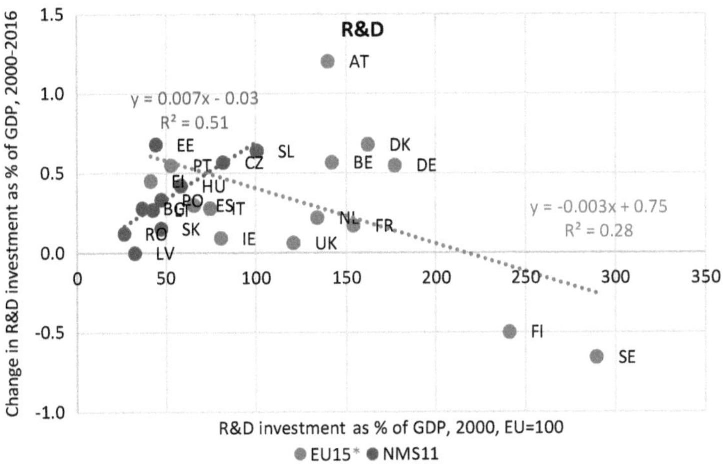

Source Own elaboration based on Eurostat data (t2020_hr)

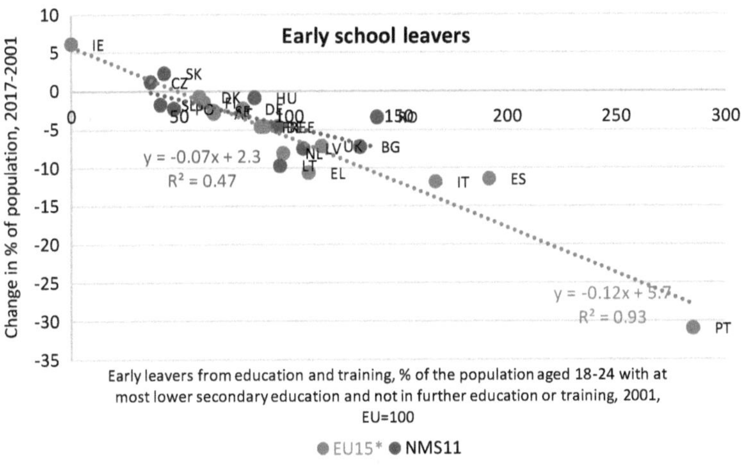

Source Own elaboration based on Eurostat data (t2020_40)

Fig. 6 Input convergence—different indicators

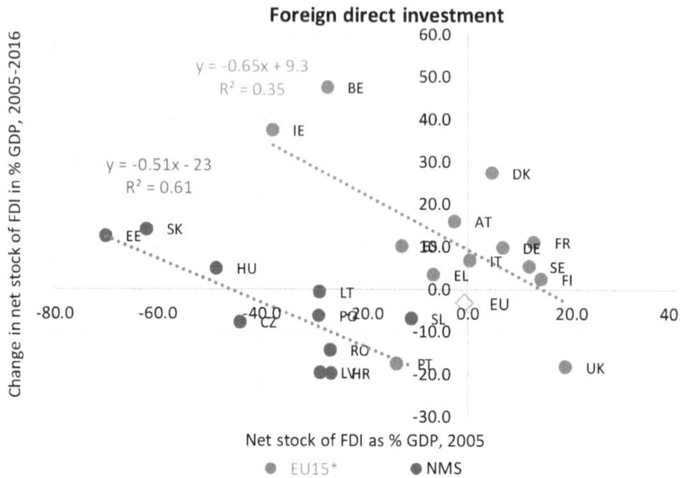

Source Own elaboration based on Eurostat data (bop_iip6_q)

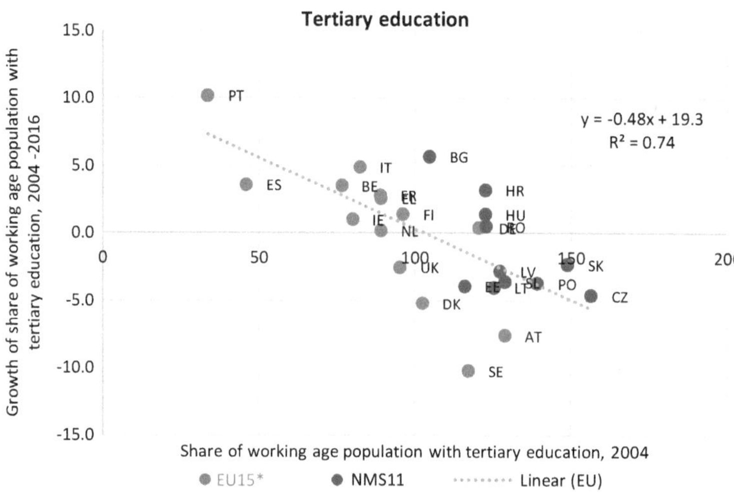

Source Own elaboration based on Eurostat (edat_lfs_9903)

Fig. 6 (continued)

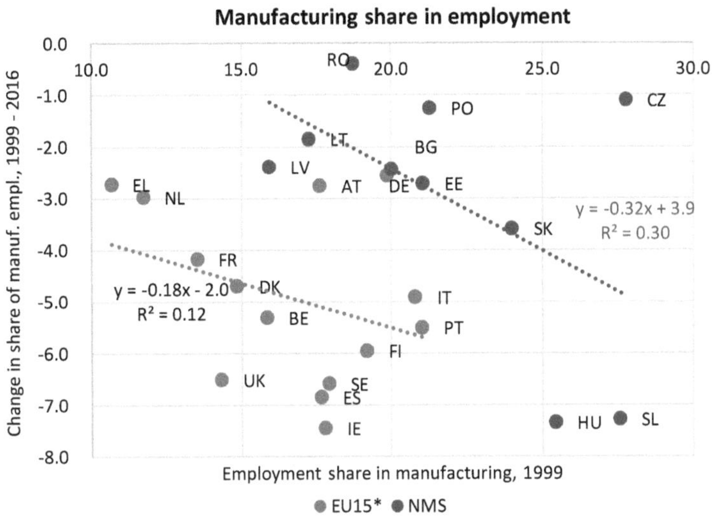

Source Own elaboration based on AMECO data (NETM)

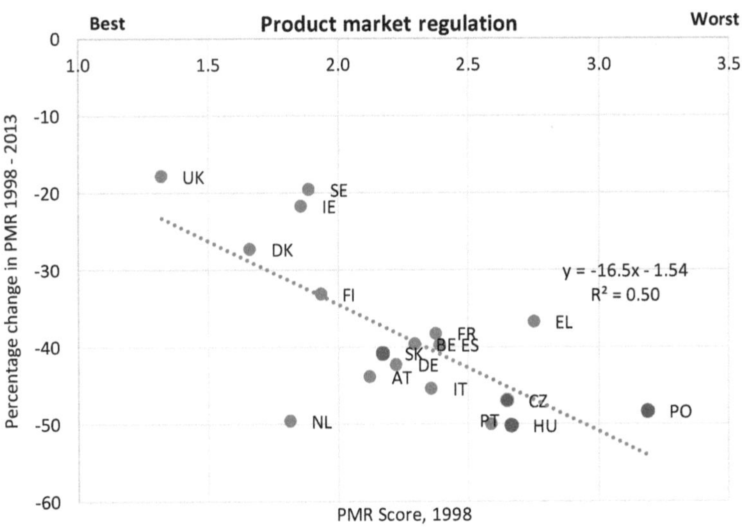

Note A reduction in the PMR signifies futher flexibilisation
Source Own elaboration based on OECD data

Fig. 6 (continued)

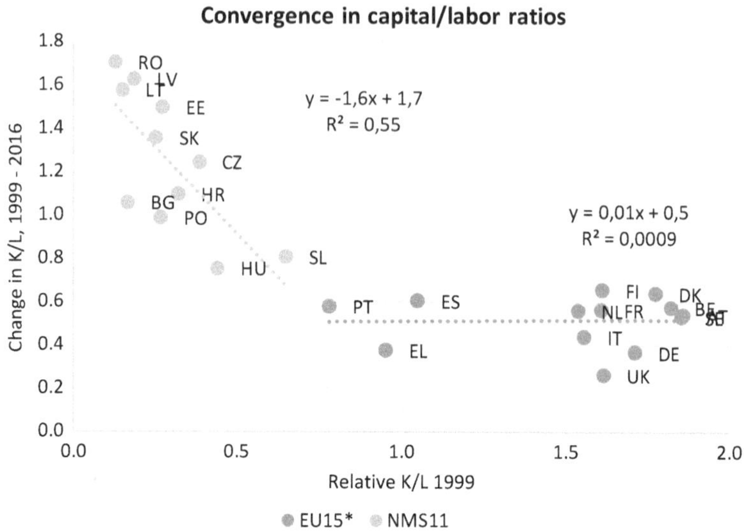

Source Own calculations based on AMECO data

Fig. 6 (continued)

Likewise, one must be careful in drawing a link between growth and FDI. For catching-up countries, large inflows of FDI can accelerate the absorption of state-of-the-art technology. But for countries aspiring to be close to the technological frontier, large outflows of FDI can be taken as a sign of success. One thus observes a link between income and the net FDI position: the higher the income per capita, the more likely the country is to have a positive FDI balance. This regularity can also be observed in Europe.

The NMS11 have been engaged mainly in catch-up growth over the last two decades and thus were natural recipients of FDI flows. This is indeed what happened on a large scale. Each of the NMS11 has a 'negative' FDI balance position, with the net inward stock of FDI now amounting to around 40% of GDP for most of them and reaching a peak of 75% of GDP for Bulgaria.

One observes some convergence among the NMS11 in terms of the accumulated stock of FDI in relation to GDP; those which had received relatively little FDI in 1998 have generally experienced a stronger increase over the last two decades. This is consistent with the income convergence among that group. By contrast, among the older MSs, there is little convergence and only a tendency of the richer ones to have a positive FDI balance.

R&D constitutes a key input into what the European Commission has called 'smart growth'. Expenditure on R&D as a percentage of GDP is one of the indicators of the EU2020 strategy. One finds that in terms of R&D expenditure there is a large gap between the old and the new MSs, which is closing only very slowly. Moreover, among the NMS11, the difference seems to be increasing as those closer to the EU average at the start of the period also expanded their R&D expenditure the most relative to the EU average.

Domestic R&D, of course, requires the availability of enough highly qualified scientists. This explains why the share of the population with a university degree is one of the Europe 2020 growth indicators.[9] Great variance exists across member states for this indicator. Most countries have improved considerably, but there is no strong tendency towards convergence. However, on the other end of the spectrum, the rate of early school leavers has witnessed some degree of convergence over the past decade.

Beyond the education and research sector, the regulatory framework can play an important role in fostering economic growth. At the turn of the century, differences in product market regulation had been marked, with many member states being tightly regulated, at least as measured by the OECD's Product Market Regulation (PMR) indicator. Although this indicator is not available for all MSs, for the ones where it is available, one observes considerable convergence over the past 15 years with most MSs becoming less regulated, especially those which initially showed the tightest regulations (see Fig. 6). There has been much less change, however, and much less convergence in labour market regulations. The OECD provides an indicator for this as well,[10] but it has shown little change over time.

A key input in growth is the accumulation of capital. Physical capital is of course not the only input in growth, but convergence in income levels would not be possible without some convergence in the capital stock.

[9] See http://ec.europa.eu/eurostat/web/europe-2020-indicators/europe-2020-strategy/headline-indicators-scoreboard.

[10] See http://www.oecd.org/eco/growth/indicatorsofproductmarketregulationhomepage.htm.

On this front, there has already been considerable convergence. Figure 6 shows that there has been a strong convergence among the NMS11 in terms of the amount of capital available per worker (indicated by the variable K/L). But nothing similar can be observed among the EU15. But one should keep in mind that convergence is still far from being achieved. In 1999, the value of the capital stock (at current exchange rates) in the richest MS was 14 times larger than in the poorest MS. Today (2017 data) this ratio has fallen to 'only' 6 times larger. Moreover, the gap is likely to be reduced further as the investment ratios remain higher in the NMS11, while it might widen among the EU15. There is, again, little difference between the euro and non-euro area participants among the NMS11.

The speed of convergence has been falling, especially since the Great Financial Crisis, which led to a permanent reduction in investment ratios of almost 2 percentage points of GDP. It is encouraging, however, that most of this decline in overall investment was due to a fall in construction activity, rather than investment in equipment. Construction investment accounts now for almost exactly the same percentage of GDP, around 10%, as in the EU15 (AMECO data). This means that during the boom years a large part of the capital flows into the NMS11 (and some peripheral euro area countries, such as Ireland, Spain and Portugal) had gone into the construction of new houses. These flows have stopped.

Investment in equipment has been less affected by the crisis. In the NMS11 it is, at over 9% of GDP, much higher than in the EU15 (6.6% of GDP) and 'only' 20% lower than during the boom years. All this indicates that capital-labour ratios are continuing to converge, especially in terms of the machines and other productive capital needed to produce industrial goods. In all these variables, we find few systematic differences between the euro and the non-euro states among the NMS11.

The data presented so far refer to overall investment, 80–90% of which is usually private and thus not directly determined by policy, which can only indirectly affect the key drivers of investment, namely growth expectations, financial market conditions and the regulatory framework. The persistence of higher private investment rates in the NMSs is not surprising given that their capital-to-labour ratios remain much lower, which implies that, *ceteris paribus*, the marginal productivity of capital should be much higher.

We do not wish to enter into a discussion here about the effectiveness of the Structural Funds (for a brief recent survey, see EEAG 2018).

But one aspect is clear: the net transfers from the EU budget allow the NMS11 to have a higher investment ratio without incurring more foreign debt (or having to support higher domestic savings ratios). This implies that EU transfers have financed, indirectly, at least part of the convergence in capital-to-income ratios observed so far. These resource transfers are substantial since many of the NMSs have a 'net balance' of about 3–4% of GDP, which should be compared to national investment rates of around 20%.

Concluding Remarks

Convergence and growth are two very complex phenomena, which cannot be fully treated in one short contribution. We thus concentrated only on one question, namely whether there is an association between euro area membership and convergence. We find that this is not the case. The key dividing line in terms of growth and convergence in the EU is between the NMS11 and the rest. The euro crisis, of course, had a strong and lasting impact on growth in some countries. But the new euro entrants from the NMS11 did not experience these problems. The two general trends of East–West convergence and the lack of convergence among the older MSs are thus independent of euro area membership.

The general argument why premature euro area membership might endanger convergence is its potential to trigger boom-bust cycles. Such cycles have occurred over the last two decades and have proven to be very destructive. But these cycles have also occurred in countries that were not in the eurozone, with Iceland possibly being the extreme example. Here again, however, it is not clear that euro area membership was a key element in creating the problem.

Moreover, the future might be different from the recent past. The euro area has now created for itself a set of institutions, which should mitigate the fall-out from financial excess and make their recurrence less likely. Completing the Banking Union and strengthening the Capital Markets Union would further contribute to financial market stability and thus convergence.

The available forecasts suggest that over the next few years the NMS11 are set to remain somewhat more dynamic than the old member states. The East–West convergence process is thus continuing but also slowing down somewhat, while it might start again among the old member states.

The example of the USA suggests that a considerable level of income differences is likely to remain in an economically diversified, continental-sized economic area. But the EU has still some way to go before reaching the US benchmark.

There is still a considerable distance between the NMS11 and the EU15 in terms of achieving the Europe 2020 indicators, but it is narrowing. Nevertheless, there is little evidence of overall convergence across all MSs in their attainment of the goals set under the Europe 2020 strategy. Any new overarching growth strategy for the EU should consider how to set more ambitious benchmarks beyond Cohesion policies.

References

Diaz del Hoyo, J. L., Dorrucci, E., Heinz, F. F., & Muzikarova, S. (2017, December). *Real Convergence in the Euro Area: A Long-Term Perspective* (ECB Occasional Paper No. 203). Frankfurt: European Central Bank.

EEAG. (2018). It's Ok to Be Different: Policy Coordination and Economic Convergence. In *What Now, with Whom, Where to—The Future of the EU* (EEAG Report on the European Economy). Munich: European Economic Advisory Group, CESifo.

European Central Bank. (2015). Real Convergence in the Euro Area: Evidence, Theory and Policy Implications. *Economic Bulletin* (5), 30–45.

European Commission. (2018a). *My Region, My Europe, Our Future* (Seventh Report on Economic, Social and Territorial Cohesion). http://ec.europa.eu/regional_policy/sources/docoffic/official/reports/cohesion7/7cr.pdf.

European Commission. (2018b, February). Sustainable Convergence in the Euro Area: A Multi-dimensional Process. *Quarterly Report on the Euro Area, 16*(3), 3–24. https://ec.europa.eu/info/sites/info/files/economy-finance/ip072_en_i_sustainable_convergence_euro_area.pdf.

Franks, J., Barkbu, B., Blavy, R., Oman, W., & Schoelermann, H. (2018, January). *Economic Convergence in the Euro Area: Coming Together or Drifting Apart?* (IMF Working Paper WP/18/10). Washington, DC: International Monetary Fund.

Goecke, H., & Hüther, M. (2016, May/June). Regional Convergence in Europe. *Intereconomics, 51*(3), 165–171.

Merler, S. (2016). *Income Convergence During the Crisis: Did the EU Funds Provide a Buffer?* (Bruegel Working Paper). Brussels: Bruegel.

Unconventional Monetary Policy in the USA and in Europe

Guerini Mattia, Lamperti Francesco and Mazzocchetti Andrea

Introduction

In the last decade, central banks around the world have reacted to the financial crisis through sets of unconventional monetary policy measures that enriched the standard ones. Such policies encompass the usage of the central bank's balance sheet to influence financial conditions beyond the short-term rate (*balance sheet policies*); the management of the expectations of the policy rate over the medium run, to provide extra stimulus when rates have reached the zero lower bound (*forward guidance*

G. Mattia (✉)
Université Côte d'Azur – GREDEG, Valbonne, France

OFCE – SciencesPo, Paris, France
e-mail: mattia.guerini@sciencespo.fr

G. Mattia · L. Francesco
Sant'Anna School of Advanced Studies, Pisa, Italy

L. Francesco
European Institute of Economics and the Environment, Milan, Italy

M. Andrea
University of Genova, Genova, Italy

V. Vlachos and A. Bitzenis (eds.), *European Union*,
https://doi.org/10.1007/978-3-030-18103-1_3

policies); and the definition of negative nominal policy rates, to incentivize the lending activity (*negative interest rate policies*).

The majority of efforts—in terms of firepower, longevity and scope—have been focused on balance sheet policies. The asset purchase programs have been implemented by the 4 major central banks with the declared objective of providing liquidity to key credit markets, restoring the lending activity to real sectors and fostering growth and employment.[1] Some of these goals have been achieved: The impacts on credit and interbank markets are usually agreed to be sizable. Other goals have not: The effects on the real economy are debatable and weak (Borio and Zabai 2016; Guerini et al. 2018; Lombardi et al. 2018). Furthermore, not all the consequences of ten years of unconventional policies have been desirable. The very institutional and structural differences between the USA and EU have contributed to such heterogeneous, somehow undesirable, effects.

Economic theory suggests four possible channels through which the unconventional policies may affect economic and financial systems. First, there is a portfolio rebalance channel, such that central banks' purchases of government securities influence the available supply of these assets to private investors (Bernanke 2010). Second, if the announcements or operations are understood by markets to signal lower future policy rates than previously expected, bond yields will adjust downward. Third, the signaling or expectation channels capture those changes in the expected path of future short-term rates that arise from perceived new information that asset purchases measures might relay about the state of the economy. Fourth, by improving market functioning and sustaining demand for certain asset classes, central banks can reduce liquidity risks and, ultimately, yields. While it is not clear which channel has worked consistently across different economies and time, there is evidence that UMPs have thawed the markets and impacted on the yields (Borio and Zabai 2016).

In the present chapter, we discuss some interlinked phenomena that have characterized unconventional monetary policy in the USA (section "The Quantitative Easing in the USA: Financial Markets Segmentation") and in Euro Area (section "The Quantitative Easing in Europe: Country Heterogeneity"). For each case, we do not focus on the identification of one particular channel but we compare the specific domain of application and rationale; we reconstruct the possible heterogeneous effects that the balance

[1] Federal Reserve, European Central Bank, Bank of England and Bank of Japan have all implemented some forms of balance sheet policies indeed (see Borio and Zabai 2016).

sheet policies have produced across assets classes (in the USA) and countries (in the EU); and finally, we aim at understanding the possible unintended consequences and future risks that are associated with the quantitative easing policies. We also introduce in section "Coordination Between Monetary Policies and Financial Stability" the concept of financial stability, which gained relevance after the recent global financial crisis. We aim at understanding how central banks have coordinated the unconventional monetary policies together with a new set of policies targeting financial stability. We provide conclusion and ideas for future discussions in section "Conclusions".

The Quantitative Easing in the USA: Financial Markets Segmentation

The Federal Reserve fiercely reacted to the financial crisis by implementing several unconventional monetary policy measures. We here focus our attention on three aspects of these measures: their variety, their heterogeneous impacts on different asset classes and the possible risks and unintended effects to them associated.

General Framework

In a first approximation, the unconventional policy measures implemented by the Federal Reserve can be divided into *liquidity provision operations* and *large-scale asset purchase* (LSAPs) programs.[2] The two differ both in their rationale and in their effects. Here, we will mainly focus on the second of the two.

In the immediate aftermath of the financial crisis (end of 2007 and beginning of 2008), the Federal Reserve underwent a series of direct lending to several distressed financial institutions. These measures aimed at spurring the availability of short-term funds used by financial institutions to finance their daily operations. In particular, after the collapse of Lehman Brothers and the consecutive shutdown of many financial market segments, vast uncertainty emerged also in the interbank market. The Federal Reserve therefore implemented a number of additional programs with the aim for providing liquidity to key credit markets in order to reduce funding pressures. All these interventions were associated with the

[2] The second operation is also commonly labeled as Quantitative Easing (QE).

central bank's role as lender of last resort and had the purpose of avoiding fire sales of assets due to liquidity shortages in the financial sector. The fire sales would have indeed implied the possible percolation of effects through the balance sheets of different institutions (Bernanke 2009).

These above-mentioned measures tackled the temporary liquidity issues, but not the solvency ones. Hence, in November 2008, the first LSAP was introduced by the Federal Reserve. Via the acquisition of mortgage-backed securities (MBS) and government-sponsored enterprises debt, the Fed aimed at cleaning the balance sheet of financial institutions, to levy them from non-performing loans and other "junk bonds," and at stabilizing the housing market and its underlying financing structure.[3] A few months later—in March 2009—the program was further extended to include treasury securities in the list of the eligible assets to be acquired via the program. Such program is commonly referred to as LSAP1 (or QE1) and had a size of about \$1.75 trillion. Following the first intervention, the Fed implemented three other major balance sheet programs. As emphasized in Fratzscher et al. (2018), the first program had the peculiarity of having been introduced with the explicit aim of reducing mortgage interest rates and stabilizing the housing markets; the major objective of the treasury purchases was instead that of stimulating the economic activity by lowering long-term rates to spur investment, to increase asset prices and, in general, to stimulate aggregate demand. In August 2010, with the LSAP2 (or QE2), the Federal Open Market Committee (FOMC) decided to stabilize the quantity of securities held by the Fed by reinvesting principal payments of agency and mortgage-backed securities into longer-term treasury bonds. The objective was that of reducing their yields. Such program has been further extended in November 2010 with the purchase of \$600 billion of longer-term US treasuries. The third phase, the so-called maturity extension program (MEP or *operation twist*), was announced in September 2011. The MEP swapped the Fed's holdings of treasuries with shorter residual maturities with treasuries having longer maturities. The fourth and final step has been the LSAP3 (or QE3) program, launched in September 2012. It had the peculiarity of not having a predetermined duration and a predetermined total size

[3]Here, financial structure is intended to indicate the intricate relationships between mortgage holders, financial institutions issuing mortgages, financial institution issuing securities backed by mortgages and all the buyers of such securities.

of asset purchases; however, every monthly purchase of treasuries and MBS was regularly preannounced. The LSAP3 ceased in October 2014 with a final size of about 1.3 trillion dollars.

Heterogeneity of the Effects

Such variegated and prolonged interventions have affected the returns of asset classes differently. On average, there is substantial empirical evidence about the role that the unconventional policies implemented by the Fed had on the improvement of financing conditions in the USA. However, the effects appear to be more important at their announcement rather than at the actual execution of the purchases (see Gagnon et al. 2011; Neely 2010). This is consistent with the idea that forward guidance and the expectations channel played a relevant role in the transmission of the unconventional monetary policies. In their survey of the empirical literature, Borio and Zabai (2016) find that the LSAPs reduced the yields of the 10 years government bonds of about 100 basis points, in line with estimates from Di Maggio et al. (2016). More precisely, the effects of LSAP1 across all surveyed studies average at around −75 basis points, while the same exercise for LSAP2+MEP and LSAP3 deliver, respectively, −30 and −10 basis points.[4] A similar impact has been registered for long-term MBS, whose yields have decreased by 115 basis points, with around 80% of the effect attributed to LSAP1. All in all, the Fed's experience with balance sheet policies suggests that there were diminishing returns over time of the asset purchases. And these effects are likely due to the important role of changing market expectations through the signaling channel (Ihrig et al. 2012). The impact of LSAP2 was indeed positive yet not large and raised some debate over whether purchasing non-treasury securities (e.g., MBS) is more effective at lowering yields (see Krishnamurthy and Vissing-Jorgensen 2011, 2013). Only few studies investigated the effects of LSAP3, but in general they seem to be lower than its antecedent versions.[5]

[4] The cumulative effect is thereby at around −120.

[5] This decreasing effect over time may also suggest that QE and asset purchases in general work better when the country implementing them is in distress and that they shall not be considered as a policy for normal times. This is also consistent with the interpretation that we offer for the EU asset purchases (see section "The Quantitative Easing in Europe: Country Heterogeneity").

Table 1 Average effects of LSAP programs' announcements on various asset classes

Asset class	*Measure*	*LSAP1*	*LSAP2*	*MEP*	*LSAP3*
2y US bonds	yield variation (p.p.)	−0.069	−0.004	0.023	−0.011
5y US bonds	yield variation (p.p.)	−0.115	−0.000	0.031	−0.036
10y US bonds	yield variation (p.p.)	−0.113	0.016	−0.024	−0.016
S&P 500	index variation (p.p.)	0.146	0.282	−1.576	0.562
VIX	yield variation (p.p.)	0.080	−0.883	1.660	−0.427
Median 10y bonds in AEs	yield variation (p.p.)	0.178	−0.010	−0.464	−0.253
Median equity in AEs	index variation (p.p.)	−0.016	0.001	−0.0158	0.002
Median 10y bonds in EMEs	yield variation (p.p.)	−0.018	0.004	−0.018	−0.020
Median equity in EMEs	index variation (p.p.)	0.196	0.113	0.195	0.365

Source Authors' elaborations on Fratzscher et al. (2018). Notation: AEs = Advanced Economies; EMEs = Emerging Market Economies

Apart from the average effects, we notice that there are large discrepancies in the effects that the Fed's LSAP programs had on yields and prices. The observation of changes on the day of asset purchases announcements shows that yields of bonds with different maturities have reduced, primarily, during the first part of the QE, while the stock market—as proxied by the S&P 500—reacted most during the LSAP3 (see Table 1). While it is not possible to draw causal conclusions with this table, such descriptive evidence supports the hypothesis that the initial stages of asset purchases have been largely effective in diminishing yields and relaxing financing conditions, while the later steps have instead substantially favoured the abnormal rising trend in US equity prices during the last five years. Table 1 provides the additional insight that announcements induced a quite large and positive impact on US equity indexes (but for the MEP, which consistently induced an opposite behavior of both prices and yields with respect to LSAPs).

According to Krishnamurthy and Vissing-Jorgensen (2011), the large and significant drop in nominal interest rates on long-term safe assets (treasuries, agency bonds and highly rated corporate bonds) is due to the peculiar market for such assets. There is indeed a unique clientele for long-term safe nominal assets, and the Fed's purchases reduce the supply of such assets, in turn increasing their safety-premium (see also Caballero and Fahri 2017). On the other side, Krishnamurthy and Vissing-Jorgensen (2011) report just small effects on nominal (default-adjusted) interest rates on riskier assets, such as Baa corporate bonds. Following such lines, if the final goal of QE is to reduce interest rates paid by the majority of corporations and households, in the hope this may eventually spur spending and economic growth, then focusing on the supply effects of treasury rates could be misleading, as most economic activities are funded by debt that is not risk-free. In line with the theoretical mechanisms analyzed in Clouse et al. (2003), Krishnamurthy and Vissing-Jorgensen (2013) argue that the large reductions in mortgage rates due to LSAP1 are driven by the fact that it involved large purchases of agency MBS (this is the *market segmentation* effect also reported by Swanson 2017). For LSAP2 instead, which involved only treasury purchases, they report a substantial impact on treasury rates, but almost no impact on MBS rates. Coherently, Di Maggio et al. (2016) observe that the Fed's purchase of MBS (rather than exclusively treasuries) during QE1 resulted in an additional $600 billions of refinancing, substantially reducing interest payments for refinancing households and leading to a boom in equity extraction (and increasing consumption by an additional $76 billion). In contrast, no such effects are found for QE2. The dependency of QE's real-side effectiveness on the compositional nature of the asset purchases provides support to the idea that the key stages of QE were limited to the LSAP1.

Unintended Consequences

The prolonged asset purchases engaged by the Fed have also increased the amount of liquidity in the balance sheet of financial institutions, which raised the demand for stocks, contributing to the rally of the US equity markets from March 2009 to January 2018. Fratzscher et al. (2018) empirically document that QE1 policy announcements as well as the liquidity operations primarily triggered a portfolio rebalancing into riskier market segments, with capital flowing mainly into US equity funds. While some part of such effect was desirable, the size and the prolonged application of LSAP programs might have induced an increase in stock prices, not compensated by a comparable boost of the real economic system. Furthermore, the increase in the size of the Federal Reserve assets portfolio has not ceased until mid-2018. To reduce its size, the Fed needs to sell government bonds. This is likely to deflate asset prices in the future, and without an adequate control over such process, this might generate dangerous busts of the asset prices.

But there are also other unintended consequences of the Fed's policies. Di Maggio and Kacperczyk (2017) provide evidence that the zero lower bound commitment of the Fed during the various phases of the QE had sizable effects in accruing risk exposures on money funds, which are pivotal actors of the shadow banking system. Being the latter obliged by regulation to invest part of their liquidity in short-term safe assets, the change in monetary policy paradigm has compressed the funds' gross profit margins by squeezing investment opportunities in the industry. As a response, money funds have been found to invest in riskier asset classes and to hold less diversified portfolios, thereby showing a resurgent appetite for credit and liquidity risk. Finally, the equity-based portfolio rebalancing experienced during QE1 was mainly directed toward US stocks. While a positive trend has been maintained even during the following stages, QE2 and to some extent also QE3 announcements and treasury purchases had the strongest impact on inflows to Emerging Market Economies (increased liquidity pushed investment in US and foreign stocks). In particular, when macroeconomic uncertainty is low and the US outlook is positive, QE announcements are found to transmit with more intensity to portfolio flows outside the USA. Besides showing evidence of the relevance of the portfolio rebalancing channel for UMPs transmission, such results show that QE2 and QE3 have favoured an increasing willingness to take risks among US investors, which may be problematic in the face of a downturn.

Overall, the Fed's recent experience with UMPs suggests that QE's various rounds have provoked heterogeneous impacts on the US financial markets, with some evidence of spillover effects toward Emerging Market Economies. The first stage of the QE (i.e., the LSAP1) has been the most effective in lowering the yields of both government bonds with different maturities (from 2 to 10 years) and less safe assets (e.g., corporate bonds). The following stages of QE have produced minor effects on the financial and real sides of the economy, while increasing the size of the Fed's balance sheet. Furthermore, the prolonged duration of the Fed LSAP programs and the relatively low macroeconomic uncertainty have induced a risk-prone portfolio rebalancing effect across a variety of financial intermediaries (from banks to money funds) during the period 2009–2018. With stock markets rising more than the economy's fundamentals over the last decade, the Fed's recent need of absorbing money from the markets should be cautiously monitored.

The Quantitative Easing in Europe: Country Heterogeneity

The ECB reaction to the crisis was less prompt than the Fed one. Coordinated unconventional policies were introduced only in 2015, five years after the outset of the European debt crisis.

General Framework

Large-scale asset purchases in the Euro Area have been triggered by two contingencies: an impairment in the transmission of standard monetary policy, in particular via the bank lending channel, and a worsening of the medium-term outlook for inflation.[6] To these two triggering contingencies correspond two objectives of QE: the restoration of the normal credit conditions (i.e., the loosening of the binding credit constraints that affected the Euro Area in 2014) and the induction of a higher inflation rate in the Euro Area (consistently with the main ECB objective of targeting an inflation rate just below 2%).

Within a monetary union, the QE might have reduced the distance between the monetary and the fiscal authorities, but asset purchases haven't formally affected the operational independence of the ECB. Indeed, even if the separating line between the central bank and the governments has become more blurred with the unconventional monetary policies, the ECB has been extremely cautious in introducing QE for the first time. As also documented by Dell'Ariccia et al. (2018), the applicability of the QE was uncertain due to the presence of the Article 123 of the Treaty of the Functioning of the European Union. It was only in 2010, after the IMF and the EU announced a bailout program, that the ECB implemented its very first Security Market Program (SMP), buying a relatively small amount of Greek, Irish, Italian, Portuguese and Spanish government debts on the secondary markets.[7] After this faint acquisition

[6]The rationale behind the introduction of QE has to be found in a speech that the president of the ECB, Mario Draghi, delivered at the Netherland central bank in 2014.

[7]The SMP is here not yet considered an unconventional monetary policy such as the QE. We consider it to be more similar to a lender of last resort operation. Furthermore, its size was limited to 60 Billions Euro, a relatively low amount with respect to the asset purchases programs implemented after 2015.

of treasuries, the ECB did not implement other unconventional monetary policy measures until 2015, when the asset purchases program (APP) has begun.[8]

But how did QE in Europe take place? The Fed has acquired a vast amount of CDOs (MBS and ABS in particular) and treasury securities, inducing lower long-term interest rates in specific markets due to the market segmentation effect. In so doing, the Fed helped reduce long-run uncertainty, improving the quality of the banks' balance sheets and reinvigorating the credit supply (especially during the first LSAP1). The ECB has begun by adopting a similar strategy—having in mind similar objectives. Therefore, the first stage of the Euro Area APP targeted mostly ABS and public bonds. However, as the inflation remained persistently below the target—with also a short deflation phase in the first quarter of 2015—the ECB announced a second phase of the QE, in which the acquisition of public sector bonds became predominant.[9] This leads to the first large substantial difference between QE in EU and in the USA. Even if in both the economies the size of the CB balance sheet has increased in size (see also Borio and Zabai 2016; Guerini et al. 2018), their compositions took quite different paths: The Fed balance sheet at the end of 2015 was almost evenly divided between MBS and mid-long-term treasury securities; the ECB one is still instead vastly composed by government bonds—as before the debt crisis—with long maturity. According to the evidence collected by Borio and Zabai (2016), the operations discussed above have helped to restore the normal conditions on the credit markets and, by decreasing interest rates and by increasing the liquidity of the European interbank market, to spur investments. All in all, they therefore accomplished the first of the QE objectives. On the other side however, the inflation level is still below the 2% target and it is only slowly increasing. Thus, the second objective of QE seems to be only partially accomplished.

[8]The ECB has since then acquired, every month, around 60 billions Euros of public bonds. Furthermore, this second phase has also been accompanied by some forms of *forward guidance* as several ECB directors publicly declared that the acquisition would stop as soon as inflation reaches the 2% target.

[9]The acquisition of government bonds is called the Public Sector Purchase Programme (PSPP). The other subsections of the APP are the Covered Bonds Purchase Programme (CBPP) and the Corporate Sector Purchase Programme (CSPP). The latter two have been, respectively, implemented since March 2015 and June 2017.

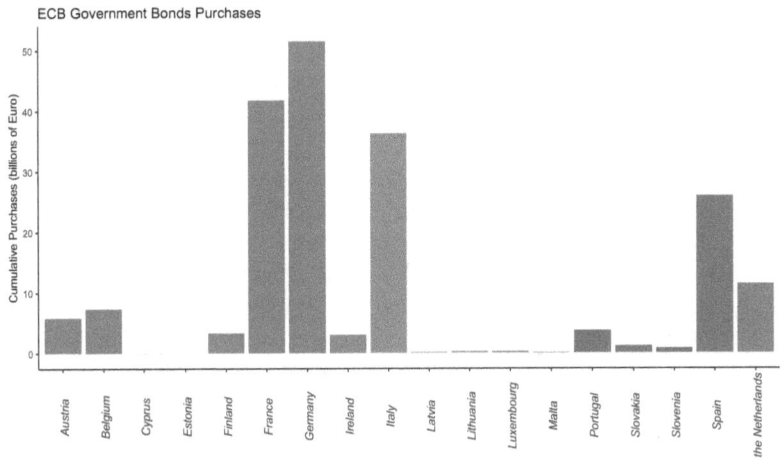

Fig. 1 European Central Bank cumulative purchases of government bonds (*Source* Authors' elaborations on ECB data)

Heterogeneity of the Effects

As observed in Fig. 1, the ECB has acquired sovereign bonds from different countries.[10] This adds another layer of complexity for the study of the effects of QE. Indeed, even if the ECB buys bonds in proportion to some structural variable (e.g., *capital keys*), it is important to understand whether the acquisition of bonds of different countries might affect their returns symmetrically or whether the relative return on government bonds is affected. This also leads to a broader question about whether the QE can be more favorable for some economies of the Euro Area rather than for others.

A first insight on the heterogeneous effects produced by monetary policy in Europe has been provided by Barigozzi et al. (2014), in a study on the effects of interest rates shocks (i.e., conventional monetary policy) on the different Eurozone economies. The evidence suggests that the effects of the same interest rate shock are quite heterogeneous across the Euro Area, especially the effects concerning the response of CPI inflation and unemployment. Such heterogeneity is intrinsically related to the structural and institutional differences of the member states, which can be offset

[10] See also https://www.ecb.europa.eu/mopo/implement/omt/html/pspp-qa.en.html.

by a complementary fiscal stance or by structural reforms. QE effects, in principle, can also be complementary to those of the conventional interest rate policies. De Santis (2016) points indeed to the fact that the large asset purchases programs of the ECB have lowered the long-term interest rates in all the Euro Area, but that such a fall have been heterogeneous across countries. In particular, consistently with the evidence brought to the fore also by Demerzis and Wolff (2016), Fratzscher et al. (2016), Koijen et al. (2018), empirical results suggest that the interest rate decrease generated by a QE shock have been stronger in southern European economies such as Portugal and Italy, while have been milder for northern economies such as Austria and Germany. Falagiarda and Reitz (2015) also find that unconventional monetary policy events had a role in reducing the spreads of most southern European economies with respect to Germany.[11] Altavilla et al. (2016) focus on the Outright Monetary Transactions (OMT) finding that also these operations had a negative effect on Spanish and Italian government bond yields but no effect on French and German ones. In general, therefore, the South of Europe has benefitted the most from the QE operations.

These empirical results constitute an important confirmation of the QE hybrid nature that links monetary and fiscal policies. Indeed, QE can favor some countries more than others. In particular, countries that have benefitted the most from QE—in terms of lower costs of debt—have been those characterized by higher stocks of public debt. Two possible mechanisms might lie behind this dynamics of the government yields. First, by means of QE, the ECB has targeted and acquired bonds from these countries in a higher proportion. Second, the expectations channel has been stronger for these economies which—without the ECB intervention—would have been perceived as riskier than their northern peers. The first channel, however, seems to be in contrast with the cumulative purchases of bonds by the ECB (see Fig. 1), since the acquisition of sovereign bonds by the ECB has not been discretional and the purchases from different countries have been proportional to the capital keys.[12] We believe that the second channel has played a more important role: complementing the asset purchases programs with some key public statement and public announcements (e.g., Draghi's *whatever it takes* statement) and with forward guidance

[11] Oddly enough, the unique country for which no effect is found is Greece, for which we also don't have data in Fig. 1.

[12] See https://www.ecb.europa.eu/ecb/orga/capital/html/index.en.html.

operations, the ECB has been able to restore investors' confidence, especially in these countries where investors' confidence has been sharply declining.

Unintended Consequences

Such an evidence could endanger the separation between monetary and fiscal authorities in the future.[13] If QE is perceived as a hybrid policy measure, by differently affecting the spread in the cost of borrowing for the various member states, it can in principle be used to reduce the government bonds interest rates for some countries more than for others. And it can therefore loosen the borrowing constraints for some member states while leaving them unaffected for others. For such reasons, different prominent economists answering to a CFM survey claimed that the degree of central bank independence has declined since the early years of the Euro experience and it is likely to be reduced even more so in the future. This might therefore be a risk that the European Union should try to regulate before the future crisis will appear.

Notwithstanding the effects on the government bonds spreads, the effects of QE on employment, inflation and output in Europe are still scant. On the one side, this is due to the fact that the structure of the monetary union makes it very difficult to estimate country-specific effects of QE—due to the presence of other institutional shocks like political events, EU regulatory changes or variations in the fiscal stances; on the other side, the asset purchase program has begun only in 2015, and hence aggregate data available for possible policy evaluation exercises are yet limited. The available literature suggests that this effect shall be in principle slightly positive. Estimates by Peersman (2011) show that an increase in the central bank balance sheet might have a positive effect on output and inflation, with a response reaching the peak around one year after the assets' purchases.[14] On a more theoretical ground instead, some evidences on the effects of the QE programs on GDP

[13]See, for example, the aggregate results and the answers of some of the participants to the CFM survey about the issue of central bank independence: http://cfmsurvey.org/surveys/future-central-bank-independence.

[14]The work by Gambacorta et al. (2014) is however an *ex-ante* investigation on the QE. The work studies indeed the effects of a possible positive increase in the balance sheet of the central bank (without specifying which types of assets are bought) employing a VAR model.

are presented either under the form of a Dynamic Stochastic General Equilibrium (DSGE) model or under the form of an Agent-based Computational Economics (ACE) model. In particular, Cincotti et al. (2010) and Andrade et al. (2016) point to some positive effect of QE on output growth, in particular during periods of distressed financial systems. But Cincotti et al. (2010)—coherently with the US evidence about the effects of QE on asset price bubbles—also suggest that the quantitative easing might become a source of instability (generating bubbles and crashes) when used for extensive time periods and that its effect might well not be positive if adopted in expansionary phases. On the other side, an empirical exercise by Blot et al. (2017) suggests that the QE in Europe doesn't seem to directly induce asset prices bubbles (neither for stock prices nor for house prices). This might signal a second important difference between EU and the USA. As observed in section "The Quantitative Easing in the USA: Financial Markets Segmentation" indeed, in the latter these effects might be significant.

Coordination Between Monetary Policies and Financial Stability

Both in the USA and in the Euro Area, monetary policy has been accompanied by other types of regulatory policies aimed at stabilizing the financial sector. Discussing the objectives, the effects and the possible drawbacks of the unconventional monetary policies without defining the aims of financial stability policies would therefore offer only an incomplete picture. In this section, we hence discuss the general issue of financial stability, which has largely broadened the scope of the central banks.

Financial Stability Overview

Central banks have always grappled with financial stability in their functions of bank supervisor, lender of last resort and payment system oversight, notably since the 1980s as frequent financial crises hit both advances and emerging economies involving large costs (see Bordo et al. 2001; Borio and White 2004). However, in the aftermath of the great financial crisis of 2007–2008, financial stability has increased in relevance and scope. The financial crisis has indeed revealed that even small shocks can amplify within the financial system and can in turn trigger catastrophic consequences on the real side of the economy. Financial shocks can also hinder the transmission mechanisms of monetary policies.[15] In particular, the crisis has unveiled the extreme complexity of the financial system and demonstrated the difficulty of capturing sound indicators of the degree of leverage or excessive risk-taking within the system, particularly as regards unregulated or slightly regulated institutions and instruments (Pozsar et al. 2010; Adrian and Shin 2010).[16] This has brought central banks to investigate more on the importance of financial stability.

Financial stability is a multifaceted concept that encompasses the interrelations between real markets, financial markets and financial institutions. Often, it refers to the smooth functioning of the financial system and its ability to absorb shocks; however, a universally agreed definition of financial stability is not yet available and the meaning of it may be different across central banks. For this reason, also the theoretical foundations of financial stability are difficult to treat and it might be cleaner to discuss separately the three interesting areas (i.e., macroeconomic fundamentals, financial system and financial institutions).

From a macroeconomic perspective, economic theories have been focusing on the interaction between private agents' financial activities and their effects on the real markets. In particular, an acceleration in credit availability and an increase in asset prices may induce to higher financial investments, which would further lead to an increase in assets prices and would contribute to the generation of financial bubbles without a parallel improvement in the economic fundamentals (see Minsky 1973). However, as soon as the bubble bursts, the fast contractions in credit supply and asset prices generate a parallel contraction of the economic activity.[17] All in all, this implies that there is an asymmetric reaction of real markets and of economic fundamentals to financial instability and financial shocks. Central banks shall therefore aim at including new tools to cope with these asymmetric relations trying to identify early warning indicators for asset price bubbles. With respect to financial markets, economic theory mainly refers to the market failures induced by informational asymmetries. This proves that markets are not efficient and that adverse selection may often occur (see Akerlof 1970; Stiglitz and Weiss 1981; Lo 2017). With the presence of market failures, asset

[15] See https://www.ecb.europa.eu/mopo/intro/transmission/html/index.en.html.

[16] See also http://www.fsb.org/wp-content/uploads/r_111027a.pdf.

[17] See, e.g., Fisher (1933), Gurley and Shaw (1955), Minsky (1986), Bernanke and Gertler (1990), Borio and Drehmann (2009).

prices may not reflect the correct underlying risks, possibly leading to excessive risk exposure in certain assets which could arise financial imbalances. Also in such area, central banks would need new tools allowing to correctly measure risk exposures and systemic risk (see Barucca et al. 2016; Battiston and Martinez-Jaramillo 2018). From the financial institutions perspective, main economic theories include issues such as bank runs (Diamond and Dybvig 1983), financial contagion (Allen and Gale 2000; Freixas et al. 2000) and the resiliency and fragility of the financial network (e.g., Haldane 2013; Battiston and Martinez-Jaramillo 2018). Nowadays, although banks remain at the core of the financial system, insurance companies, shadow banks and institutional investors (e.g., pension, investment and hedge funds) play an increasingly important role, building up a framework where systemic risk may arise from multiple sources.

Institutional Framework

In the aftermath of the great financial crisis, central banks and governments increased their efforts to monitor financial institutions and their linkages in order to capture sound indicators of the degree of leverage and excessive risk exposure within the system, thus taming the complexity and the interconnectedness of the financial system. In particular, the G20 summit in 2009 set in motion global efforts to strengthen institutional framework by creating more effective overview of key financial players, products and markets.[18]

In the USA, the Dodd-Frank Wall Street Reform and Consumer Protection Act was introduced in 2010 as part of a massive financial reform legislation, with the aim of promoting the financial stability of the USA by improving accountability and transparency in the financial system. The Dodd–Frank Act led to the creation of the Financial Stability Oversight Council (FSOC) and of the Office of Financial Research (OFR) and increased the competencies of the Board of Governors of the Fed along many dimensions pertaining to the supervision and operation

[18] See the declaration on strengthening the financial system from the leaders of the G20: https://www.g20.org/profiles/g20/modules/custom/g20_beverly/img/timeline/ReinoUnido/G20-financialsystem-london-2009-en.pdf. Also, in the summit the Financial Stability Board was established as an expansion of the Financial Stability Forum, with a broadened mandate to promote financial stability, and with a strong institutional basis and enhanced capacity.

of systemically important financial institutions. In particular, under the Dodd–Frank Act, financial institutions with $50 billions or more in assets are subject to enhanced prudential regulatory standards to reduce the effects of a bank's failure or material weakness on the financial system and on the economy at large.

In the European Union, the institutional framework was improved with the establishment of the European Systemic Risk Board in 2010 with the objective to oversee the financial system of the EU and to prevent and mitigate systemic risk; of the Single Supervisory Mechanism in 2014, which placed significant banks in participating countries under the direct supervision of the European Central Bank; and of the Single Resolution Mechanism in 2015, endowed with formal supervisory and resolution competences at the European Level. This reinforced legislative framework reflects the fact that financial stability policies might have many dimensions and can include policy development, the definition of new rules, supervisory activities and that the responsibility for many of these dimensions is shared between central banks and other agencies. For this reasons, given the importance and the complexity to tackle financial instability, a prompt exchange of information, data and a smoother coordination between different policymakers is pivotal for the future stability of the financial system.

Focusing on central banks, nowadays their interest in financial stability goes far beyond the mere lender of last resort function. The Fed is not endowed with an official mandate, though it includes a division of financial stability, which "*identifies and analyzes potential threats to financial stability; monitors financial markets, institutions, and structures; and assesses and recommends policy alternatives to address these threats.*"[19] To provide a description of the role of financial stability for the Fed, it may be useful to recall the speech of the former Fed chairman Ben S. Bernanke in February of 2009 at the National Press Club where he stated that: "*the Federal Reserve has done, and will continue to do, everything possible within the limits of its authority to assist in restoring our nation to financial stability and economic prosperity.*"[20]

With this speech, the Fed has explicitly included financial stability into the list of the central bank objectives, together with the dual mandate of price stability and low unemployment. The Governing Council of the

[19] See https://www.federalreserve.gov/econres/fsprstaff.htm.

[20] See https://www.federalreserve.gov/newsevents/speech/bernanke20090218a.htm.

ECB instead clearly declares that the Eurosystem's mission statement also involves a commitment "*... to safeguard financial stability and promote European financial integration.*"[21]

Furthermore, the ECB's financial stability objective is based on the Article 127 of the Lisbon Treaty, which requires the European System of Central Banks (ESCB) to "*contribute to the smooth conduct of policies pursued by competent authorities relating to the prudential supervision of credit institutions and the stability of the financial system.*"

All in all, the pursuing of financial stability represents de facto an inherent mandate for modern central banks, which operate to safeguard it mainly by means of three interrelated policy areas: microprudential supervision, which focuses on the health and stability of individual financial institutions; macroprudential policy, which takes into account the systemic aspects of financial stability entailed by contagion and amplification mechanisms in order to ensure the stability of the financial system as a whole; and monetary policy, which can affect the financial stability of the system in different indirect manners.

Monetary Policy and Financial Stability

Financial stability is interlinked with monetary policy. Following the price stability objective, in the first years of the 2000s the short-term interest rates have been kept at low levels by the Fed and the ECB. This low rate environment stimulated the demand for loans for prolonged periods. On the supply side instead, financial innovations have allowed financial institutions to distribute the risk-weighted loans and mortgages off their own balance sheets and have allowed financial institutions to "escape" capital requirements regulation, reducing their incentives to screen the creditworthiness of the borrowers. But such a process has increased systemic risk. Inflation has been low and macroeconomic fundamentals looked sound. But the overborrowing that led to asset price bubbles and to the financial crash was emerging unnoticed.

This transmission mechanism of the monetary policy identifies the existence of a long-run link between financial and monetary stability. In the future, central banks might need to take a longer-run perspective while conducting monetary policy. Even when inflation is below target,

[21] See https://www.ecb.europa.eu/ecb/orga/escb/eurosystem-mission/html/index.en.html.

monetary policy might not necessarily need to be extremely loose if there exists a probability of generating future financial instability that hits back on the monetary conditions.

The great financial crisis also came as a reminder to central bankers about the fact that the ZLB can be reached, and it is not only a textbook hypothetical situation. And as we have seen in the previous sections, unconventional measures are needed in such a situation. Financial stability therefore is a necessary condition to be highly regarded by central banks in order to avoid this situation. However, there is no policy instrument that has been uniquely designed to tackle financial stability. Among the tools that might have influenced the stability of the financial system, a primary role has been played by the interest rate policies (affecting it via the asset price stability channel) and prudential supervision (affecting it via the restoration of sound financial conditions for individual institutions). Not diverting such instruments from their principal purpose inevitably has involved trade-offs and a risk of unintended consequences, as we have seen also for the unconventional monetary policy. However, most of the central bank directives were silent on how to balance the risks arising from the potential trade-offs between monetary and financial stability objectives, mainly due to the lack of knowledge of the underlying mechanisms involved, and the complex dimension that this trade-off might have over time.

Furthermore, a key question concerns the interaction between financial stability and unconventional monetary policies. Undoubtedly, the QE helped to counteract the liquidity shortage of financial institutions (both in the USA and in Europe) by creating a massive amount of liquidity which was used to buy illiquid assets and government bonds.[22] However, even assuming that there may be no conflict between financial and monetary stability in the midst of the crisis and during the application of QE, the potential for such a conflict reappears in times where a central bank might decide to end the unconventional expansionary monetary policy packages. A too early withdrawal from the stimulus measures could delay the resumption of normal financial market functioning; a too late withdrawal could instead end up generating asset price bubbles and excess credit to untrustworthy borrowers. The Federal Reserve combined the end of LSAP programs with forward guidance announcements

[22] See sections "The Quantitative Easing in the USA: Financial Markets Segmentation" and "The Quantitative Easing in Europe: Country Heterogeneity".

in 2013, that anyway led to a sharp market decline (Mishra et al. 2014). This process of winding down the QE was also referred to as the *tapering*. Ultimately, the program ended at the end of 2014 as the economic data began to improve to a point at which the market appears to be able to bear the end of QE without disruptions. Furthermore, the Fed started to increase the interest rate at the end of 2015 and has been shrinking its balance sheet since 2018. Also the ECB is approaching the tapering phase using the forward guidance: The APP will end in December 2018, but the practice of reinvesting principal payments from maturing securities purchased under the APP will continue for an extended period.[23] In addition, announcements have been made about the fact that the interest rates for the main refinancing operations will remain unchanged at the present low level at least until the summer of 2019.

However, potential risks for the financial stability in the aftermath of the QE may build up from different sources. For instance, Yu (2016) states that with yields on long-term assets very low, investors may allot a greater share of their portfolios to riskier assets, such as stocks or high-yield corporate junk bonds. Such a *reaching for yield* behavior might leave investors' portfolios more sensitive to interest rate variations increasing in turn the market volatility. Furthermore, Caldentey (2017) argues that QE contributed to the growth of the international bond market, facilitating the expansion of the debt both for the financial sector and for the nonfinancial corporate sector, reinforcing the role of the asset management industry. Due to its concentration, interconnectedness, illiquidity and procyclicality, the asset management industry may therefore entail important risks to financial stability.

Hence, how to evaluate when unconventional policies shall be ended? And how to evaluate whether or not financial stability has been (temporarily) reached? While inflation and unemployment are quantifiable, it is more difficult to provide a synthetic indicator of the (in)stability of the financial sector. Also, even if on the one side the quantification of financial stability might provide a clearer framework for policy guidance and might make the central banks' activity accountable, on the other side a quantifiable numerical objective risks to reduce the discretionary activity of a central bank. And this discretionality is particularly relevant when the economy is in distress and when the complex disequilibrium

[23] See https://www.ecb.europa.eu/press/pr/date/2018/html/ecb.mp181213.en.html.

processes underlying the economic system are expressing themselves (see also Gaffard 2018). Besides those difficulties, experts and scholars are trying to assess the effects of the QE termination and of a rise of interest rate on financial stability, while central banks are strengthening their efforts to monitor financial stability by releasing periodical financial stability reports. Withdrawing from unconventional policy seems therefore at the moment more of a discretionary choice.

Conclusions

The use of unconventional monetary policies in the USA and Europe has been characterized by commonalities and differences. In particular, both in USA and EU the quantitative easing injected massive amounts of money into the economy, increasing the total assets of the central banks by a factor of around 4. However, the securities targeted by the two central banks have been heterogeneous, reflecting only a partial overlap between the objectives. In the USA, the set of four balance sheet programs implemented by the Fed starting from 2008, which encompasses LSAP1, LSAP2, Operational Twist and LSAP3, targeted at first mortgage-backed securities and government agencies debt with the major objective of stabilizing the housing market; only later they have been extended to mid- and long-term treasury securities with the aim to stimulate the economic activity by lowering long-term interest rates. In EU instead, the QE was introduced only in 2015 and it targeted mostly public bonds and asset-backed securities. But as inflation remained below target over the medium run, the acquisition of long-term public sector bonds became the dominant operation. Concerning the effects, QE in the USA prevented the economy from falling into a deflationary spiral and the financial sector from displaying a cascade of defaults; in Europe, it preserved the existence of the euro system itself by reducing the cost of debt the most for southern economies. Notwithstanding this possible asymmetric effects that reduce government spreads, at the moment QE has not been used as a policy that explicitly aims at solving the high debt problems.

From a broad perspective, the QE demonstrated to be quite useful at tackling the purposes they have been designed for: supporting the financial markets, promoting the credit activity in periods of distress and inducing upward pressure to prices. Nevertheless, the prolonged use of QE or a bad timing of withdrawal may entail unintended consequences.

In the USA, the liquidity injected by QE raised the demand for stocks, possibly contributing to the increase of US equity markets from 2009 to January 2018. Such a stock price rally has not been compensated by a growth of the real economy however. This induced several financial actors to rebalance their portfolios toward riskier assets since the yields of safer assets have been reduced by Fed purchases; this could be a source of instability in the face of a downturn. Furthermore, having the QE pushed up asset prices, we believe that the tapering of the Fed balance sheet should be carefully monitored to avoid asset prices crashes. In Europe, instead, the most evident issue concerns the effects that the end of QE will have on the sustainability of debt of southern countries, which have benefited the most from the public asset purchase program. Without the protection of the QE, changes in market expectations could increase again the spreads and in turn debt sustainability concerns.

References

Adrian, T., & Shin, H. S. (2010). The Changing Nature of Financial Intermediation and the Financial Crisis of 2007–2009. *Annual Review of Economics, 2*(1), 603–618.

Akerlof, G. (1970). The Market for “Lemons”: Quality Uncertainty and the Market Mechanism. *The Quarterly Journal of Economics, 84*(3), 488–500.

Alesina A., & Summers L. (1993). Central Bank Independence and Macroeconomic Performance: Some Comparative Evidence. *Journal of Money Credit and Banking, 25*(2), 151–162.

Allen, F., & Gale, D. (2000). Financial Contagion. *Journal of Political Economy, 108*(1), 1–33.

Altavilla, C., Giannone, D., & Lenza, M. (2016, September). The Financial and Macroeconomic Effects of the OMT Announcements. *International Journal of Central Banking.*

Andrade, P., Breckenfelder, J., De Fiore, F., Karadi, P., Tristani, O. (2016). The ECB’s Asset Purchase Programme: An Early Assessment (ECB Working Paper Series, No. 1956).

Barucca, P., Bardoscia, M., Caccioli, F., D’Errico, M., Visentin, G., Battiston, S., & Caldarelli, G. (2016). Network Valuation in Financial Systems. *Available at SSRN.*

Barigozzi, M., Conti, A. M., Luciani, M. (2014). Do Euro Area Countries Respond Asymmetrically to the Common Monetary Policy? *Oxford Bulletin of Economics and Statistics, 76*(5), 693–714.

Battiston, S., & Martinez-Jaramillo, S. (2018). Financial Networks and Stress Testing: Challenges and New Research Avenues for Systemic Risk Analysis and Financial Stability Implications. *Journal of Financial Stability, 35*, 6–16.

Bernanke, B. S. (2009). Reflections on a Year of Crisis. In *Speech at the Federal Reserve Bank of Kansas City's Annual Economic Symposium, Jackson Hole*. Wyoming.

Bernanke, B. S. (2010). Opening Remarks: The Economic Outlook and Monetary Policy. In *Proceedings-Economic Policy Symposium-Jackson Hole* (pp. 1–16). Federal Reserve Bank of Kansas City.

Bernanke, B., & Gertler, M. (1990). Financial Fragility and Economic Performance. *The Quarterly Journal of Economics, 105*(1), 87–114.

Blot, C., Creel, J., Hubert, P., Labondance, F., & Ragot, X. (2017). *Financial Stability and the ECB Sciences Po publications.*

Bordo, M., Eichengreen, B., Klingebiel, D., & Marinez-Peria, M. S. (2001). Is the Crisis Problem Growing More Severe? *Economic Policy, 32*, 53–75.

Borio, C., & Drehmann, M. (2009). *Assessing the Risk of Banking Crises—Revisited.* Bank of International Settlements: BIS quarterly review.

Borio, C., & White, W. (2004). Whither Monetary and Financial Stability? The Implications of Evolving Policy Regimes. *BIS Working Paper Series*, no. 147.

Borio, C., & Zabai, A. (2016). Unconventional Monetary Policies: A Re-appraisal (*BIS Working Paper Series*, No. 570).

Caballero, R., & Farhi, E. (2017). The Safety Trap. *The Review of Economic Studies, 85*(1), 223–274.

Caldentey, E. P. (2017). Quantitative Easing (QE), Changes in Global Liquidity, and Financial Instability. *International Journal of Political Economy, 46*(2), 91–112.

Cincotti, S., Raberto, M., & Teglio, A. (2010). Credit Money and Macroeconomic Instability in the Agent-Based Model and Simulator Eurace. *Economics: The Open-Access Open-Assessment E-Journal, 4*(26), 1–32.

Clouse, J., Henderson, D., Orphanides, A., Small, D. H., & Tinsley, P. A. (2003). Monetary Policy When the Nominal Short-Term Interest Rate Is Zero. *The B.E. Journal of Macroeconomics, 3*(1), 1–65.

De Santis, R. A. (2016). *Impact of the Asset Purchase Programme on Euro Area Government Bond Yields Using Market News* (ECB Working Paper Series, No. 1939).

Dell'Ariccia, G., Rabanal, P., & Sandri, D. (2018). Unconventional Monetary Policies in the Euro Area, Japan, and the United Kingdom. *Journal of Economic Perspectives, 32*(4), 147–172.

Demerzis, M., & Wolff, G. B. (2016). *What Impact Does the ECB's Quantitative Easing Policy Have on Bank Profitability?* (*Bruegel Policy Contribution*, No. 20).

Diamond, D. W., & Dybvig, P. H. (1983). Bank Runs, Deposit Insurance, and Liquidity. *Journal of Political Economy, 91*(3), 401–419.

Di Maggio, M., & Kacperczyk, M. (2017). The Unintended Consequences of the Zero Lower Bound Policy. *Journal of Financial Economics, 123*(1), 59–80.

Di Maggio, M., Kermani, A., & Palmer, C. (2016). How Quantitative Easing Works: Evidence on the Refinancing Channel (*National Bureau of Economic Research Working Papers*, No. 22638).

Falagiarda, M., & Reitz, S. (2015). Announcements of ECB Unconventional Programs: Implications for the Sovereign Spreads of Stressed Euro Area Countries. *Journal of International Money and Finance, 53,* 276–295.

Fisher, I. (1933). The Debt-Deflation Theory of Great Depressions. *Econometrica, 1,* 337–357.

Fratzscher, M., Lo Duca, M., & Straub, R. (2016). ECB Unconventional Monetary Policy: Market Impact and International Spillovers. *IMF Economic Review, 64*(1), 36–74.

Fratzscher, M., Lo, Duca M., & Straub, R. (2018). On the International Spillovers of US Quantitative Easing. *The Economic Journal, 128*(608), 330–367.

Freixas, X., Parigi, B. M., & Rochet, J. C. (2000). Systemic Risk, Interbank Relations, and Liquidity Provision by the Central Bank. *Journal of Money, Credit and Banking, 32*(3), 611–638.

Gaffard, J.-L. (2018). *Le débat de théorie et de politique monétaires revisité* (Sciences Po OFCE Working Paper, No. 39).

Gagnon, J., Raskin, M., Remache, J., & Sack, B. (2011). The Financial Market Effects of the Federal Reserve's Large-Scale Asset Purchases. *International Journal of central Banking, 7*(1), 3–43.

Gambacorta, L., Hofmann, B., Peersman, G. (2014). The Effectiveness of Unconventional Monetary Policy at the Zero Lower Bound: A Cross-Country Analysis. *Journal of Money, Credit and Banking, 46*(4), 615–642.

Guerini, M., Lamperti, F., & Mazzocchetti, A. (2018). Unconventional Monetary Policy: Between the Past and Future of Monetary Economics. *European Journal of Economics and Economic Policy, 15*(2), 122–131.

Gurley, J., & Shaw, E. (1955). Financial Aspects of Economic Development. *The American Economic, 45*(4), 515–538.

Haldane, A. G. (2013). Rethinking the Financial Network. In S. A. Jansen, E. Schörter, & N. Stehr (Eds.), *Fragile Stabilität - stabile Fragilität* (pp. 243–278).Wiesbaden: Springer Fachmedien Wiesbaden.

Ihrig, J., Klee, E., Li, C., Schulte, B., & Wei, M. (2018, March). Expectations About the Federal Reserve's Balance Sheet and the Term Structure of Interest Rates. *International Journal of Central Banking.*

Koijen, R. S., Koulisher, F., Nguyen, B., & Yogo, M. (2018). Quantitative Easing in the Euro Area: The Dynamics of Risk Exposures and the Impact on Asset Price (*Bank de France Working Papers,* Revised wp. 601).

Krishnamurthy, A., & Vissing-Jorgensen, A. (2011). The Effects of Quantitative Easing on Long-Term Interest Rates: Channels and Implication for Policies. *Brookings Papers on Economic Activity, 2,* 215–265.

Krishnamurthy, A., & Vissing-Jorgensen, A. (2013). The Ins and Outs of LSAPs, in: *Kansas City Federal Reserve Symposium on Global Dimensions of Unconventional Monetary Policy* (pp. 57–111).

Lo, A. (2017). *Adaptive Markets: Financial Evolution at the Speed of Thought.* Princeton and Oxford: Princeton University Press.

Lombardi, D., Siklos, P., & St. Amand, S. (2018). A Survey of the International Evidence and Lessons Learned About Unconventional Monetary Policies: Is a 'New Normal' in Our Future? *Journal of Economic Surveys, 32*(5), 1229–1256.

Mishra, P., Moriyama, K., & N'Diaye, P. (2014). *Impact of Fed Tapering Announcements on Emerging Markets* (IMF Working Paper No. 14/109).

Minsky, H. (1973). *The Financial Instability Hypothesis: An Alternative View* (Hyman P. Minsky Archive. Paper No. 355).

Minsky, H. (1986). *Stabilizing an Unstable Economy: A Twentieth Century Fund Report.* New Haven, CT and London: Yale University Press.

Neely, C. J. (2010). *The Large Scale Asset Purchases Had Large International Effects.* Research Division: Federal Reserve Bank of St. Louis.

Peersman, G. (2011). Macroeconomic Effects of Unconventional Monetary Policy in the Euro Area (*ECB Working Paper Series,* No. 1397).

Pozsar, Z., Adrian, T., Ashcraft, A. B., & Boesky, H. (2010). *Shadow Banking* (Federal Reserve Bank of New York Staff Reports, No. 458).

Swanson, E. T. (2017). *Measuring the Effects of Federal Reserve Forward Guidance and Asset Purchases on Financial Markets* (NBER Working Papers, No. 23311).

Stiglitz, J., & Weiss, A. (1981). Credit Rationing in Markets with Imperfect Information. *American Economic Review, 71*(3), 393–410.

Yu, E. (2016). Did Quantitative Easing Work? *Economic Insights, 1*(1), 5–13.

Time to Tidy Up EU Competition Law on Information Exchange Object Restriction Concerted Practices?

Mark Clough QC

Outline

In the beginning was "the word" and "the word" became "flesh", we are told the Evangelist Saint John wrote in his New Testament Gospel.[1] This article attempts to unravel the equally cryptic words "object and effect"

[1] John 1:1–18.

(1) In the beginning was the Word, and the Word was with God, and the Word was God. (2) He was in the beginning with God. (3) All things came into being through him, and without him not one thing came into being. What has come into being. (4) in him was life, and the life was the light of all people.

(5) The light shines in the darkness, and the darkness did not overcome it. (6) There was a man sent from God, whose name was John. (7) He came as a witness to testify to

The chapter is based on an article that was published in *Competition Law Insight*, Volume 17, Issue 6, June 2018 (www.competitionlawinsight.com).

M. Clough QC (✉)
Dentons Europe, Brussels, Belgium
e-mail: Mark.Clough@dentons.com

V. Vlachos and A. Bitzenis (eds.), *European Union*,
https://doi.org/10.1007/978-3-030-18103-1_4

in Article 101 TFEU[2] as they have been given life by Commission Guidelines and the decisions of the EU Courts. The discussion has to be seen against the background of the philosophical debate that still divides competition policy makers, if not competition lawyers and economists: the debate between the formalistic ordo-liberal interventionist approach and that of the effects-based economics approach developed over the last twenty years.[3] It concludes that new guidelines should be adopted by the Commission to restore legal certainty regarding the conditions to be met for an object infringement in the context of information exchange concerted practices, and to reconcile the apparent conflict between recent case law and past guidelines.

The purpose of this article is first to identify from the Commission Guidelines and recent case law the principles applicable to establishing when an information exchange between competitors constitutes an object restriction of competition under Article 101(1) TFEU, and in particular where the information exchange takes the form of a concerted practice. Second, it seeks to demonstrate from these principles that the apparent problem is one of a need for clarification because there is no fundamental contradiction between the guidelines and cases despite some apparent differences in emphasis as they all require a finding that the behaviour on a case-by-case basis is sufficiently harmful

the light, so that all might believe through him. (8) He himself was not the light, but he came to testify to the light. (9) The true light, which enlightens everyone, was coming into the world. (10) He was in the world, and the world came into being through him; yet the world did not know him. (11) He came to what was his own, and his own people did not accept him. (12) But to all who received him, who believed in his name, he gave power to become children of God. (13) who were born, not of blood or of the will of the flesh or of the will of man, but of God. (14) And the Word became flesh and lived among us, and we have seen his glory, the glory as of a father's only son, full of grace and truth.

(15) John testified to him and cried out, "This was he of whom I said, 'He who comes after me ranks ahead of me because he was before me.'" (16) From his fullness we have all received, grace upon grace. (17) The law indeed was given through Moses; grace and truth came through Jesus Christ. (18) No one has ever seen God. It is God the only Son.

[2] Consolidated version of the Treaty on the Functioning of the European Union (2012).

[3] See, the instructive history and discussion in "The EU Law of Competition", edited by Jonathan Faull, Ali Nikpay, and Deirdre Taylor, 1 March 2014, Part I General Principles, 3 Article 101, C Article 101(1), (7) The Notion of Restriction of Competition under EU Competition law, at paragraphs 3.160 to 3.183; as well as generally, (8) Restriction by Object, at paragraphs 3.184 to 3.218.

to competition by its nature that it will result in competition between undertakings being restricted, on the basis of an analysis of its legal and economic context including its contents and objectives. Third, it advocates that the Commission should amend the 2010 Horizontal Guidelines so that they are consistent with the *Cartes* Bancaires decision and related case law going further than the *T-Mobile* case.

Guidelines and Case Law

In Article 101 TFEU, the concepts of agreement, concerted practice and decision by an association all contemplate that an infringement may have either the object or effect of restricting competition. The Commission has published guidelines on the basis of the cases available at the time, which are cited, on object restrictions, concerted practices and horizontal information exchange between competitors. In particular, these include the 2004 "Commission Communication (Guidelines on application of Article 81(3), OJ C101/97, 27.4.2004), paras 20 to 23 on object restrictions" and the 2010 "Commission Communication (Guidelines on the applicability of Article 101 of the Treaty on the Functioning of the European Union to horizontal co-operation agreements ('Horizontal Guidelines'), OJ C11/1, 11.1.2011), paras 24 to 25 on object restrictions, 55 to 110 on information exchange" (see Annex below for extracts from Guidelines and case law).

The 2010 Horizontal Guidelines understandably borrow substantially from the EUCJ 2009 preliminary ruling in Case C-8/08, *T-Mobile Netherlands* [2009] ECR I-4529. However, in 2014, the EUCJ overturned on appeal the decision of the General Court in Case C-67/13P, *Groupement des Cartes Bancaires v Commission* [2014] ECR I-2204, where the General Court had upheld the Commission Decision on an object infringement effectively applying the principles laid down in the *T-Mobile* case without adopting the different language used for the object restriction test in some newer EUCJ cases, such as Case C-32/11, *Allianz Hungaria Biztozito and Others* [2013] ECR II-160. In particular, the EUCJ held that the General Court erred in law in paragraph 125 of its judgment by failing to refer to the settled case law set out in paragraphs 49 to 52 of the EUCJ judgment, citing paragraphs 34 to 36 of the *Allianz Hungaria* case, summarized as requiring a finding that such coordination reveals in itself a sufficient degree of harm to competition (paragraph 57).

The *Cartes Bancaires* case makes it clearer, therefore, that the object restriction test requires that the behaviour in question is sufficiently harmful to competition by its very nature that it will result in competition between undertakings being restricted: "the essential legal criterion for ascertaining whether coordination between undertakings involves such a restriction of competition 'by object' is the finding that such coordination reveals in itself a sufficient degree of harm to competition" (paragraph 57). Ironically, the outcome of applying this test is similar to the way the criteria were described in the 2004 Guidelines.

Paragraph 21 of the 2004 Commission Guidelines on Article 81(3) defines "Restrictions of competition by object as those that ...have such a high potential of negative effects on competition that it is unnecessary for the purposes of applying Article 81(1) to demonstrate any actual effects on the market".

This definition can be seen to be consistent with the later guidelines and case law of the EUCJ and not to exclude the consideration of effects on competition. The test set by the Commission does not require a demonstration of any actual effects on the market but does oblige the Commission to assess the agreement or practice sufficiently, given the economic context, to conclude that the economic effect (or restriction of competition) is so self-evident that it does not need to be established. It is a kind of chicken and egg situation, but in the context of the debate between ordo-liberal formalism and consumer welfare, favours the economic effects-based approach before any presumption can be made. Paragraph 22 of the Guidelines further explains that it may be necessary to examine the facts underlying the agreement and the specific circumstances in which it operates.

Paragraphs 26 to 31 of Case C-8/08, *T-Mobile Netherlands et al.*, 4 June 2009 summarize the criteria which the Court says it has already provided for establishing the existence of a concerted practice. For example, "close regard must be paid in particular to the objectives which it is intended to attain and to its economic and legal context" (paragraph 27).

Paragraph 29 makes it clear that "certain forms of collusion between undertakings may be regarded, by their very nature, as being injurious to the proper functioning of normal competition".

Paragraph 29 and its reference to object restrictions being harmful to competition "by their very nature" must be read as qualifying the suggestion in paragraph 31 that the object test is satisfied as long as the practice has the potential for a negative impact on competition.

However, the Court makes it clear in paragraph 31 itself, in its overview of the criteria for assessing a concerted practice in general, that a concerted practice must be shown to result in the restriction of competition to qualify as an object restriction: "In other words, the concerted practice must simply be capable in an individual case, having regards to the specific legal and economic context, of resulting in the prevention, restriction or distortion of competition within the common market". Paragraphs 32 to 35 deal with exchange of information, leading up to the answer to the Dutch Court's first question in paragraph 43. In paragraph 33, the Court appears to suggest that information exchanges may infringe competition law when they simply reduce uncertainty. However, in paragraph 35, the Court clarifies the test by concluding that "it follows that the exchange of information between competitors is liable to be incompatible with the competition rules if it reduces or removes the degree of uncertainty as to the operation of the market in question, with the result that competition between undertakings is restricted".

The language dealing with information exchange as an object infringement, therefore, makes it even clearer by requiring "the result that competition between undertakings is restricted". It can be seen that the T-Mobile decision recognizes the need to apply an effects-based test in the same way as the 2004 Guidelines.

The Apparent Problem

The main cause of uncertainty is the complexity of the concepts involved in establishing the conditions for the application of Article 101 TFEU to an object infringement consisting of the exchange of commercially sensitive information in the form of a concerted practice.

The EUCJ decisions require an impact on the market test for all three concepts to be satisfied. What is not so clear is how those concepts work together, and in particular how the market impact test of one removes the need to establish a market impact test for the others. The extracts of the guidelines and cases set out in the Annex below indicate that the test may be the same in so far as it consists of a condition to be met requiring that the behaviour in question will have a result of a restriction of competition on a case-by-case basis. In particular, to this extent object restrictions require an analysis of their effects on the market to establish that they are restrictions which are "by their very nature" injurious to competition.

The conflict arises from the EUCJ's implied criticism of the legal tests applied by the Court itself in the 2006 *T-Mobile* case, which was reflected in the European Commission's 2010 Horizontal Guidelines on object infringements and information exchange, when the EUCJ changed its position in its decision on the appeal from the General Court's decision in the 2014 *Cartes Bancaires* case.

The extracts from the Commission's Guidelines and the EUCJ case law in the Annex below demonstrate that the Commission understands the tests of the case law which are to be met to establish an object restriction as a concerted practice in the context of information exchange between competitors. In particular, the tests require an assessment of the restrictions to show that they have a high potential for negative effects on competition.

This test recognized in the 2004 Guidelines, and as discussed above, is consistent with the EUCJ case law including the *Cartes Bancaires* case. As will be illustrated in the next section, the language of paragraphs 49 to 52 and 57 of that case may differ from the wording of the Guidelines, but their effect is similar, with the consequence that is arguable that the problem centred on the *T-Mobile* case is merely apparent. It is also relevant to recall that there is no doctrine of precedence applicable to the judgments of the EUCJ in EU Law.

Potential Solutions from Recent Cases

A solution to the apparent problem, or the need to understand how the different concepts should be applied cumulatively, can be illustrated by the UK Competition Appeal Tribunal's judgment in the Balmoral Tanks Appeal[4] against the CMA's decision fining it for unlawfully exchanging commercially sensitive pricing information with its competitors by means of a concerted practice in the form of an object infringement. (The competitors were themselves found to be operating a price-fixing cartel regarding cylindrical galvanized steel tanks, in a separate decision.)

For example, as the CAT rehearsed in paragraphs 37 to 51, at the top of the conceptual hierarchy, a concerted practice requires a form of coordination between competitors which "knowingly substitutes practical

[4]Case No. 1277/1/12/17 (1) *Balmoral Tanks Limited* and (2) *Balmoral Group Holdings Limited v CMA* [2017] CAT 23, 6 October 2017, and in particular at paragraphs 40 and 119.

cooperation between them for the risks of competition" (see, Case 48/69, *ICI v Commission* [1972] ECT 70, paragraph 64). The EUCJ also held that in order to establish a concerted practice it was not enough to prove that the parties concerted together, there must also be conduct on the market pursuant to those collusive practices and a "relationship of cause and effect (see, Case C-92/99P, *Commission v Anic Partecipazioni* [1999] ECR 356 at paragraph 11)" (paragraph 40).

As the CAT held, the EUCJ case law on concerted practices in the context of information exchange establishes that "it is inherent in the concept of a concerted practice that the information exchanged has some effect on the subsequent conduct of the parties, even where the concerted practice is an object infringement so that there is no need to show any actual effect on competition" (paragraph 119). This condition for establishing a concerted practice must be sufficient to meet the similar test for an object infringement in the case law on object or effect.

However, there is a further complication. The CAT continues: "We also referred to the legal presumption that the information exchanged will affect the conduct on the market of the parties where they remain active suppliers following the exchange: see paragraph 40, above" (paragraph 119), which is already cited above.

This appears to mean that where the legal presumption is applicable, although rebuttable, it replaces any need to consider the effects on the market of the information exchange to show the result of a restriction of competition. The simplest conclusion is that the presumption can be applied without offending the principles of the Cartes Bancaires case applicable to object restrictions, because that case did not concern a concerted practice or information exchange. The presumption, therefore, can be a creature limited to the information exchange context.

Another case that illustrates a solution to the apparent problem, or which rather shows how the EUCJ principles following the Cartes Bancaires case should be applied in practice to an object infringement exchange of information in the form of a concerted practice, is the European Commission's decision on price signalling in "Container Shipping" of 7 July 2016.[5] In paragraphs 35 to 36, the Commission sets out similar principles to those above relied upon by the CAT for

[5] Commission Decision of 7 July 2016 relating to a proceeding under Article 101 of the Treaty on the Functioning of the European Union and Article 53 of the EEA Agreement, Case AT. 39850 Container Shipping, C(2016) 4215 final.

an information exchange as a concerted practice. In particular, the Commission found:

> Although in terms of Article 101(1) of the Treaty, the concept of a concerted practice requires not only concertation but also conduct on the market resulting from the concertation and having a causal connection with it, it may be presumed, subject to proof to the contrary, that undertakings taking part in such concertation and remaining active in the market will take account of the information exchanged with competitors in determining their own commercial conduct on the market, all the more so when the concertation occurs on a regular basis and over a long period. Such a concerted practice is caught by Article 101(1) of the Treaty, even in the absence of anti-competitive effects on the market ('restriction by object', see Section 3.3.4). (paragraph 36)

It came to the provisional conclusion (as it is a Commitments Decision, so not legally binding) that: "every party was in a position to take account of the information published in the GRI (General Rate Increases) announcements of the other parties when determining its own conduct on the market and therefore took part in the concerted practice by making GRI announcements itself" (paragraph 47).

In Section 3.3.4 on restriction of competition by object, the Commission applies the tests laid down by the EUCJ in the Cartes Bancaires[6] and Dole[7] cases:

> Certain types of coordination between undertakings reveal a sufficient degree of harm to competition that they may be considered a restriction of competition by object and that there is no need to examine their effects. To determine whether this is the case, regard must be had inter alia to:
>
> (a) its content,
> (b) the objectives it seeks to attain, and
> (c) the economic and legal context of which it forms part. (emphasis added, paragraph 48)

[6] Case C-67/13 P, *Groupement des cartes bancaires v Commission* [2014] ECR II 2204, paragraph 53.

[7] Case C-286/13 P, *Dole v European Commission* [2015] ECR II 184, paragraph 117.

The Commission continues to address the above three factors of the GRI information exchange in paragraphs 49 to 55, finding in particular in paragraph 50:

> The information disseminated by way of GRI announcements in this case includes the amount of the intended price increase, the intended implementation date and the geographic area concerned. In line with the case law of the Court of Justice, "*an exchange of information which is capable of removing uncertainty between participants as regards timing, extent and details of the modifications to be adopted by the undertakings concerned in their conduct on the market must be regarded as pursuing an anticompetitive object*".[8]

This approach of the Commission in the Liner Shipping Case is consistent with the Opinion of AG Wahl, followed by the EUCJ in the Cartes Bancaires Case, where he said that the concept of object restriction should be reserved for "conduct whose harmful nature is proven and easily identifiable, in the light of experience and economics".[9]

In his Opinion in the Intel Case,[10] AG Wahl suggests a parallel between the assessment of loyalty rebates under Article 102 TFEU and the assessment of restrictions of competition by object under Article 101(1) TFEU. In this context, he introduces a probability test by equating "capability" with "likelihood", and with the standard of proof being significantly beyond the mere balance of probabilities.[11]

He applies a similar two-step approach to loyalty rebates under Article 102 as to object restrictions under Article 101(1) TFEU, when he says with regard to the former: "the assessment of capability as concerns presumptively unlawful behaviour must be understood as seeking to ascertain that, having regard to all the circumstances, the behaviour in question does not just have ambivalent effects on the market..., but that

[8] Referencing the Dole case, paragraph 122; and see, Horizontal Guidelines 2010, paragraphs 73 and 74.

[9] Case C-67/13 P, *Groupement des Cartes Bancaires (CB) v European Commission* [2014] ECR I-1958, Opinion delivered on 27 March 2014.

[10] Case C-413 P, *Intel Corporation Inc v European Commission*, Opinion of AG Wahl, delivered on 20 October 2016.

[11] Ibid., paragraphs 114 to 119.

its presumed restrictive effects are in fact confirmed. Absent such a confirmation, a fully-fledged analysis has to be performed".[12]

The approach taken by AG Wahl to Article 102 TFEU in the Intel Case provides, therefore, another useful guide for the Commission to introduce into its own new guidelines on object restrictions, when he says: "in a somewhat similar fashion to the enforcement shortcut concerning restrictions by object under Article 101 TFEU, the assessment of all circumstances under Article 102 TFEU involves examining the context of the impugned conduct to ascertain whether it can be confirmed to have an anti-competitive effect. If any of the circumstances thus examined cast doubt on the anti-competitive nature of the behaviour, a more thorough effects analysis becomes necessary".[13]

Conclusion

In the light of the above analysis, it is suggested that the Liner Shipping Decision could form the basis of new guidelines on horizontal information exchange object restrictions in the form of a concerted practice.

Annex

Commission Guidelines

Commission Communication (Guidelines on application of Article 81(3), OJ C101/97, 27.4.2004), paras 20 to 23 on object restrictions

"20. The distinction between restrictions by object and restrictions by effect is important. Once it has been established that an agreement has as its object the restriction of competition, there is no need to take account of its concrete effects (25). In other words, for the purpose of applying Article 81(1) no actual anti-competitive effects need to be demonstrated where the agreement has a restriction of competition as its object. Article 81(3), on the other hand, does not distinguish between agreements that restrict competition by object and agreements that restrict competition by effect. Article 81(3) applies to all agreements that fulfil the four conditions contained therein (26)."

[12] Ibid., paragraph 120.

[13] Ibid., paragraph 135.

"(25) See e.g. Case C-49/92 P, Anic Partecipazioni, [1999] ECR I-4125, paragraph 99."

"21. Restrictions of competition by object are those that by their very nature have the potential of restricting competition. These are restrictions which in light of the objectives pursued by the Community competition rules have such a high potential of negative effects on competition that it is unnecessary for the purposes of applying Article 81(1) to demonstrate any actual effects on the market. This presumption is based on the serious nature of the restriction and on experience showing that restrictions of competition by object are likely to produce negative effects on the market and to jeopardise the objectives pursued by the Community competition rules. Restrictions by object such as price fixing and market sharing reduce output and raise prices, leading to a misallocation of resources, because goods and services demanded by customers are not produced. They also lead to a reduction in consumer welfare, because consumers have to pay higher prices for the goods and services in question."

"22. *The assessment of whether or not an agreement has as its object the restriction of competition is based on a number of factors. These factors include, in particular, the content of the agreement and the objective aims pursued by it. It may also be necessary to consider the context in which it is (to be) applied and the actual conduct and behaviour of the parties on the market (27). In other words, an examination of the facts underlying the agreement and the specific circumstances in which it operates may be required before it can be concluded whether a particular restriction constitutes a restriction of competition by object. The way in which an agreement is actually implemented may reveal a restriction by object even where the formal agreement does not contain an express provision to that effect. Evidence of subjective intent on the part of the parties to restrict competition is a relevant factor but not a necessary condition.* (rebuttable presumption not assumption)."

"(27) See Joined Cases 29/83 and 30/83, CRAM and Rheinzink, [1984] ECR 1679, paragraph 26, and Joined Cases 96/82 and others, ANSEAU-NAVEWA, [1983] ECR 3369, paragraphs 23 to 25."

"23. Non-exhaustive guidance on what constitutes restrictions by object can be found in Commission block exemption regulations, guidelines and notices. Restrictions that are black-listed in block exemptions or identified as hardcore restrictions in guidelines and notices are generally considered by the Commission to constitute restrictions by object. In the case of horizontal agreements restrictions of competition by object include price fixing, output limitation and sharing of markets and customers (28). As regards vertical agreements the category of restrictions by object includes, in particular, fixed and minimum resale price maintenance and restrictions providing absolute territorial protection, including restrictions on passive sales (29)."

"PRINCIPLES IN HORIZONTAL GUIDELINES OJ C11/1, 11.1.2011), PARAS 24 TO 25 ON OBJECT RESTRICTIONS, 55 TO 110 ON INFORMATION EXCHANGE, AND CASE LAW"

Object Restrictions

"24. Restrictions of competition *by object* are those that by their very nature have the potential to restrict competition within the meaning of Article 101(1) ([27]). It is not necessary to examine the actual or potential effects of an agreement on the market once its anti-competitive object has been established ([28])."

"([27]) See, for example, Case C-209/07, *BIDS*, [2008] ECR I-8637, paragraph 17."

"([28]) See, for example, Joined Cases C-501/06 P and others, *GlaxoSmithKline*, paragraph 55; Case C-209/07, *BIDS*, paragraph 16; Case C-8/08, *T-Mobile Netherlands*, ECR [2009] I-4529, paragraph 29 *et seq.*; Case C-7/95 P, *John Deere*, paragraph 77."

"25. According to the settled case-law of the Court of Justice of the European Union, in order to assess whether an agreement has an anti-competitive object, regard must be had to the content of the agreement, the objectives it seeks to attain, and the economic and legal context of which it forms part. In addition, although the parties' intention is not a necessary factor in determining whether an agreement has an anti-competitive object, the Commission may nevertheless take this aspect into account in its analysis ([29])."

"([29]) See, for example, Joined Cases C-501/06 P and others, *GlaxoSmithKline*, paragraph 58; Case C-209/07, *BIDS*, paragraphs 15 *et seq.*"

Concerted Practice

"form of coordination between undertakings by which, without it having been taken to the stage where an agreement properly so-called has been concluded, practical cooperation between them is knowingly substituted for the risks of competition": Case C-8/08, *T-Mobile Netherlands*, paras 23, 26, 33; Case 48/69, *ICI v Commission*, para 64; Woodpulp, Joined Cases C-89 et al., *Ahlstrom et al. v Commission*, para 63; and para 71: "parallel conduct cannot be regarded as furnishing proof of concertation unless concertation constitutes the only plausible explanation for such conduct". OECD Unilateral disclosure of Information and anti-competitive Effects, [2012] paras 12–13.

Horizontal Guidelines Information Exchange Concerted Practice, 60–63.

"61. This does not deprive companies of the right to adapt themselves intelligently to the existing or anticipated conduct of their competitors. It does, however, preclude any direct or indirect contact between competitors, the object or effect of which is to create conditions of competition which do not correspond to the normal competitive conditions of the market in question, regard being had to the nature of the products or services offered, the size and number of the undertakings, and the volume of the said market (44). This precludes any direct or indirect contact between competitors, the object or effect of which is to influence conduct on the market of an actual or potential competitor, or to disclose to such competitor the course of conduct which they themselves have decided to adopt or contemplate adopting on the market, thereby facilitating a collusive outcome on the market (45)."

"Hence, information exchange can constitute a concerted practice if it reduces strategic uncertainty (46) in the market thereby facilitating collusion, that is to say, if the data exchanged is strategic. Consequently, sharing of strategic data between competitors amounts to concertation, because it reduces the independence of competitors' conduct on the market and diminishes their incentives to compete."

"(44) Case C-7/95 P, *John Deere*, paragraph 87."

"(45) See Cases 40/73 and others, *Suiker Unie*, [1975] ECR 1663, paragraph 173 *et seq*."

"(46) Strategic uncertainty in the market arises as there is a variety of possible collusive outcomes available and because companies cannot perfectly observe past and current actions of their competitors and entrants."

"62. *A situation where only one undertaking discloses strategic information to its competitor(s) who accept(s) it can also constitute a concerted practice (47). Such disclosure could occur, for example, through contacts* via *mail, emails, phone calls, meetings etc.* It is then irrelevant whether only one undertaking unilaterally informs its competitors of its intended market behaviour, or whether all participating undertakings inform each other of the respective deliberations and intentions. When one undertaking alone reveals to its competitors strategic information concerning its future commercial policy, that reduces strategic uncertainty as to the future operation of the market for all the competitors involved and increases the risk of limiting competition and of collusive behaviour (48). *For example, mere attendance at a meeting (49) where a company discloses its pricing plans to its competitors is likely to be caught by Article 101, even in the absence of an explicit agreement to raise prices (50).*"

"*When a company receives strategic data from a competitor (be it in a meeting, by mail or electronically), it will be presumed to have accepted the information and adapted its market conduct accordingly unless it responds with a clear statement that it does not wish to receive such data* (51)."

"(47) See, for example, Joined Cases T-25/95 and others, *Cimenteries*, [2000] ECR II-491, paragraph 1849: '[…] the concept of concerted practice does in fact imply the existence of reciprocal contacts […]. That condition is met where one competitor discloses its future intentions or conduct on the market to another when the latter requests it or, at the very least, accepts it'."

"(48) See Opinion of Advocate General Kokott, Case C-8/08, *T-Mobile Netherlands*, [2009] ECR I-4529, paragraph 54."

"(49) See Case C-8/08, *T-Mobile Netherlands*, paragraph 59: 'Depending on the structure of the market, the possibility cannot be ruled out that a meeting on a single occasion between competitors, such as that in question in the main proceedings, may, in principle, constitute a sufficient basis for the participating undertakings to concert their market conduct and thus successfully substitute practical cooperation between them for competition and the risks that that entails.'"

"(50) See Joined Cases T-202/98 and others, *Tate & Lyle v Commission*, [2001] ECR II-2035, paragraph 54."

"(51) See Case C-199/92 P, *Hüls*, [1999] ECR I-4287, paragraph 162; Case C-49/92 P, *Anic Partezipazioni*, [1999] ECR I-4125, paragraph 12."

Information Exchange

"Each undertaking must determine independently the commercial policy it intends to adopt in the internal market: *T-Mobile*, para 32; Case 172/80, *Zuchner*, para 13; Case T-279/02, *Degussa*, para 132."

"Exchange of information 'which is capable of removing uncertainties between participants as regards timing, extent and details of the modifications to be adopted by the undertaking concerned must be regarded as pursuing an anti-competitive object.' *T-Mobile*, para 41."

"Horizontal Guidelines, paras 58, 77–85, and 86–94: consider whether (1) information is strategic; (2) the market coverage of the undertakings publishing the data; (3) the age of the data; (4) the frequency of the publication of the data; and the relevant market context."

"58. However, the exchange of market information may also lead to restrictions of competition in particular in situations *where it is liable to enable undertakings to be aware of market strategies of their competitors* (41). The competitive outcome of information exchange depends on the *characteristics of the market* in which it takes place (such as concentration, transparency, stability, symmetry, complexity etc.) as well as on the *type of information* that is exchanged, which may modify the relevant market environment towards one liable to coordination."

"*77–85, Market characteristics*: collusive outcome more likely in markets which are sufficiently transparent, concentrated, non-complex, stable and symmetric (77)."

"*86–94, Characteristics of the information exchange*: Strategic data reduces strategic uncertainty, market coverage, aggregated/ individualised, age, frequency, public/non-public and exchange."

HORIZONTAL GUIDELINES INFORMATION EXCHANGE OBJECT RESTRICTIONS, 72–74:

"72. Any information exchange with the objective of restricting competition on the market will be considered as a restriction of competition by object. *In assessing whether an information exchange constitutes a restriction of competition by object, the Commission will pay particular attention to the legal and economic context in which the information exchange takes place. To this end, the Commission will take into account whether the information exchange, by its very nature, may possibly lead to a restriction of competition.*"

Case Law

"Case C-8/08, T-Mobile Netherlands [2009] ECR I-4529"

"The first question"

"23 As a preliminary point, the definitions of 'agreement', 'decisions by associations of undertakings' and 'concerted practice' are intended, from a subjective point of view, to catch forms of collusion having the same nature which are distinguishable from each other only by their intensity and the forms in which they manifest themselves (see, to that effect, *Commission v Anic Partecipazioni*, paragraph 131)."

"24 It follows, as the Advocate General stated in essence at point 38 of her Opinion, that the criteria laid down in the Court's case-law for the purpose of determining whether conduct has as its object or effect the prevention, restriction or distortion of competition are applicable irrespective of whether the case entails an agreement, a decision or a concerted practice."

"25 In that regard, it should be noted that the Court has already provided a number of criteria on the basis of which it is possible to ascertain whether an agreement, decision or concerted practice is anti-competitive."

"26 With regard to the definition of a concerted practice, the Court has held that such a practice is a form of coordination between undertakings by which, without it having been taken to the stage where an agreement properly so-called has been concluded, practical cooperation between them is knowingly substituted for the risks of competition (see Joined Cases 40/73 to 48/73, 50/73, 54/73 to 56/73, 111/73, 113/73 and 114/73 *Suiker Unie and Others v Commission* [1975] ECR 1663, paragraph 26, and Joined Cases C-89/85, C-104/85, C-114/85, C-116/85, C-117/85 and C-125/85 to C-129/85 *Ahlström Osakeyhtiö and Others v Commission* [1993] ECR I-1307, paragraph 63)."

"27 With regard to the assessment as to whether a concerted practice is anti-competitive, close regard must be paid in particular to the objectives which it is intended to attain and to its economic and legal context (see, to that effect, Joined Cases 96/82 to 102/82, 104/82, 105/82, 108/82 and 110/82 *IAZ International Belgium and Others v Commission* [1983] ECR 3369, paragraph 25, and Case C-209/07 *Beef Industry Development Society and Barry Brothers* [2008] ECR I-0000, paragraphs 16 and 21). Moreover, while the intention of the parties is not an essential factor in determining whether a concerted practice is restrictive, there is nothing to prevent the Commission of the European Communities or the competent Community judicature from taking it into account (see, to that effect, *IAZ International Belgium and Others v Commission*, paragraphs 23 to 25)."

"28 As regards the distinction to be drawn between concerted practice having an anti-competitive object and those with anti-competitive effects, it must be borne in mind that an anti-competitive object and anti-competitive effects constitute not cumulative but alternative conditions in determining whether a practice falls within the prohibition in Article 81(1) EC. It has, since the judgment in Case 56/65 *LTM* [1966] ECR 235, 249, been settled case-law that the alternative nature of that requirement, indicated by the conjunction 'or', means that it is necessary, first, to consider the precise purpose of the concerted practice, in the economic context in which it is to be pursued. Where, however, an analysis of the terms of the concerted practice does not reveal the effect on competition to be sufficiently deleterious, its consequences should then be considered and, for it to be caught by the prohibition, it is necessary to find that those factors are present which establish that competition has in fact been prevented or restricted or distorted to an appreciable extent (see, to that effect, *Beef Industry Development Society and Barry Brothers*, paragraph 15)."

"29 Moreover, in deciding whether a concerted practice is prohibited by Article 81(1) EC, there is no need to take account of its actual effects once it is apparent that its object is to prevent, restrict or distort competition within the common market (see, to that effect, Joined

Cases 56/64 and 58/64 *Consten and Grundig v Commission* [1966] ECR 299, 342; Case C-105/04 P *Nederlandse Federatieve Vereniging voor de Groothandel op Elektrotechnisch Gebied v Commission* [2006] ECR I-8725, paragraph 125; and *Beef Industry Development Society and Barry Brothers*, paragraph 16). The distinction between 'infringements by object' and 'infringements by effect' arises from the fact that certain forms of collusion between undertakings can be regarded, by their very nature, as being injurious to the proper functioning of normal competition (*Beef Industry Development Society and Barry Brothers*, paragraph 17)."

"30 Accordingly, contrary to what the referring court claims, there is no need to consider the effects of a concerted practice where its anti-competitive object is established."

"31 With regard to the assessment as to whether a concerted practice, such as that at issue in the main proceedings, pursues an anti-competitive object, it should be noted, first, as pointed out by the Advocate General at point 46 of her Opinion, that in order for a concerted practice to be regarded as having an anti-competitive object, it is sufficient that it has the potential to have a negative impact on competition. In other words, the concerted practice must simply be capable in an individual case, having regard to the specific legal and economic context, of resulting in the prevention, restriction or distortion of competition within the common market. Whether and to what extent, in fact, such anti-competitive effects result can only be of relevance for determining the amount of any fine and assessing any claim for damages."

"32 Second, with regard to the exchange of information between competitors, it should be recalled that the criteria of coordination and cooperation necessary for determining the existence of a concerted practice are to be understood in the light of the notion inherent in the Treaty provisions on competition, according to which each economic operator must determine independently the policy which he intends to adopt on the common market (see *Suiker Unie and Others v Commission*, paragraph 173; Case 172/80 *Züchner* [1981] ECR 2021, paragraph 13; *Ahlström Osakeyhtiö and Others v Commission*, paragraph 63; and Case C-7/95 P *Deere v Commission* [1998] ECR I-3111, paragraph 86)."

"33 While it is correct to say that this requirement of independence does not deprive economic operators of the right to adapt themselves intelligently to the existing or anticipated conduct of their competitors, it does, none the less, strictly preclude any direct or indirect contact between such operators by which an undertaking may influence the conduct on the market of its actual or potential competitors or disclose to them its decisions or intentions concerning its own conduct on the market where the object or effect of such contact is to create conditions of competition which do not correspond to the normal conditions of the market in question, regard being had to the nature of the products or services offered, the size and number of the undertakings involved and the volume of that market (see, to that effect, *Suiker Unie and Others v Commission*, paragraph 174; *Züchner*, paragraph 14; and *Deere v Commission*, paragraph 87)."

"34 At paragraphs 88 et seq. of *Deere v Commission*, the Court therefore held that on a highly concentrated oligopolistic market, such as the market in the main proceedings, the exchange of information was such as to enable traders to know the market positions and strategies of their competitors and thus to impair appreciably the competition which exists between traders."

"35 It follows that the exchange of information between competitors is liable to be incompatible with the competition rules if it reduces or removes the degree of uncertainty as to the operation of the market in question, with the result that competition between undertakings is restricted (see *Deere v Commission*, paragraph 90, and Case C-194/99 P *Thyssen Stahl v Commission* [2003] ECR I-10821, paragraph 81)."

"36 Third, as to whether a concerted practice may be regarded as having an anti-competitive object even though there is no direct connection between that practice and consumer prices, it is not possible on the basis of the wording of Article 81(1) EC to conclude that only concerted practices which have a direct effect on the prices paid by end users are prohibited."

"37 On the contrary, it is apparent from Article 81(1)(a) EC that concerted practices may have an anti-competitive object if they 'directly or indirectly fix purchase or selling prices or any other trading conditions'. In the present case, as the Netherlands Government submitted in its written observations, as far as concerns postpaid subscriptions, the remuneration paid to dealers is evidently a decisive factor in fixing the price to be paid by the end user."

"38 In any event, as the Advocate General pointed out at point 58 of her Opinion, Article 81 EC, like the other competition rules of the Treaty, is designed to protect not only the immediate interests of individual competitors or consumers but also to protect the structure of the market and thus competition as such."

"39 Therefore, contrary to what the referring court would appear to believe, in order to find that a concerted practice has an anti-competitive object, there does not need to be a direct link between that practice and consumer prices."

"40 Fourth, as regards Vodafone's argument that the object of the concerted practice at issue in the main proceedings cannot be to restrict competition because standard dealer remunerations should, in any event, have been reduced as a result of market conditions, it is, admittedly, clear from paragraph 33 above that the requirement that economic operators should be free to act independently does not deprive them of the right to adapt themselves intelligently to the existing or anticipated conduct of their competitors."

"41 However, as the Advocate General observed at points 66 to 68 of her Opinion, while not all parallel conduct of competitors on the market can be traced to the fact that they have adopted a concerted action with an anti-competitive object, an exchange of information which is capable of removing uncertainties between participants as regards the timing, extent and details of the modifications to be adopted by the undertaking concerned must be regarded as pursuing an anti-competitive object, and that extends to situations, such as that in the present case, in which the modification relates to the reduction in the standard commission paid to dealers."

"42 It is for the referring court to determine whether, in the dispute in the main proceedings, the information exchanged at the meeting held on 13 June 2001 was capable of removing such uncertainties."

"43 In the light of all the foregoing considerations, the answer to the first question must be that a concerted practice pursues an anti-competitive object for the purpose of Article 81(1) EC where, according to its content and objectives and having regard to its legal and economic context, it is capable in an individual case of resulting in the prevention, restriction or distortion of competition within the common market. It is not necessary for there to be actual prevention, restriction or distortion of competition or a direct link between the concerted practice and consumer prices. An exchange of information between competitors is tainted with an anti-competitive object if the exchange is capable of removing uncertainties concerning the intended conduct of the participating undertakings."

"C-67/13P, Groupement des Cartes Bancaires v Commission [2014] ECR I-2204, 11 September 2014".

"49 In that regard, it is apparent from the Court's case-law that certain types of coordination between undertakings reveal a sufficient degree of harm to competition that it may be found that there is no need to examine their effects (see, to that effect, judgments in *LTM*, 56/65, EU:C:1966:38, paragraphs 359 and 360; *BIDS*, paragraph 15, and *Allianz Hungária Biztosító and Others*, C-32/11, EU:C:2013:160, paragraph 34 and the case-law cited)."

"50 That case-law arises from the fact that certain types of coordination between undertakings can be regarded, by their very nature, as being harmful to the proper functioning of normal competition (see, to that effect, in particular, judgment in *Allianz Hungária Biztosító and Others* (EU:C:2013:160) paragraph 35 and the case-law cited)."

"51 Consequently, it is established that certain collusive behaviour, such as that leading to horizontal price-fixing by cartels, may be considered so likely to have negative effects, in particular on the price, quantity or quality of the goods and services, that it may be considered redundant, for the purposes of applying Article 81(1) EC, to prove that they have actual effects on the market (see, to that effect, in particular, judgment in *Clair*, 123/83, EU:C:1985:33, paragraph 22). Experience shows that such behaviour leads to falls in production and price increases, resulting in poor allocation of resources to the detriment, in particular, of consumers."

"52 Where the analysis of a type of coordination between undertakings does not reveal a sufficient degree of harm to competition, the effects of the coordination should, on the other hand, be considered and, for it to be caught by the prohibition, it is necessary to find that factors are present which show that competition has in fact been prevented, restricted or distorted to an appreciable extent (judgment in Allianz Hungária

Biztosító and Others (EU:C:2013:160), paragraph 34 and the case-law cited)."

"53 According to the case-law of the Court, in order to determine whether an agreement between undertakings or a decision by an association of undertakings reveals a sufficient degree of harm to competition that it may be considered a restriction of competition 'by object' within the meaning of Article 81(1) EC, regard must be had to the content of its provisions, its objectives and the economic and legal context of which it forms a part. When determining that context, it is also necessary to take into consideration the nature of the goods or services affected, as well as the real conditions of the functioning and structure of the market or markets in question (see, to that effect, judgment in *Allianz Hungária Biztosító and Others* (EU:C:2013:160), paragraph 36 and the case-law cited)."

"54 In addition, although the parties' intention is not a necessary factor in determining whether an agreement between undertakings is restrictive, there is nothing prohibiting the competition authorities, the national courts or the Courts of the European Union from taking that factor into account (see judgment in *Allianz Hungária Biztosító and Others* (EU:C:2013:160), paragraph 37 and the case-law cited)."

"55 In the present case, it must be noted that, when the General Court defined in the judgment under appeal the relevant legal criteria to be taken into account in order to ascertain whether there was, in the present case, a restriction of competition by 'object' within the meaning of Article 81(1) EC, it reasoned as follows, in paragraphs 124 and 125 of that judgment:

- 124 According to the case-law, the types of agreement covered by Article 81(1)(a) to (e) EC do not constitute an exhaustive list of prohibited collusion and, accordingly, the concept of infringement by object should not be given a strict interpretation (see, to that effect, [judgment in *BIDS*], paragraphs 22 and 23).
- 125 In order to assess the anti-competitive nature of an agreement or a decision by an association of undertakings, regard must be had *inter alia* to the content of its provisions, its objectives and the economic and legal context of which it forms a part. In that regard, it is sufficient that the agreement or the decision of an association of undertakings has the potential to have a negative impact

on competition. In other words, the agreement or decision must simply be capable in the particular case, having regard to the specific legal and economic context, of preventing, restricting or distorting competition within the common market. It is not necessary for there to be actual prevention, restriction or distortion of competition or a direct link between [that agreement or decision] and consumer prices. In addition, although the parties' intention is not a necessary factor in determining whether an agreement is restrictive, there is nothing prohibiting the Commission or the Community judicature from taking it into account (see, to that effect, [judgments in *T-Mobile Netherlands and Others*, C-8/08, EU:C:2009:343], paragraphs 31, 39 and 43, and [*GlaxoSmithKline Services v Commission*, C-501/06 P, C-513/06 P, C-515/06 P and C-519/06 P, EU:C:2009:610] paragraph 58 and the case-law cited)."

"56 It must be held that, in so reasoning, the General Court in part failed to have regard to the case-law of the Court of Justice and, therefore, erred in law with regard to the definition of the relevant legal criteria in order to assess whether there was a restriction of competition by 'object' within the meaning of Article 81(1) EC."

"57 First, in paragraph 125 of the judgment under appeal, when the General Court defined the concept of the restriction of competition 'by object' within the meaning of that provision, it did not refer to the settled case-law of the Court of Justice mentioned in paragraphs 49 to 52 of the present judgment, thereby failing to have regard to the fact that the essential legal criterion for ascertaining whether coordination between undertakings involves such a restriction of competition 'by object' is the finding that such coordination reveals in itself a sufficient degree of harm to competition."

"58 Secondly, in the light of that case-law, the General Court erred in finding, in paragraph 124 of the judgment under appeal, and then in paragraph 146 of that judgment, that the concept of restriction of competition by 'object' must not be interpreted 'restrictively'. The concept of restriction of competition 'by object' can be applied only to certain types of coordination between undertakings which reveal a sufficient degree of harm to competition that it may be found that there is no need to examine their effects, otherwise the Commission would be exempted from the obligation to prove the actual effects on the market of agreements which are in no way established to be, by their very nature, harmful to the proper functioning of normal competition. The fact that the types of agreements covered by Article 81(1) EC do not constitute an exhaustive list of prohibited collusion is, in that regard, irrelevant."

References

Case No. 1277/1/12/17 (1) *Balmoral Tanks Limited* and (2) *Balmoral Group Holdings Limited v Competition and Markets Authority* [2017] CAT 23.

Communication from the Commission—Guidelines on the applicability of Article 101 of the Treaty on the Functioning of the European Union to horizontal co-operation agreements. Text with EEA relevance, OJ C11, 14.1.2011, p. 1–72.

Communication from the Commission—Notice—Guidelines on the application of Article 81(3) of the Treaty (Text with EEA relevance), OJ C101, 27.4.2004, p. 97–118.

Consolidated version of the Treaty on the Functioning of the European Union, OJ C326, 26.10.2012, p. 47–390.

Faull, J., Nikpay, A., & Deirdre, T. (2014). *The EU Law of Competition*. Oxford: Oxford University Press.

Judgment of the Court of 14 July 1972. *Imperial Chemical Industries Ltd. v Commission of the European Communities*. Case 48–69. ECLI identifier: ECLI:EU:C:1972:70.

Judgment of the Court (Sixth Chamber) of 8 July 1999. *Commission of the European Communities v Anic Partecipazioni SpA*. Appeal—Commission's Rules of Procedure—Procedure for the adoption of a decision by the College of Members of the Commission—Competition rules applicable to undertakings—Concepts of agreement and concerted practice—Responsibility of an undertaking for an infringement as a whole—Attachment of liability for the infringement—Fine. Case C-49/92 P. *European Court Reports 1999 I-04125*. ECLI identifier: ECLI:EU:C:1999:356.

Judgment of the Court (Third Chamber) of 4 June 2009. *T-Mobile Netherlands BV, KPN Mobile NV, Orange Nederland NV and Vodafone Libertel NV v Raad van bestuur van de Nederlandse Mededingingsautoriteit*. Reference for a preliminary ruling: College van Beroep voor het bedrijfsleven—Netherlands. Reference for a preliminary ruling—Article 81(1) EC—Concept of 'concerted practice'—Causal connection between concerted action and the market conduct of undertakings—Appraisal in accordance with the rules of national law—Whether a single meeting is sufficient or whether concerted action on a regular basis over a long period is necessary. Case C-8/08. *European Court Reports 2009 I-04529*. ECLI identifier: ECLI:EU:C:2009:343.

Judgment of the Court (First Chamber) of 14 March 2013. *Allianz Hungária Biztosító Zrt. and Others v Gazdasági Versenyhivatal.* Request for a preliminary ruling from the Magyar Köztársaság Legfelsőbb Bírósága. Competition—Article 101(1) TFEU—Application of similar national regulations—Jurisdiction of the Court—Bilateral agreements between an insurance company and car repairers relating to hourly repair charges—Charges paid depending on the number of insurance contracts concluded for the insurance company by those repairers in their capacity as brokers—Concept of 'agreement having as its object the restriction of competition'. Case C-32/11. *Digital reports (Court Reports—General).* ECLI identifier: ECLI:EU:C:2013:160.

Judgment of the Court (Third Chamber) of 11 September 2014. *Groupement des cartes bancaires (CB) v European Commission.* Appeal—Competition—Agreements, decisions and concerted practices—Article 81(1) EC—Payment cards system in France—Decision by an association of undertakings—Issuing market—Pricing measures applicable to 'new entrants'—Membership fee, mechanism for 'regulating the acquiring function' and 'dormant member "wake-up"' mechanism—Concept of restriction of competition 'by object'—Examination of the degree of harm to competition. Case C-67/13 P. *Digital reports (Court Reports—General).* ECLI identifier: ECLI:EU:C:2014:2204.

Judgment of the Court (Second Chamber) of 19 March 2015. *Dole Food Company, Inc. and Dole Fresh Fruit Europe v European Commission.* Appeals—Competition—Agreements, decisions and concerted practices—European banana market—Coordination in the setting of quotation prices—Obligation to state reasons—Belated statement of reasons—Belated submission of evidence—Rights of defence—Principle of equality of arms—Principles governing the establishment of the facts—Distortion of the facts—Assessment of the evidence—Market structure—Requirement for the Commission to specify those aspects of the exchange of information which constitute a restriction of competition by object—Burden of proof—Calculation of the fine—Whether sales made by subsidiaries not involved in the infringement are to be taken into account—Sales of the same bananas counted twice. Case C-286/13 P. *Digital reports* (*Court Reports—General*). ECLI identifier: ECLI:EU:C:2015:184.

Judgment of the Court (Grand Chamber) of 6 September 2017. *Intel Corp. v European Commission.* Appeal—Article 102 TFEU—Abuse of a dominant position—Loyalty rebates—Commission's jurisdiction—Regulation (EC) No 1/2003—Article 19. Case C-413/14 P. *Digital reports (Court Reports—General).* ECLI identifier: ECLI:EU:C:2017:632.

Summary of Commission Decision of 7 July 2016 relating to a proceeding under Article 101 of the Treaty on the Functioning of the European Union and Article 53 of the EEA Agreement (Case AT. 39850—Container Shipping) (notified under document C[2016] 4215). OJ C327, 6.9.2016, p. 4–6.

European Union Transport Policy

Post-crisis Challenges

Tania Pantazi and Vasileios Vlachos

Introduction

The European Union (EU) has emerged as an area of free movement of persons and goods between member states. The global financial and economic crisis (henceforth crisis) hit EU member states in the end of the previous decade and has affected since then all sectors of economic activities. This chapter gives an overview of the economic effects of the crisis in the transport sector and examines the response of the European legal order to the new challenges. The next section looks into macroeconomic indicators of the transportation and storage sector performance in the EU. The rest of the chapter is devoted to the objectives of the European transport policy as presented in recent official policy documents.

T. Pantazi (✉)
Hellenic Civil Aviation Authority, Thessaloniki, Greece

Aristotle University, Thessaloniki, Greece

V. Vlachos
Department of International and European Studies,
University of Macedonia, Thessaloniki, Greece

V. Vlachos and A. Bitzenis (eds.), *European Union*,
https://doi.org/10.1007/978-3-030-18103-1_5

Unlike other economic sectors, transport is an extremely complex field, where both public and private undertakings interfere for the provision of services that aim to the transportation of passengers and goods. Transport is very much dependent on infrastructure, since in all transport modes, it is impossible for carriers to pursue their economic activities without the existence of the appropriate facilities: roads, railways, airports and ports.

This chapter inevitably focuses on issues concerning the functioning of the internal market, which can stimulate or impede growth from an institutional and economic point of view. As recognized by the European Commission in the 2011 White Paper (2011a, p. 10) "obstacles to a smooth functioning and effective competition in the internal market persist. The objective for the next decade is to create a genuine single European transport area by eliminating all residual barriers between modes and national systems, easing the process of integration and facilitating the emergence of multinational and multimodal operators." In this regard, European policy in the field of transport infrastructure is not specifically examined in this chapter. Moreover, there are branches of transport modes, such as urban transport and short-haul national passenger transport, that remain entirely within the competence of the State or they are a public monopoly, in which the interference of European regulation is very limited: These issues will are not addressed in this chapter.

A short overview of EU's policy documents on transport reveals that the primary issue which preoccupies the European institution is the environmental impact of transport, particularly with regard to greenhouse gas emissions. The detailed examination of a European strategy and the legal framework on environmental protection in the field of transport falls outside the scope of this chapter. It should be acknowledged, though, that the principal objective of European policy is to enhance mobility that is sustainable, energy-efficient and respectful of the environment, a consideration that can be found underlying in most initiatives and in all transport modes.

Similarly, social issues such as working conditions, employment and gender equality in the field of transport will not be specifically addressed. With regard to consumer protection, however, it is noteworthy that the EU has introduced specialized rules for the protection of passengers in all transport modes: air, railway, coach and maritime transport. The EU aims at achieving a high level of consumer protection in the field of transport. Relevant legislation establishes common rules regarding the rights of the passenger in the event of delays and cancellations, such as the right to information, reimbursement, re-routing or compensation.

Finally, another general policy issue which should be mentioned before looking into the objectives of the European transport policy and rather falls within the notion of infrastructure is the "Trans-European Transport Network" program. The program aims at creating a transportation network that effectively connects the European continent, between East and West, North and South. For this reason, it has defined a number of trans-European "corridors" that include primary roads, railways, inland waterways, airports, seaports, inland ports and traffic management systems between specific points of the continent and has the intention to promote and fund a large number of projects (studies or works) cohesion, interconnection and interoperability of the network.[1]

An Overview of the EU Transportation and Storage Sector Performance

Information about the performance of the transportation and storage services sector can be found in Eurostat's Web site (Eurostat Statistics Explained). The statistics available from Eurostat focus on transport services provided to clients for hire and reward, and the information about the sector's performance is based on data for 2015. In particular, it is stated that the sector accounted for 7.9% of the total workforce and for 5.1% of the total number of enterprises in the EU in 2015. The discussion in this section presents information of the sector's performance over a 12-year span, before the crisis.

A considerable share of economic activity in the EU belongs to the services sector of transportation and storage. Data from Eurostat reveal that the total gross value added of transportation and storage in EU28 for the period 2005–2016, ranged between 4.6 and 4.9% of total NACE activities. The total size of transportation and storage in EU28 (in terms of gross value added) was the 8th (from larger to smaller) of the 21 sectors of NACE Rev. 2 (Eurostat 2008) in 2007 (the peak of 2005–2016 period) and the 9th in 2016 (most recent data available from Eurostat).

[1]For information about the EU transport infrastructure policy, the reader may refer to Ponti et al. (2013) and "The Pillars of the TEN-T policy" (available online at https://ec.europa.eu/transport/themes/infrastructure/ten-t-guidelines_en, accessed 15 January 2019).

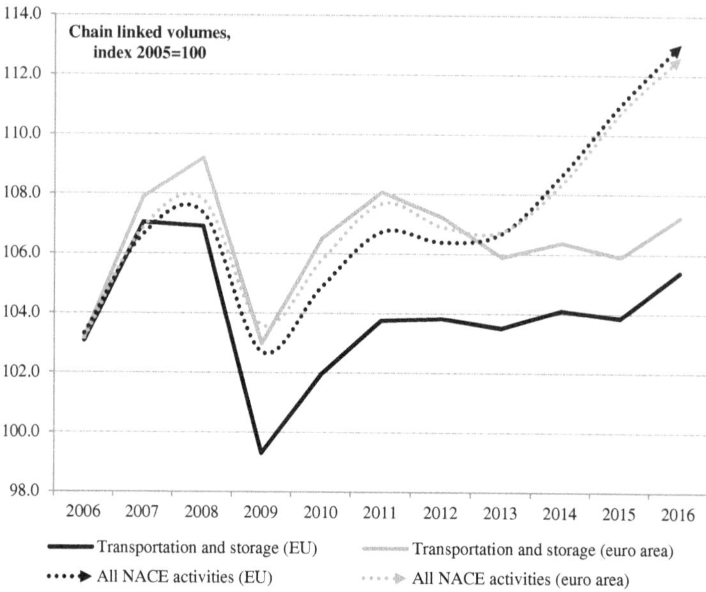

Fig. 1 Transportation and storage gross value added in the EU (*Source* Eurostat database. *Notes* [1] Chain linked volumes index calculated by authors with data on chain linked volumes [2005], million euro. [2] EU28 for all years. EA12 in 2005–2006, EA13 in 2007, EA15 in 2008, EA16 in 2009–2010, EA17 in 2011–2013, EA18 in 2014, EA19 in 2015–2016)

Figure 1 presents the changes of gross value added of the transportation and storage services sector and of all NACE activities in both EU and the euro area for the period 2005–2016 (2005 = 100). The euro area (whose composition is changing throughout the period in Fig. 1) and the EU (whose composition is fixed) data have similar trends and those of the euro area are less volatile. It can be assumed that the similarity of trends in data is an indication that a smaller EU (with less member states) data set would also have a similar trend. The EU and euro area data trends are also similar in the rest of figures in this chapter. For that reason, data for the euro area are not depicted henceforth.

Figure 1 indicates that gross value added of the EU transportation and storage services sector peaked in 2007, declined in 2008 and bottomed in 2009 as a result of the crisis. The sector did not reach the peak of 2007 but managed to recover a great part of the loss until 2016.

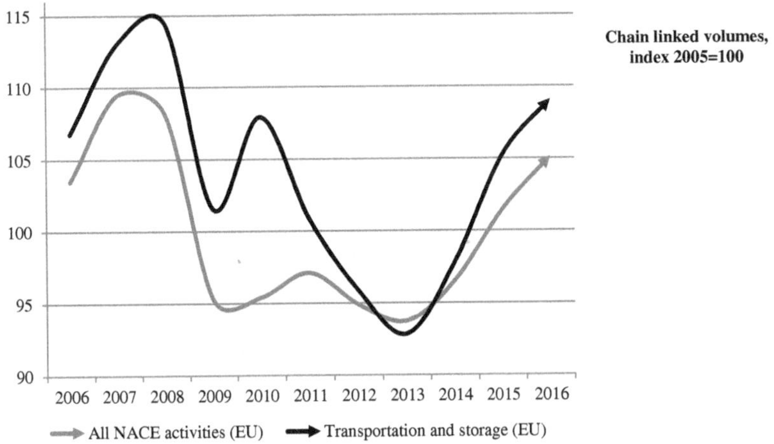

Fig. 2 Transportation and storage total fixed assets (gross) in the EU (*Source* Eurostat database. *Notes* [1] Chain linked volumes index calculated by authors with data on chain linked volumes [2005], million euro. [2] EU25 for all years. Data not available for Croatia, Cyprus and Poland)

Gross value added of all NACE activities in the EU peaked in 2008 and fully recovered the loss from the crisis in 2014. In addition, the trend of all NACE activities gross value added in the EU is more volatile than the respective of transportation and storage (also true for the euro area). The difference in data trends indicates that transportation and storage belongs to the group of sectors of NACE Rev. 2 which have not yet fully recovered from the crisis.

Figure 2 illustrates the change in fixed assets. The pace of recovery in investment, which has been very slow and has raised several concerns in the EU (see European Commission 2017a), gains extra importance under the consideration of the critical role of the transportation and storage services sector in the functioning of the internal market. Figure 2 shows that transportation and storage total fixed assets peaked in 2008, declined in 2009 and bottomed in 2013 and ultimately did not reach the pre-crisis peak until 2016. The trend in data on fixed assets of all NACE activities in the EU is similar, but peaks a year earlier and is less volatile nonetheless. The comparison indicates that (unlike the case of value added) transportation and storage belongs to the group of sectors of NACE Rev. 2 whose fixed assets have grown (and recovered

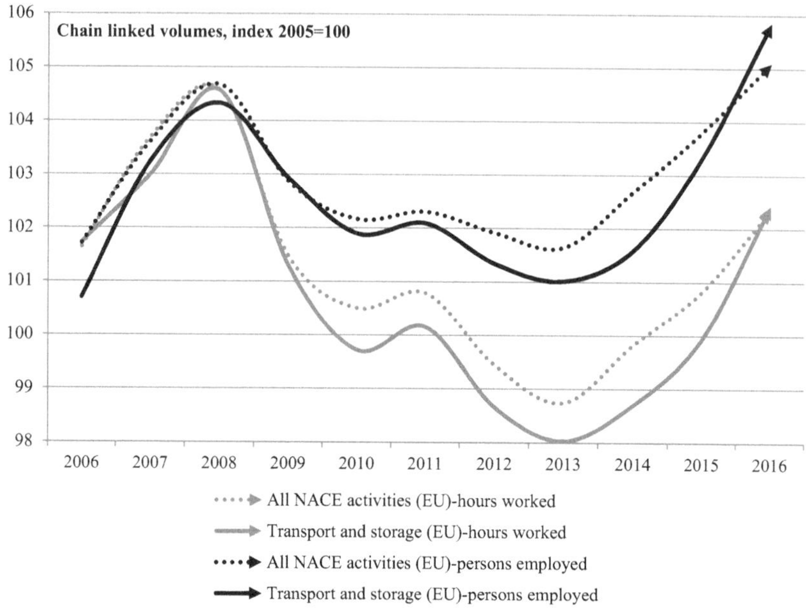

Fig. 3 Transportation and storage employment in the EU (*Source* Eurostat database. *Notes* [1] Chain linked volumes index calculated by authors with data on thousand hours worked and thousand persons employed [total employment domestic concept]. [2] EU28 for all years)

from the crisis) much faster than the average pace. A report published by the European Commission (2018a, p. 34) indicates that the increase in EU28 gross value added from 2008 to 2017 in the non-financial business sector has been 23% for large enterprises and 14.3% for small- and medium-sized enterprises. The transportation and storage services sector includes activities (e.g., postal services, air and rail transport services) which are dominated by very large enterprises. Eurostat data reveal that EU28 transportation and storage services sector gross value added in 2016 has been 54.6% for large enterprises. The performance of large enterprises may well have contributed to the above average growth rate of the sector's fixed assets.

Figure 3 presents employment in terms of hours worked and persons employed. Figure 3 indicates that the number of persons employed in transportation and storage in 2016 was well over the 2008 peak point.

The trend in data of all NACE activities in the EU is similar, and the comparison indicates that transportation and storage belongs to the group of sectors of NACE Rev. 2 whose employment rate has grown (and recovered from the crisis) faster than the average (in 2016). In contrast to the number of persons employed, the indicator of employment in terms of number of hours worked in Fig. 3 reveals that post-crisis recovery means jobs with fewer working hours (for both transportation and storage services sector and all NACE activities average).

Information about the performance of the transportation and storage services sector in Eurostat's Web site (Eurostat Statistics Explained) indicates that the wage-adjusted labor productivity ratio was almost equal to the average of the non-financial business economy in 2015. Figure 3 implies that labor productivity would be greater if measured in terms of hours worked. In addition, information in Eurostat's Web site (Eurostat Statistics Explained) indicates that the gross operating rate for the transportation and storage services sector was well above the non-financial business economy average in 2015.

Table 1 presents the main changes in gross value added and employment of the 5 divisions (subsectors) of EU transportation and storage services sector. The values in Table 1 refer to the following conditions:

a. the year before their decline due to the crisis,
b. the year that they reached their minimum and
c. the year with most recent data available from Eurostat.

Table 1 Gross value added and employment in the divisions of EU transportation and storage industry

	Gross value added (billion euro)			*Employment (million persons)*		
Subsector/year	*2007*	*2009*	*2016*	*2008*	*2013*	*2015*
Land transport and transport via pipelines	246.40	229.31	242.73	6.35	6.12	6.26
Water transport	40.31	39.62	31.28	0.27	0.26	0.26
Air transport	38.98	31.82	32.10	0.40	0.37	0.36
Warehousing and support activities for transportation	166.31	155.62	182.72	2.63	2.64	2.78
Postal and courier activities	55.79	51.36	47.95	1.85	1.75	1.74

Source Eurostat database

In value added terms, the largest subsector in the transportation and storage services sector is that of land transport and transport via pipelines, followed by warehousing and support activities for transportation. Both subsectors comprise approximately 80% of the sector's total gross value added. In terms of number of persons employed, the largest subsectors and their comprised percentage are the same, and postal and courier activities recorded a double-digit sectoral share in 2015. Equally in Table 1, only in the case of warehousing and support activities for transportation the values of condition "c" have been greater than those of "a." The recovery of the particular subsector in terms of number of persons employed has been driving the full recovery of the whole sector (see Fig. 3).

Information about the performance of the transportation and storage services sector in Eurostat's Web site (Eurostat Statistics Explained) indicates that also this subsector recorded the highest wage-adjusted labor productivity ratio among the transportation and storage services subsectors for which data are available in 2015 (data not available for water transport). It was followed by land transport and transport via pipelines, air transport, and postal and courier activities. In addition, tables in Eurostat's Web site (Eurostat Statistics Explained) indicate that the highest gross operating rate was recorded in 2015 by the warehousing and support activities for transportation. It was followed by land transport and transport via pipelines, water transport, postal and courier activities, and air transport.

A conclusion to the preceding discussion is that transportation and storage is an important sector of economic activity in the EU, which did not recover fully in terms of value added after 8 years from the eruption of the crisis. Nevertheless, the fact that the European economy experienced consecutive years of economic growth in the 2010s and the positive forecasts (from all major international organizations/institutions) for annual GDP growth over 1.5% until 2020, imply that the transportation and storage services sector will (like all other sectors) soon grow beyond pre-crisis levels of economic activity. An issue of concern is the yet uncertain impact of the UK leaving the EU on the sector's economic activity. Eurostat data reveal that the UK contributed 14.7% to the sector's total gross value added in 2016. In addition, the UK is one of the 4 EU members with the largest size of value added across all subsectors. As Brexit would be likely to affect the cost of transporting passengers and goods between the UK and the EU, the particular subsectors and the economic activity that they support would also be materially affected.[2]

Another issue is the impact of the global concern for climate change on the demand for new technologies, which are energy saving and reduce greenhouse gas emissions. If the economy and the transport sector change to this trajectory (e.g., electric vehicles), it seems probable that the additional market forces which will emerge will foster the technological change toward even more sustainable production and transport (e.g., see Rothengatter 2011). The strength of the market forces that foster technological change toward sustainable production and transport will also affect the subsectors of the transportation and storage services sector.

A final point is that the significance of the transportation and storage services sector should not only be discussed in terms of size of economic activity but also and most importantly in terms of investment in infrastructure required to support a minimum level of activity. The development of efficient, integrated and reliable logistics networks guarantee the smooth functioning of the internal market, and thereby, the full realization of the efficiency and competitiveness gains from integration. A report from the European Investment Bank published in 2016 indicates that the crisis has negatively affected transport infrastructure investment in Europe. It is estimated in this report that annual investment expenditure in transport and logistics infrastructure should double until 2020 to address the backlog and regain the historic investment levels of about 1% of GDP (European Investment Bank 2016, p. 30). The timeframe to achieve this target becomes unrealistic, as Eurostat data reveal that only 13 EU member states had increased the size of gross fixed capital formation in 2017 above their pre-crisis value (i.e., greater than the value of gross fixed capital formation recorded in the year before the member state was hit by the crisis). In addition, a recent report of the European Commission (2018b) indicates that the EU still suffers from low levels of investment in transport infrastructure and that quality and availability of transport infrastructure are particularly a problem for the eastern part of Europe.

[2]The reader may refer to the announcements of the European Commission about Brexit and the transport sector (see https://ec.europa.eu/transport/transport-modes/news/2017-12-11-brexit-notice-stakeholders_en, accessed 23 January 2019).

The Legal Grounds for EU Action in the Field of Transport

The functioning of the single market in the EU relies to a great deal on the application of the so-called four fundamental freedoms: the free movement of goods, the free movement of capital, the freedom of establishment and to provide services and the free movement of persons. It is evident that uniform regulation in the field of transport is crucial for the materialization of the fundamental rights granted to European citizens.

The provisions on a European common transport policy date back to the Treaty of Rome of 1957. These provisions have remained more or less unchanged, although EU policy and legislative intervention in the transport sector have evolved dramatically throughout the years. The principal instrument of the European legal order is currently the Treaty on the Functioning of the EU (TFEU), signed at Lisbon in 2007. Under Article 4 TFEU, transport is a sector of shared competence between the EU and the member states, along with other sectors of vital importance, such as the internal market, the environment, energy and consumer protection. This means that both the EU (on a supranational level) and the member states (on a national level) have the mandate to intervene in order to regulate the sector, as long as their actions can be justified by general European policies of by national exigencies (Colangelo et al. 2016, pp. 1–26).

Provisions on common transport policy are included in Articles 90–100 TFEU. In brief, the EU is authorized to introduce common rules on international transport between member states, on the conditions under which non-resident carriers may operate transport services within a member state and may establish measures to improve transport safety, as well as any other appropriate provisions. The Treaty also mentions state aid in the field of transport and prohibits discriminations of carriers with regard to country of origin. According to Article 100, par. 1, the rules of Articles 90–100 apply to transport by rail, road and inland waterway. Especially for air and sea transport, Article 100 par. 2 states that "The European Parliament and the Council, acting in accordance with the ordinary legislative procedure, may lay down appropriate provisions." The practical consequence is that, for EU action in the field of air and maritime transport, unanimity is not required and decisions may be taken by majority vote (Colangelo et al. 2016, pp. 1–26).

However, the majority of Treaty rules that have promoted advancements in the transport sector can rather be found in provisions outside those concerning the common transport policy, in the general rules of the Treaty on freedom to provide services and competition, as developed by the European Court of Justice throughout the years (see Colangelo et al. 2016, pp. 1–26; Kassim et al. 2010, part II for the air transport sector in particular).

The principal legal instruments for rulemaking in the European legal system are Directives and Regulations. Regulations are directly applicable to all national legal orders, while Directives require the introduction of implementing national law that clarifies its provisions. While in the early days the intervention of the Community in the transport sector took the form of Directives, in recent years it is observed that there is a shift toward the more binding choice of Regulation.

Apart from the binding legal instruments, information on EU's views and intentions can be derived from "soft law" documents, such as green and white papers, studies, legislative proposals and Commission communications. In the field of transport, white papers were adopted from the European Commission in 2001 and 2011, setting the main goals for future European policy and serving as preparatory work for legislative proposals.

Policy Issues for Each Transport Mode

Air Transport

Air transport is the only transport sector in the EU which has undergone full liberalization. The process took place in the early 1990s, after similar developments in the USA with the deregulation of the aviation market. Under Regulation 1008/2008 "on common rules for the operation of air services in the Community" (*OJ L 293, 31.10.2008*, p. 3) which constitutes the core legal instrument for the operation of air transport, European airlines enjoy freedom of establishment and freedom to provide passenger and freight air transport services in all national as well and international routes within the EU. The above-mentioned Regulation also establishes the rules for "public service obligation": Member states may subsidy certain routes between airports, provided that this service is considered vital for economic or social development of certain regions and that specific procedures are followed and supervised by the European institutions.

Following the establishment of the internal air transport market, prices have fallen dramatically, in particular on the most popular routes. The number of intra-EU routes between EU member states increased from 874 in 1992 to 3522 in 2015. This policy has led to more activity, new routes and airports, greater choice and lower prices to the benefit of consumers, airlines, airports and employees (Burghouwt et al. 2015; European Commission 2017b). The liberalization and deregulation of international air transport have fostered unprecedented competition within the EU market and globally. Global competition is expected to further intensify in coming years with projected international aviation growth of around 5% per year until 2030 (European Commission 2017b).

Under these circumstances, the attention of EU has shifted to other issues with regard to air transport. The most important problem to be envisaged by the authorities in the near future will probably be congestion; both major airports and airspace corridors are reaching their capacity limits. According to the European Commission (2018b), popular European airports are likely to face a capacity crunch in the next few years: Estimation shows that by 2035, there will be an additional annual demand of about two million flights, which European airports will be unable to accommodate due to capacity shortages. The countries forecasted to have the highest unaccommodated demand in 2035 are Benelux countries, Germany and the UK.

In order to mitigate airspace capacity problems, as well as high—in comparison with other markets—operational costs of Air Traffic Management services in Europe, in 1999 the EU introduced the project of "Single European Sky": a legislative initiative, the primary aim of which is to meet future capacity and safety needs. The initiative involves the separation of airspace into "functional blocks" and the coordination of Air Traffic Management service providers of the member states, under a European network coordinator. Full implementation of the Single European Sky is a constant challenge for the EU due to the resistance of many member states, particularly due to social concerns. Moreover, the Commission observes that the implementation of functional airspace blocks is still not satisfactory in most of the EU countries and there are ongoing infringement procedures against a large number of member states (European Commission 2018b). Functional airspace blocks should have been implemented by 2012, according to 2011 White Paper. It is argued that the removal of airspace fragmentation and full interoperability of the European ATM Network is vital for Europe to be united (Fox 2016). A more efficient Air Traffic Management system would also contribute to gas emissions reduction, which is the primary aim of the 2011 White Paper.

Increasing airport capacity, which would satisfy increased demand and stimulate further growth of air traffic, is another complex problem. Development of new airports in regions where existing infrastructure has reached its limits remains in general a matter of public policy. The right of an airline to use a busy airport for a particular period of time is called a "slot." In 1993, the EU introduced rules in order to ensure that slots in busy airports are allocated by independent government bodies in each member state and that airlines enjoy equal treatment when trying to access a congested airport. The European Commission has proposed amendments to the existing legal framework in order to improve capacity of congested airports (European Commission 2011b). However, this proposal is still pending for approval from the competent European institutions.

According to 2011 White Paper, one of the aims of the European transport policy is for the EU to become the world's safest region for aviation. In order to do so, the EU expressed its will to develop a comprehensive European aviation safety strategy, building on the work of the European Aviation Safety Agency (EASA). EASA, established is 2002, has become the EU's leading organization in the field of implementing uniform standards and monitoring national authorities of the member states in the field of aviation safety. To fulfill its purposes, the Agency has contributed to the development of an extensive legal framework for issues such as certification of aircraft and maintenance organizations, pilot licenses, aerodrome safety and Air Traffic Management.

Another issue currently envisaged by the European institutions that affects the functioning of the internal market in air transport sector is competition by third-country air carriers. As already said, in the EU all carriers are granted the same rights and same opportunity of accessing air transport-related services. However, European airlines are facing competition from some third-country carriers, which may be given competitive advantage by discriminatory practices and subsidies in their country of origin (Burghouwt et al. 2015). The EU has tried to protect the interests of European air carriers, launching a Regulation Proposal in 2017 "on safeguarding competition in air transport," after the failure of an earlier

Regulation to resolve the issue (European Commission 2017b). In brief, the proposal establishes a procedure for the Commission to investigate allegations for competition distortion by third-country air carriers and to impose redressive measures.

The environmental impact of aviation traffic is another topic which should be given special attention. Unlike other sectors, aviation emissions are forecast to increase dramatically as air traffic increases worldwide. CO_2 emissions have increased by about 80% between 1990 and 2014 and are forecast to grow by a further 44% between 2014 and 2035 (European Commission 2018b).

Rail Transport

Unlike air transport, rail transport sector in the EU has remained very much "public." The main reason for this is the fact that rail transport has traditionally been organized on a purely national basis, both from a regulatory and from a technical point of view (Knieps 2013; Colangelo et al. 2016, pp. 89–122). Since rail transport was historically the first mode of public transport to be developed, infrastructure as well as service providers were introduced and owned by the state. In 2015, two-thirds of all passenger rail services in the EU were still provided under public service contracts, with some member states (namely Denmark, Ireland, Greece, Croatia and Luxembourg) lacking any involvement of private sector in the field (European Commission 2018b). Coordination between national authorities and rail service providers of the member states has proved to be complex. Activity of the EU in this field has been limited until recently and a great deal of reforms is still in progress.

In the 2011 White Paper, the European Commission confirmed that the area where bottlenecks are still most evident is the internal market for rail services, which must be completed as a priority in order to achieve a single European railway area. This includes the abolishment of technical, administrative and legal obstacles which still impede entry to national railway markets. One of the goals of the 2011 White Paper was to "ensure effective and non-discriminatory access to rail infrastructure, including rail-related services, in particular through structural separation between infrastructure management and service provision" (European Commission 2011a, p. 11). However, in 2018 the European Commission finds that rail transport has been still struggling to achieve its potential, despite its comparative advantages (notably speed and comfort for passengers and economies of scale for freight) over medium to long distances and the significant contribution it can make to both the decarbonization of transport and socially inclusive mobility. The lack of effective competition may explain why in many EU countries rail transport has not developed customer-oriented services, innovative business models and costs/price reductions that can be witnessed after market opening in other transport modes (European Commission 2018b, p. 15). Indeed, opening of rail transport market in Sweden and UK in the early 1990s, without particular binding actions of the EU has proved to have very positive results (Ponti et al. 2013).

Directive 2012/34 (*OJ L 343, 14.12.2012*, p. 32) "establishing a single European railway" area brought about a number of important innovations. The Directive introduces the obligation of the member states to separate management of infrastructure from operational activities, i.e., transport services per se. Moreover, it has granted all railway undertakings who wish to perform international transport services within the EU the right to access railway infrastructure. Each member state should establish a national regulatory body for the railway sector, whose responsibilities will include the issuing of operating licenses to railway service providers and the monitoring of the railway sector (see Colangelo et al. 2016, pp. 89–122).

National and international freight transport has been fully open to competition since 2007. Similarly, operators have been granted open access rights to international passenger rail transport—including cabotage[3]—since 2010 (see Knieps 2013). The Fourth Railway Package of 2016 is a set of rules (Directives and Regulations) that aim to further harmonize technical oversight and interoperability of railway networks and place the conditions for market opening in domestic passenger transport services.[4] One of the issues addressed is also the conditions under which member states are permitted to subsidy railway undertakings and impose "public service obligations." As the European Commission notes (2018b), the opening of rail transport market is an objective currently pursued by several EU countries, in view of the obligations imposed by

[3]Cabotage is the transport of goods or passengers between two places in the same country by a transport operator from another country.

[4]The reader may refer for more information to the "Fourth railway package of 2016" (available online at https://ec.europa.eu/transport/modes/rail/packages/2013_en, accessed 15 January 2019).

European legislation. However, new commercial operators still face serious difficulties in entering the rail transport market and experience discriminations with regard to access to infrastructure and service facilities.

Road Transport

With regard to road transport, the most significant aspect for the EU seems to be its environmental impact. Transport in general is a major contributor to Europe's greenhouse gas emissions, second only to energy. Road transport alone is responsible for almost a fifth of EU emissions (European Commission 2017c). One of the primary goals for future transport policy defined in the 2011 White Paper was to reduce greenhouse gas emissions by 60% by 2050. In order to achieve this goal, a significant number of targets concerned road transport:

- the use of "conventionally-fuelled" cars in urban transport should be reduced by 50% until 2030 and gradually abolished by 2050, and
- 30% of road freight over 300 km should shift to other modes such as rail or waterborne transport by 2030, and more than 50% by 2050. It is recognized that appropriate infrastructure will be required in order to reach this target.

Between 2011 and 2018, a great number of initiatives were taken up for the reduction of the use of oil fuels, the promotion of environmentally friendly vehicles and the control of greenhouse emissions in general.

With regard to the functioning of the internal market in the road transport sector, the provision of international haulage services (i.e., the transport of goods between member states or between a member state and a third country) is practically open to competition. Relevant rules can be found in Regulation 1072/2009 on "common rules for access to the international road haulage market" (*OJ L 300, 14.11.2009*, p. 72), which also establishes the conditions for the issuing of a Community license or driver attestation for truck drivers to be permitted to work in the EU. Furthermore, Regulation 1071/2009 (*OJ L 300, 14.11.2009*, pp. 51–71) introduces common rules on admission to the occupation of road haulage operator or road passenger transport operator. Perhaps the most remarkable aspect of legislation on the provision of road freight transport services is the restriction of cabotage: Under Regulation

1072/2009, cabotage is permitted only as continuance of an international journey and for three operations within 7 days only. Rules of the "host" member state should apply. Improvement of the rules for cabotage could optimize road transport operations (European Commission 2018b) and minimize greenhouse gas emissions from road transport.

Passenger bus and coach services within the EU fall within the scope of Regulation 1073/2009 (*OJ L 300, 14.11.2009*, p. 88). Again, carriers are free to provide international services between member states or between a member state and a third country, provided that they meet the common standards described in the Regulation and they have issued a Community license. Here, too, the provision of passenger cabotage services is permitted, as with freight haulage, provided that cabotage is not the main aim of the transport service.

All three Regulations (1071–1073/2009) are under revision from the European institutions, with the proposals announced in 2017.[5] Particularly with regard to cabotage in road haulage, the new proposed rule is to permit unlimited cabotage operations within five days from the last unloading of an international journey.

According to a European Commission's study (2017d), road freight transport in the EU still had not fully recovered from the impact of the economic and financial crisis, but has shown signs of steady growth since 2012. National transport accounts for around two-thirds of total transport activity in the EU and is still predominantly carried out by domestic carriers. Finally, there is no measurable modal shift in the last 10 years examined, which means that the target of shifting to other transport modes is not yet accomplished.

Maritime Transport

The importance of maritime transport for Europe is evident: The supply of energy, food and commodities to and from the EU is in principal conducted by sea, as almost 90% of the EU's external freight trade is seaborne.[6]

[5] For more information, the reader may refer to "Europe on the move: A well-functioning internal market" (available online at https://ec.europa.eu/transport/modes/road/road-initiatives/well-functioning-internal-market-for-road-transport_en, accessed 15 January 2019).

[6] For more information, the reader may refer to "Mobility and Transport: Maritime" (available online at https://ec.europa.eu/transport/modes/maritime_en, accessed on 15 January 2019).

Since 1986, member state nationals, as well as ships registered in a member state and controlled by member state nationals, have the right to carry passengers or goods between ports of different member states, as well as between ports of the same member state or to a third country.[7] European rules also exist to protect EU carriers from unfair pricing practices of non-EU ship owners and from actions of non-EU countries that impede free access to the transport of liner cargoes, bulk cargoes or other cargoes (free access to ocean trades).[8] State aid in maritime transport is generally permitted, under guidelines of the European Commission.[9]

Port services are vital to the efficient operation of maritime transport. In general, port ownership and funding in the EU is complex, and the current situation is thought to present obstacles for the full exploitation of ports to the benefit of maritime transport operators and passengers (Colangelo et al. 2016, pp. 123–130). Most ports in Europe are under the control of the state or government-appointed authorities, and this seems to impede the enhancement of competition (Ponti et al. 2013). A recent Regulation introduces a new legal framework for the provision of port services.[10] The Regulation sets the minimum requirements for the provision of port services, with regard to safety and environment protection, introduces common rules on the transparency of public funding and of charging for the use of port infrastructure and services and also defines a new mechanism for complaint handling between stakeholders. Moreover, the "Blue Belt" initiative is a mechanism that aims to minimize port formalities and particularly customs controls for ships traveling between European ports.

The environmental dimension of maritime transport is another issue which has attracted the attention of European institutions: In the 2011 White Paper, the EU has stated as an objective that CO_2 emissions from maritime transport should be reduced by 40% (if feasible by 50%) by 2050 compared to 2005 levels (European Commission 2011a).

[7] Council Regulation (EEC) No. 4055/86, p. 1.

[8] Council Regulation (EEC) No. 4057/86, p. 14 and Council Regulation (EEC) No. 4058/86, p. 21.

[9] Commission Communication C (2004, p. 3).

[10] Regulation (EU) 2017/352, p. 1.

Concluding Remarks

Transport policy has been one of the EU's common policies since the establishment of the European Community. The EU has a coherent legal framework for action in the field of transport, based on the provisions of the Treaty, particularly with regard to international transport and elimination of discriminations against transport operators.

The vision of EU, as expressed in the White Paper of 2011 (European Commission 2011a), was to promote a "Single European Transport Area" until 2021. According to the Commission, this would mean the creation of a competitive transport system, the removal of barriers and the stimulation of growth and employment.

Progress in the transport sector has been remarkable, especially in the last decades, since many initiatives were taken toward development of networks and enhancement of competition. Nevertheless, barriers to the full growth of the transport sector still persist. Advancements have been diverse in the various transport modes. The air transport sector operates in circumstances of full liberalization, and competition has grown in the field to the benefit of consumers and operators. However, some issues, such as congestion in air corridors and in major airports, have not been successfully addressed. Rail transport, which is still predominantly under state control, has a potential not yet accomplished. Market opening is the primary aim currently pursued by the EU, and it is expected to bring positive results. The removal of some restrictions in the road transport sector could further enhance competition and growth. In the maritime sector, the internal market has been to a great extent established and improvements are needed in infrastructure.

Beyond the developments for the establishment of an internal market in the transport sector, the environmental impact of transport is an aspect to be taken into consideration for all future policy initiatives. The EU is working toward the development of a transport network which is sustainable, energy-efficient and respectful of the environment, and the reduction of oil dependency and greenhouse gas emissions is its primary objective in this respect.

EU transport faces growing competition from extra-EU transport markets and the realization of Brexit would be likely to affect the cost of transporting passengers and goods between the UK and the EU, and as such, the economic activity and competition of EU transport.

Another major challenge for European transport is the development of infrastructure. Even infrastructure quality across the EU guarantees the smooth functioning of the internal market, and thereby, the full realization of the efficiency and competitiveness gains from integration. Transport is very much dependent on infrastructure, and it is acknowledged that levels of investment in transport infrastructure have remained low since the outbreak of the crisis in the end of 2000s. Since EU still suffered from low levels of investment in transport infrastructure in 2018, the target of regaining the historic investment (expenditure in transport and logistics infrastructure) levels of about 1% of GDP by 2020 becomes unrealistic.

Finally, the transportation and storage sector is of vital importance in the EU, not only because it is indispensable for the functioning of the internal market, but also because of its contribution to the activity of the European economy. Although the sector (overall) did not reach its pre-crisis levels of economic activity (in terms of employment, investment and value added) in 2017, estimates and forecasts imply that all loss caused by the crisis will be fully recovered by 2019. However, forecasts are not optimistic for the pace of investment in transport infrastructure.

References

Burghouwt, G., Mendes de Leon, P., & De Wit, J. (2015). *EU Air Transport Liberalization: Process, Impacts and Future Considerations* (International Transport Forum Discussion Paper No. 2015-04). Paris: International Transport Forum/OECD.

Colangelo, M., & Zeno-Zencovich, V. (2016). *Introduction to European Union Transport Law* (2nd ed.). Rome: RomaTrE-Press.

Commission Communication C. (2004). 43—Community Guidelines on State Aid to Maritime Transport. *OJ C 13, 17.1.2004*, pp. 3–12.

Council Regulation (EEC) No. 4055/86 of 22 December 1986 Applying the Principle of Freedom to Provide Services to Maritime Transport Between Member States and Between Member States and Third Countries. *OJ L 378, 31.12.1986*, pp. 1–3.

Council Regulation (EEC) No. 4057/86 of 22 December 1986 on Unfair Pricing Practices in Maritime Transport. *OJ L 378, 31.12.1986*, pp. 14–20.

Council Regulation (EEC) No. 4058/86 of 22 December 1986 Concerning Coordinated Action to Safeguard Free Access to Cargoes in Ocean Trades. *OJ L 378, 31.12.1986*, pp. 21–23.

Directive 2012/34/EU of the European Parliament and of the Council of 21 November 2012 Establishing a Single European Railway Area Text with EEA Relevance. *OJ L 343, 14.12.2012*, pp. 32–77.

European Commission. (2011a). *White Paper Roadmap to a Single European Transport Area—Towards a Competitive and Resource Efficient Transport System*. COM/2011/0144 Final. Available Online at https://eur-lex.europa.eu/legal-content/EN/ALL/?uri=CELEX:52011DC0144. Accessed 20 January 2019.

European Commission. (2011b). *Proposal for a Regulation of the European Parliament and of the Council on Common Rules for the Allocation of Slots at European Union Airports*. COM/2011/0827 Final—2011/0391 (COD). Available Online at https://eur-lex.europa.eu/legal-content/EN/TXT/?uri=CELEX%3A52011PC0827. Accessed 20 January 2019.

European Commission. (2017a). *Investment in the EU Member States: An Analysis of Drivers and Barriers* (European Economy Institutional Paper No. 62). Luxembourg: Publications Office of the European Union.

European Commission. (2017b). *Proposal for a Regulation of the European Parliament and of the Council on Safeguarding Competition in Air Transport* (Repealing Regulation (EC) No. 868/2004). COM/2017/0289 Final—2017/0116 (COD). Available Online at https://eur-lex.europa.eu/legal-content/EN/TXT/?uri=CELEX%3A52017PC0289. Accessed 20 January 2019.

European Commission. (2017c). *Communication from the Commission to the European Parliament, the Council, the European Economic and Social Committee and the Committee of the Regions Europe on the Move an Agenda for a Socially Fair Transition Towards Clean, Competitive and Connected Mobility for All*. COM/2017/0283 Final. Available Online at https://eur-lex.europa.eu/legal-content/EN/TXT/?uri=CELEX%3A52011PC0827. Accessed 20 January 2019.

European Commission. (2017d). *An Overview of the EU Road Transport Market in 2015*. Brussels: European Commission, Directorate-General Mobility and Transport.

European Commission. (2018a). *Annual Report on European SMEs 2017/2018: SMEs Growing Beyond Borders*. Luxembourg: Publications Office of the European Union.

European Commission. (2018b). *Transport in the European Union—Current Trends and Issues*. Brussels: European Commission, Directorate-General Mobility and Transport.

European Investment Bank. (2016). *Restoring EU Competitiveness*. 2016 Updated Version. Available Online at http://www.eib.org/attachments/efs/restoring_eu_competitiveness_en.pdf. Accessed 15 January 2019.

Eurostat. (2008). *NACE Rev. 2: Statistical Classification of Economic Activities in the European Community*. Luxembourg: Office for Official Publications of the European Communities.

Eurostat. (n.d.). *Eurostat Database*. Available Online at https://ec.europa.eu/eurostat/data/database. Accessed 10 January 2019.

Eurostat Statistics Explained. *Transportation and Storage Statistics—NACE Rev. 2*. Available Online at https://ec.europa.eu/eurostat/statistics-explained/index.php/Transportation_and_storage_statistics_-_NACE_Rev._2#Size_class_analysis. Accessed 15 January 2019.

Fox, S. J. (2016). Single European Skies: Functional Airspace Blocks—Delays and Responses. *Air & Space Law, 41*(3), 201–228.

Kassim, H., & Stevens, H. (2010). *Air Transport and the European Union: Europeanization and Its Limits*. Basingstoke: Palgrave Macmillan.

Knieps, G. (2013). Competition and the Railroads: A European Perspective. *Journal of Competition Law & Economics, 9*(1), 153–169.

Ponti, M., Boitani, A., & Ramella, F. (2013). The European Transport Policy: Its Main Issues. *Case Studies on Transport Policy, 1*(1–2), 53–62.

Regulation (EC) No. 1008/2008 of the European Parliament and of the Council of 24 September 2008 on Common Rules for the Operation of Air Services in the Community (Recast) (Text with EEA Relevance). *OJ L 293, 31.10.2008*, pp. 3–20.

Regulation (EC) No. 1071/2009 of the European Parliament and of the Council of 21 October 2009 Establishing Common Rules Concerning the Conditions to Be Complied with to Pursue the Occupation of Road Transport Operator and Repealing Council Directive 96/26/EC (Text with EEA Relevance). *OJ L 300, 14.11.2009*, pp. 51–71.

Regulation (EC) No. 1072/2009 of the European Parliament and of the Council of 21 October 2009 on Common Rules for Access to the International Road Haulage Market (Text with EEA Relevance). *OJ L 300, 14.11.2009*, pp. 72–87.

Regulation (EC) No. 1073/2009 of the European Parliament and of the Council of 21 October 2009 on Common Rules for Access to the International Market for Coach and Bus Services, and Amending Regulation (EC) No. 561/2006 (Text with EEA Relevance). *OJ L 300, 14.11.2009*, pp. 88–105.

Regulation (EU) 2017/352 of the European Parliament and of the Council of 15 February 2017 Establishing a Framework for the Provision of Port Services and Common Rules on the Financial Transparency of Ports (Text with EEA Relevance). *OJ L 57, 3.3.2017*, pp. 1–18.

Rothengatter, W. (2011). Economic Crisis and Consequences for the Transport Sector. In W. Rothengatter, Y. Hayashi, & W. Schade (Eds.), *Transport Moving to Climate Intelligence*. New York, NY: Springer.

Size of the Shadow Economies of 28 European Union Countries from 2003 to 2018

The Latest Development

Friedrich Schneider

Introduction

Fighting (reducing) the shadow economy or tax evasions have been important policy goals all over the world for a long time. In light of the last financial and worldwide economic crises, governments are in even greater need to achieve this goal as they have to bring back macroeconomic stability. However, doing so requires profound knowledge about the size and development of the shadow economy. Hence, in this short paper, some remarks about the estimation methods are made and the latest results about the size and development of the 28 European shadow economies are presented.[1]

[1] The calculation of the size and development of the shadow economy is done with the Multiple Indicators and Multiple Causes (MIMIC) estimation procedure. For a detailed

F. Schneider (✉)
Johannes Kepler University, Linz, Austria
e-mail: friedrich.schneider@jku.at

V. Vlachos and A. Bitzenis (eds.), *European Union*,
https://doi.org/10.1007/978-3-030-18103-1_6

Econometric Methodology and Estimation Procedure

Definition of the Shadow Economy

To define the shadow economy in a common way is a difficult task, because it is done in many different ways, but the most common definition is the following[2]: The shadow economy includes all legal production and provision of goods and services that are deliberately concealed from public authorities for the following four reasons:

1. To avoid payment of income, value-added, or other taxes,
2. To avoid payment of social security contributions,
3. To avoid having to meet certain legal standards such as minimum wages, maximum working hours, safety standards, etc., and
4. To avoid complying with certain administrative procedures, such as completing statistical questionnaires or other administrative forms.

Hence, the shadow economy is something different from the traditional underground (classical crime) economy and the informal household economy:

i. *Underground (classical crime)* activities are all *illegal actions* that fit the characteristics of classical crime activities like burglary, smuggling, drug dealing, etc.
ii. *Informal household and do-it-yourself activities* are household actions that are not registered officially under various specific forms of national legislation, this includes neighbors, or friends help, too.
iii. *These two sectors* ([i] classical crime and [ii] household production) *are not included* in the shadow economy activities. However, there are overlapping areas (e.g., for [i] prostitution and for [ii] do-it-yourself activities).

explanation of these calculation methods, see Schneider (2011), Schneider and Williams (2013), Williams and Schneider (2016), and Medina and Schneider (2018).

[2] This is the most used definition, for references see footnote 1.

Methods to Estimate the Size of the Shadow Economy

Estimating the size of a shadow economy is a difficult and challenging task. Only a sketch of the various procedures for estimating the size of a shadow economy is provided here. For a detailed discussion, see Williams and Schneider (2016) and Medina and Schneider (2018). Three different categories of measurement methods are most widely used and each is briefly discussed. All references can be found in Williams and Schneider (2016) and Medina and Schneider (2018).

Direct Approaches

These are microeconomic approaches that either employ well-designed surveys and samples based on voluntary replies, or tax auditing and other compliance methods. Sample surveys designed to estimate the shadow economy are widely used. The main disadvantages of this method are the flaws inherent in all surveys. For example, the average precision and results depend greatly on the respondent's willingness to cooperate, it is difficult to assess the amount of undeclared work from a direct questionnaire, most interviewees hesitate to confess to fraudulent behavior, and responses are of uncertain reliability.

Indirect Approaches

These approaches, which are also called indicator approaches, are mostly macroeconomic and use various economic and other indicators that contain information about the development of the shadow economy over time. Relating them to the definition of the shadow economy, they provide value added figures. In most cases, legally bought material is often included; hence, they provide upper-bound estimates with the danger of a double counting problem due to the inclusion of the legally bought material. Therefore, a wide (broad) definition of the shadow economy is applied, especially as some criminal activities like human trafficking are also included. Currently, five indicators leave some traces of the shadow economy.

1. *The discrepancy between national expenditure and income statistics*: This approach is based on discrepancies between income and expenditure statistics. In national accounting, the income measure of GNP should be equal to the expenditure measure of GNP.

Thus, if an independent estimate of the expenditure side of the national accounts is available, the gap between the expenditure measure and the income measure can be used as an indicator of the extent of the shadow economy.

2. *The discrepancy between the official and actual labor force*:
   A decline in participation in the labor force in the official economy can be seen as an indication of increased activity in the shadow economy. If total labor force participation is assumed constant, then a decreasing official rate of participation can be seen as an indicator of increased shadow economic activities, ceteris paribus.
3. *The transactions approach*:
   This approach has been fully developed by Feige (1979). It is based on the assumption that there is a constant relation over time between the volume of transactions and official GNP, as summarized by the well-known Fisher quantity equation or $M^* V = p^* T$ (with M money, V velocity, p prices, and T total transactions). Assumptions also have to be made about the velocity of money and about the relationships between the total value of transactions $p^* T$ and total (official + unofficial) nominal GNP. Relating total nominal GNP to total transactions, the GNP of the shadow economy can be calculated by subtracting official GNP from total nominal GNP.
4. *The currency demand approach*:
   Tanzi, who econometrically estimated a currency demand function for the USA for the period 1929–1980 in order to calculate the size of the shadow economy, first developed the currency demand approach. His approach assumes that shadow (or hidden) transactions are undertaken in the form of cash payments so as to leave no observable traces for the authorities. An increase in the size of the shadow economy will therefore increase the demand for currency. To isolate the resulting excess demand for currency, an equation for currency demand is estimated over time. All possible conventional factors, such as the development of income, payment habits, interest rates, credit, and other debit cards as a substitute for cash and so on, are controlled for. Additionally, variables such as direct and indirect tax burdens, government regulation, etc., which are assumed to be major factors causing people to work in the shadow economy, are included in the estimation equation.

5. *The physical input (electricity consumption) method*:
   i. *The Kaufmann–Kaliberda Method*:
   To measure overall (official and unofficial) economic activity in an economy, Kaufmann and Kaliberda (1996) assume that electric power consumption is regarded as the single best physical indicator of overall (or official plus unofficial) economic activity. Overall, economic activity and electricity consumption have been empirically observed throughout the world to move in lockstep with an electricity-to-GDP elasticity usually close to one. This means that the growth of total electricity consumption is an indicator for growth of overall (official and unofficial) GDP. By having this proxy measurement for the overall economy and then subtracting from this overall measure the estimates of official GDP, Kaufmann and Kaliberda (1996) derive an estimate of unofficial GDP.
   iii. *The Lackó method*:
   Lackó (1998, 1999) assumes that a certain part of the shadow economy is associated with the household consumption of electricity. This part comprises so-called household production, do-it-yourself activities, and other non-registered production and services. Lackó further assumes that in countries where the portion of the shadow economy associated with household electricity consumption is high, the rest of the hidden economy (or the part Lackó cannot measure) will also be high. Lackó (1998) assumes that in each country a part of the household consumption of electricity is used in the shadow economy.
6. *The MIMIC Approach*:
   The Multiple Indicators and Multiple Causes (MIMIC) approach is based on the idea that the shadow economy is not a directly observable figure. However, it is possible to approximate it using quantitatively measurable causes of working in the underground economy (such as the tax burden and amount of regulation) and using indicators (such as cash, official working hours, etc.), in which shadow economic activities are reflected. As the MIMIC method only enables relative orders of magnitude of the underground economy of individual countries to be calculated, some values that were calculated with the help of the cash approach are necessary to convert the shadow economy quantities into absolute values (in percentage of official GDP or in billions of Euros).

Final Remarks

There is a long and controversial discussion with estimation method is the most appropriate one. Up to day no conclusion is reached, all estimation methods have their strengths and weaknesses. The best strategy is to use several and compare the results, if possible. In this paper estimations using the MIMIC method are presented, one reliable but also criticized macromethod; for the strengths and weaknesses, see Medina and Schneider (2018).

Results

In Table 1, the size and development of 28 European shadow economies over the period 2003–2018 are presented. First, as an example of a large European economy the results for France are presented: In 2003, the French shadow economy was 14.7% of official GDP; it declined continuously to 9.9% of the official GDP up to 2013 (except for 2009, where an increase of 0.5 percentage points took place due to the world economic crises). From 2014 up to 2017, the French shadow economy increased again from 10.8% to 12.8% of official GDP, the reasons where missing economic reforms in France and low increase of the GDP in the official economy. For this year (2018) and for the first time since 2013, a decrease of 0.5 percentage points is forecasted due to the attempts of undertaking major economic reforms in France.

Second if one considers the results of the average size of the shadow economy of the 28 European Union countries (presented in Table 1), one realizes that the shadow economy in the year 2003 was 22.6% (of official GDP), which decreased to 19.6% in 2008 and increased to 20.1% in 2009 and then decreased again to 16.8% in 2018.[3] With respect to a decrease or increase in 2018, the development of the shadow economy in the individual countries will again not be uniform. In most EU-countries (23 out of 28), the shadow economy will further decrease but in the remaining 5 countries it will increase. The 23 EU-countries where the shadow economy will further

[3]The calculated values for 2017 are projections for some countries, for 2018 they are projections for all countries, based on the forecasts of the official figures (GDP, unemployment, etc.) of these countries.

Table 1 Size of the shadow economy of the 28 EU-countries over 2003–2018 (in % of official GDP)

Country/year	*2003*	*2004*	*2005*	*2006*	*2007*	*2008*	*2009*	*2010*	*2011*	*2012*	*2013*	*2014*	*2015*	*2016*	*2017*	*2018*
Austria	10.8	11.0	10.3	9.7	9.4	8.1	8.5	8.2	7.9	7.6	7.5	7.8	8.2	7.8	7.1	6.72
Belgium	21.4	20.7	20.1	19.2	18.3	17.5	17.8	17.4	17.1	16.8	16.4	16.1	16.2	16.1	15.6	15.42
Bulgaria	35.9	35.3	34.4	34.0	32.7	32.1	32.5	32.6	32.3	31.9	31.2	31.0	30.6	30.2	29.6	30.84
Croatia	32.3	32.3	31.5	31.2	30.4	29.6	30.1	29.8	29.5	29.0	28.4	28.0	27.7	27.1	26.5	27.43
Czech Republic	19.5	19.1	18.5	18.1	17.0	16.6	16.9	16.7	16.4	16.0	15.5	15.3	15.1	14.9	14.1	13.61
Denmark	17.4	17.1	16.5	15.4	14.8	13.9	14.3	14.0	13.8	13.4	13.0	12.8	12.0	11.6	10.9	9.32
Estonia	30.7	30.8	30.2	29.6	29.5	29.0	29.6	29.3	28.6	28.2	27.6	27.1	26.2	25.4	24.6	23.21
Finland	17.6	17.2	16.6	15.3	14.5	13.8	14.2	14.0	13.7	13.3	13.0	12.9	12.4	12.0	11.5	11.02
France	14.7	14.3	13.8	12.4	11.8	11.1	11.6	11.3	11.0	10.8	9.9	10.8	12.3	12.6	12.8	12.32
Germany[a]	16.7	15.7	15.0	14.5	13.9	13.5	14.3	13.5	12.7	12.5	12.1	11.6	11.2	10.8	10.4	9.74
Greece	28.2	28.1	27.6	26.2	25.1	24.3	25.0	25.4	24.3	24.0	23.6	23.3	22.4	22.0	21.5	20.81
Hungary	25.0	24.7	24.5	24.4	23.7	23.0	23.5	23.3	22.8	22.5	22.1	21.6	21.9	22.2	22.4	22.70
Ireland	15.4	15.2	14.8	13.4	12.7	12.2	13.1	13.0	12.8	12.7	12.2	11.8	11.3	10.8	10.4	9.70
Italy	26.1	25.2	24.4	23.2	22.3	21.4	22.0	21.8	21.2	21.6	21.1	20.8	20.6	20.2	19.8	19.51
Latvia	30.4	30.0	29.5	29.0	27.5	26.5	27.1	27.3	26.5	26.1	25.5	24.7	23.6	22.9	21.3	20.24
Lithuania	32.0	31.7	31.1	30.6	29.7	29.1	29.6	29.7	29.0	28.5	28.0	27.1	25.8	24.9	23.8	22.96
Luxembourg (Grand-Duché)	9.8	9.8	9.9	10.0	9.4	8.5	8.8	8.4	8.2	8.2	8.0	8.1	8.3	8.4	8.2	7.94
Malta	26.7	26.7	26.9	27.2	26.4	25.8	25.9	26.0	25.8	25.3	24.3	24.0	24.3	24.0	23.6	23.21
Netherlands	12.7	12.5	12.0	10.9	10.1	9.6	10.2	10.0	9.8	9.5	9.1	9.2	9.0	8.8	8.4	7.51
Poland	27.7	27.4	27.1	26.8	26.0	25.3	25.9	25.4	25.0	24.4	23.8	23.5	23.3	23.0	22.2	21.74
Portugal	22.2	21.7	21.2	20.1	19.2	18.7	19.5	19.2	19.4	19.4	19.0	18.7	17.6	17.2	16.6	16.13
Romania	33.6	32.5	32.2	31.4	30.2	29.4	29.4	29.8	29.6	29.1	28.4	28.1	28.0	27.6	26.3	26.66
Slovenia	26.7	26.5	26.0	25.8	24.7	24.0	24.6	24.3	24.1	23.6	23.1	23.5	23.3	23.1	22.4	22.16

(continued)

Table 1 (continued)

Country/year	*2003*	*2004*	*2005*	*2006*	*2007*	*2008*	*2009*	*2010*	*2011*	*2012*	*2013*	*2014*	*2015*	*2016*	*2017*	*2018*
South-Cyprus	28.7	28.3	28.1	27.9	26.5	26.0	26.5	26.2	26.0	25.6	25.2	25.7	24.8	24.2	23.6	23.21
Spain	22.2	21.9	21.3	20.2	19.3	18.4	19.5	19.4	19.2	19.2	18.6	18.5	18.2	17.9	17.2	16.61
Slovakia	18.4	18.2	17.6	17.3	16.8	16.0	16.8	16.4	16.0	15.5	15.0	14.6	14.1	13.7	13.0	12.83
Sweden	18.6	18.1	17.5	16.2	15.6	14.9	15.4	15.0	14.7	14.3	13.9	13.6	13.2	12.6	12.1	11.63
United Kingdom	12.2	12.3	12.0	11.1	10.6	10.1	10.9	10.7	10.5	10.1	9.7	9.6	9.4	9.0	9.4	9.80
28 EU-countries/ Average (unweighted)	22.6	22.3	21.8	21.1	20.3	19.6	20.1	19.9	19.6	19.3	18.8	18.6	18.3	17.9	17.3	16.8

Source Own calculations, April 2018; values for some countries in 2017 and 2018 are projections on the basis of preliminary values

[a]The shadow economy values for Germany have been adjusted due to a change in the official GDP statistics of the German national accounts

decrease are Austria, Belgium, the Czech Republic, Denmark, Estonia, Finland, France, Germany, Greece, Ireland, Italy, Latvia, Lithuania, Luxembourg, Malta, the Netherlands, Poland, Portugal, Slovenia, South-Cyprus, Spain, Slovakia, and Sweden, whereas the shadow economy will increase in Croatia, Bulgaria, Hungary, Romania and UK. The strongest increase will take place in Croatia from 26.5% of official GDP (2017) to 27.4% in 2018 and in the UK from 9.4% of GDP in 2017 to 9.8% in 2018; the strongest decrease will be in Estonia from 24.6% (2017) to 23.1% in 2018.

To sum up: In the vast majority of the 28 EU-countries, the shadow economy will further decrease, averaging to 16.8% of official GDP in 2018.

If one considers the size of the shadow economies over the last 2 years (2017 and 2018) and compare them with the years 2008/2009, one realizes that, in most countries, one will again have a decrease in the size and development of the shadow economy, which is due to the recovery from the worldwide economic and financial crises. Hence, the most important reason for this decrease is that, if the official economy is recovering or booming, people have fewer incentives to undertake additional activities in the shadow economy and to earn extra "black" money.

Summary and Conclusions

To summarize: There are three different developments with respect to the size of the shadow economy of these 28 countries:

1. In general, one has a further decline of the shadow economy in 30 out of the 36 OECD countries. The main reason is a further recovery of the official economy. In 6 countries, one observes an increase due to a sluggish official economy or due to policy decisions which increased the shadow economy.
2. The eastern or central European countries and/or the "new" European Union members, such as Bulgaria, Cyprus, the Czech Republic, Latvia, Lithuania, and Poland have higher shadow economies than the "old" European Union countries, like Austria, Belgium, Germany, and Italy. Hence, one has an increase of the size of the shadow economy from west to east.
3. Also, one observes an increase in the size and development of the shadow economy from north to south. On average, the southern

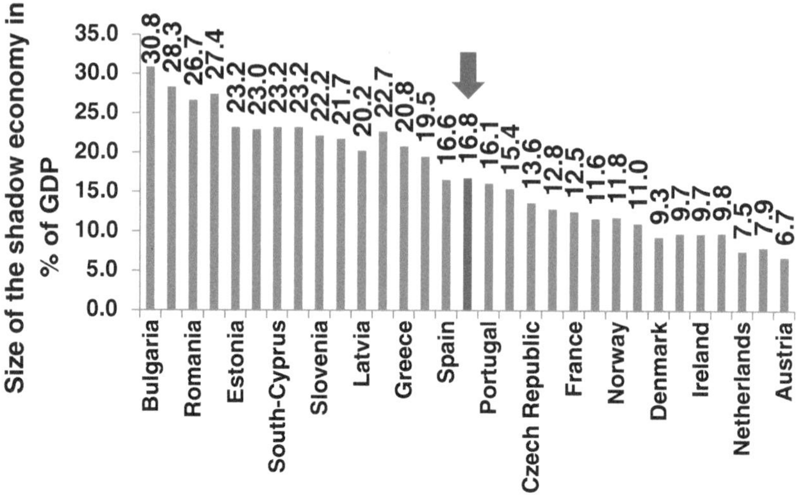

Fig. 1 Size of the shadow economy of 28 European countries in 2018 (in % of official GDP) (*Source* Own calculations, April 2018)

European countries have considerably higher shadow economies than those of Central and Western Europe. This can also be demonstrated by Fig. 1.

References

Feige, E. (1979). How Big Is the Irregular Economy? *Challenge, 22*(5), 5–13.

Kaufmann, D., & Kaliberda, A. (1996). Integrating the Unofficial Economy into the Dynamics of Post Socialist Economies: A Framework of Analyses and Evidence. In B. Kaminski (Ed.), *Economic Transition in Russia and the New States of Eurasia* (pp. 81–120). London: M.E. Sharpe.

Lackó, M. (1998). The Hidden Economies of Visegrad Countries in International Comparison: A Household Electricity Approach. In L. Halpern and C. Wyplosz (Eds.), *Hungary: Towards a Market Economy* (pp. 128–148). Cambridge, MA: Cambridge University Press.

Lackó, M. (1999). Electricity Intensity and the Unrecorded Economy in Post-Socialist Countries. In E. Feige & K. Ott (Eds.), *Underground Economies in Transition* (pp. 102–142). Aldershot: Ashgate.

Medina, L., & Schneider, F. (2018). *Shadow Economies Around the World: What Did We Learn Over the Last 20 Years?* (IMF Working Paper WP/18/17). Washington, DC: International Monetary Fund.

Schneider, F. (Ed.). (2011). *Handbook on the Shadow Economy*. Cheltenham, UK: Edward Elgar.

Schneider, F., & Williams, C. C. (2013). *The Shadow Economy*. London: The Institute of Economic Affairs (IEA).

Williams, C. C., & Schneider, F. (2016). *Measuring the Global Shadow Economy*. Cheltenham, UK: Edward Elgar.

Evaluating the Prevalence and the Working Conditions of Dependent Self-Employment in the European Union

Colin C. Williams and Adrian V. Horodnic

Introduction

In recent decades, it has been widely recognised that the so-called standard employment relationship (SER) of formal, full-time and permanent waged employment is becoming ever less the SER. This is problematic. The SER has been the main means of allocating rights and social protection, and its demise raises issues regarding working conditions, rights and benefits. The SER is being replaced not only by non-standard forms of employment (NSEs), including part-time, fixed-term and agency employment (Eichhorst et al. 2013; Hatfield 2015; Pedersini and Coletto 2010), but also self-employment, where workers have a contract for services or civil contract with those to whom they supply their labour, and therefore do not normally have the same protective rights as dependent employees (Fondeville et al. 2015; ILO 2016).

C. C. Williams (✉)
University of Sheffield, Sheffield, UK
e-mail: C.C.Williams@sheffield.ac.uk

A. V. Horodnic
"Grigore T. Popa" University of Medicine and Pharmacy, Iasi, Romania

V. Vlachos and A. Bitzenis (eds.), *European Union*,
https://doi.org/10.1007/978-3-030-18103-1_7

In recent years, furthermore, there is a growing concern that many employees are being falsely classified as self-employed by their employers in order to circumvent collective agreements, labour laws (e.g. minimum wages, working time legislation), employment tax and other employer liabilities implied in the standard contract of employment, and that the emergent 'platform' economy is accelerating this trend (European Commission 2014; European Parliament 2013; Fehringer 2014; Williams and Horodnic 2017). 'Dependent self-employment' is therefore seen to exist where workers are self-employed but have a de facto employment relationship, if not de jure, in the sense that they either only work for one employer, do not have the authority to hire staff, and/or the authority to make strategic decisions about how to run the business (Eurofound 2016a, b; Williams and Lapeyre 2017).

The aim of this paper is to advance understanding of such dependent self-employment by evaluating its scale and distribution in the European Union. This will put under the spotlight the dominant depiction of dependent self-employment as a precarious form of work, conducted by marginalised groups of workers with poorer working conditions than the rest of the employed population. To do so, this paper reports the only major data source available on the prevalence of dependent self-employment in the European Union, namely the European Working Conditions Survey (EWCS). To commence, the next section briefly reviews the emergent literature to reveal a series of dominant depictions about its prevalence, distribution and the job quality. Section "Methods and Data" introduces the EWCS; section "Findings" reports the findings on the prevalence of dependent self-employment in the European Union, who engages in this form of work and their working conditions. The last section then addresses what can be done about dependent self-employment and the implications for the future of work.

Dominant Depictions of Dependent Self-Employment: Prevalence, Distribution and Working Conditions

Reviewing the literature, there is no universally accepted definition of dependent self-employment (Mühlberger and Bertolini 2008), not least because the legislation varies across countries in terms of what constitutes self-employment and dependent employment (ILO 2015). Moreover, even within countries, self-employment is defined differently in labour law, tax law, trade law and social security law (Spasova et al. 2017) or not even defined at all in some countries such as the UK (Jorens 2008). When it is also recognised that some authors try to differentiate between dependent self-employment and bogus self-employment, defining what is meant by dependent self-employment becomes even more problematic. Indeed, analysing the 35 ESPN (European Social Policy Network) national expert's reports, the conclusion is that 'currently no single, unambiguous definition applicable in any of the countries (except for Slovenia) drawing a clear-cut distinction between 'genuine', 'dependent' and 'bogus' self-employed' exists (Spasova et al. 2017: 11).

However, the consensus in literature is that both forms belong to the 'grey zone' of employment relationships that exists between genuine self-employment and pure dependent employment. To denote the disguised employment relationships in this grey zone, various terms have been used including 'bogus', 'fake', 'false', 'sham', 'involuntary' or 'misclassified' self-employment, or 'disguised employment' (Böheim and Mühlberger 2006; Eichhorst et al. 2013; Harvey and Behling 2008; Kautonen et al. 2009, 2010; Mandrone et al. 2014; Pedersini and Coletto 2010). Examining the most common criteria used to define genuine self-employment, Eurofound (2013, 2016b) defines the dependent self-employed as workers who report themselves as self-employed without employees and meet two or more of the following characteristics: they do not have more than one client; they do not have the authority to hire staff, and/or do not have the authority to make important strategic decisions about how to run the business. Based on these criteria, therefore, dependent self-employment is in this chapter defined as an employment relationship where workers are self-employed but have a de facto employment relationship, if not de jure, because they either only work for one employer, do not have the authority to hire staff, and/or do not have the authority to make important strategic decisions about how to run the business.

The widespread assumption is that employment relationships in this 'grey zone' between genuine self-employment and pure dependent employment are growing. This is mainly because it is cheaper for employers to hire self-employed persons to perform work than it is to hire employees. Indeed, in the UK, the incentive for employers to hire self-employed workers through outsourcing and sub-contracting arrangements is at least 13.8% of labour costs because employer national insurance contributions do not need to be paid (Taylor 2017). This, however, is not the only benefit of hiring on a self-employed basis or firing employees and re-hiring them as self-employed to perform the same work. Doing so also allows employers to evade minimum wage rates, compensation in the case of dismissal, higher wages based on seniority, holiday payments and the right of an employee to be paid if sick and incapable of work. This practice thus circumvents collective agreements, labour laws, employment tax and other employer liabilities that would otherwise apply.

Indeed, in a study covering 29 countries (European Union member states and Norway) which analysed the fraudulent use of various forms of non-standard working arrangements (e.g. self-employees, freelancers, temporary workers, on-call workers), the finding was that in 23 out of 29 countries, the experts reported a 'significant' fraudulent use of self-employment and freelance work (Eurofound 2016a: 1). At the EU27 level, using data from the 2010 EWCS and the criteria above (i.e. they do not have more than one client; they do not have the authority to hire staff, and/or do not have the authority to make important strategic decisions about how to run the business), Eurofound (2013) estimated that the share of dependent self-employment was at around 0.9% of the total EU workforce. Meanwhile, using the same data and the same methodology, the OECD (2014) estimates the dependent self-employed as a share of dependent workers to have its highest prevalence in Turkey and Greece (5%). In 2015, Eurofound (2016b) analysed the next wave of EWCS, conducted in 2015, and concluded that dependent self-employment in the European member states is around 1% but there is an additional grey area of about 30% of the self-employed without employees who fail to comply with one of the three criteria. However, using a slightly different method (i.e. changing one of the three criteria) by adding whether the self-employed without employees get paid an agreed fee on a weekly or monthly basis (rather than their ability to make important decisions regarding how their business is run), the result is that 2.4% of the labour market in the EU28 can be classified as dependent self-employment (Eurofound 2018a, b).

It is not just the prevalence but also the distribution of dependent self-employment that will be investigated in this chapter. Dependent self-employment is sometimes portrayed as a 'precarious' form of employment. This is because by employing somebody as self-employed rather than as a dependent employee, employers can evade employment rights and entitlements (e.g. holiday/sickness pay) attached to the employment of an employee, as well as taxes, which leads this practice to be considered a type of precarious work (Congregado et al. 2012; Fehringer 2014; Thörnqvist 2014). On the other hand, and following on from the depiction of dependent self-employment in the grey area as precarious work conducted by precarious workers, the widespread view is that marginalised workers are most affected by this employment relationship. Indeed, previous studies consider the following populations more likely to be in dependent self-employment: women (European Institute for Gender Equality 2015), older populations and lower-educated persons (Böheim and Mühlberger 2006; Eurofound 2018a, b) and migrants (Spasova et al. 2017).

Similarly, there is a view that those in lower-skilled occupations are most affected by employment in the grey zone between genuine self-employment and dependent employment (Congregado et al. 2012; Fehringer 2014; Thörnqvist 2014). The results of previous studies, however, are mixed. Some find dependent self-employment as prevalent in lower-skilled occupations and sectors such as: construction (Echihorst et al. 2013; European Commission 2018; Spasova et al. 2017), transport (European Commission 2018; Echihorst et al. 2013; Pulignano et al. 2016; Spasova et al. 2017), wholesale, retail and repair of motor vehicles (European Commission 2018), parcel delivery industry (Moore and Newsome 2018), elementary occupations and services, sales workers (Eurofound 2013), agricultural, forestry and fishing sector (Eurofound 2018b; Williams and Horodnic 2018; Williams and Lapeyre 2017) and food processing sector (Spasova et al. 2017), household services (Williams and Horodnic 2018) and cleaning services (Spasova et al. 2017). However, other studies identify a large share of dependent self-employment in higher-skilled occupations. As such, dependent self-employment has been also found in accountancy, insurance, architecture and creative industry (Echihorst et al. 2013), financial and insurance activities (European Commission 2018), financial, insurance and facility services, media, IT, airlines (Spasova et al. 2017), arts, entertainment, recreation and other service activities (Williams and Horodnic 2018) and platform work (Suárez Corujo 2017).

Grounded in the belief that employers can use dependent self-employment to evade the protective rights linked to dependent employment, and that this is precarious work undertaken by precarious workers, the widespread view has been that the working conditions of the dependent self-employed are poorer. Precarious work refers to employment which 'involves instability, a lack of labour protection, insecurity, and social and economic vulnerability' (Eichhorst et al. 2013: 14). Indeed, in general, those in self-employment, regardless of whether they are genuine or dependent self-employed, enjoy less social protection, fewer employment rights and less training (Broughton et al. 2016; OECD 2018; Social Security Advisory Committee 2014). While open-ended full-time employment contracts (SER) are perceived as the working arrangement with the lowest level of precariousness (Broughton et al. 2016), bogus self-employment is one of the working arrangements most often associated with precarity, alongside informal and casual work (Mckay et al. 2012; Thörnqvist 2014). Indeed, some 82% of the employment experts surveyed in 12 European Union member states (Bulgaria, France, Germany, Greece, Ireland, Italy, Latvia, the Netherlands Poland, Spain, Sweden, and the UK) concluded that dependent self-employed persons are at risk of precarious work (Mckay et al. 2012). Meanwhile, a study by ILO (2016) concluded that for both dependent and bogus self-employment, it is common to witness labour market transition and employment insecurity, lower earnings, extended working hours, risks related to occupational safety and health, low social security coverage, poor training and representation insecurity.

Indeed, several studies have highlighted the poorer working conditions of those in dependent self-employment, such as: working longer hours (ILO 2016; Millán et al. 2018; Walby 2009), experiencing higher economic risk than dependent employed drivers (Eichhorst et al. 2013); the unpaid work associated with essential activities of the dependent self-employed in parcel delivery (Moore and Newsome 2018), and low income or insufficient income to compensate for the lack of entitlement to public pensions (Eichhorst et al. 2013).

Using descriptive statistics at the EU27 level, based on the fifth EWCS conducted in 2010, Eurofound (2013) provides an extensive comparison between the working conditions of the dependent self-employed, genuine self-employed and dependent employees. The finding is that for some working conditions, those in dependent self-employment are more similar to dependent workers than the genuine self-employment (intrinsic rewards such as feeling that their work is useful, work-life balance, working time and pace dependency), for other working conditions they are more similar to the genuine self-employed (irregular working time patterns, the possibility to take time off during working time for solving a personal or family issue), and on yet other working conditions, they sit in between dependent employees and the genuine self-employed (autonomy, working during free time and exposure to physical risk). Few, if any, differences are identified in relation to their perception of their safety and health at work, regardless of their employment status. However, as far as the household ability to make ends meet, perceived job security and career prospects, and mental well-being, those in dependent self-employment are found to suffer more than the genuine self-employed and dependent employees (Eurofound 2013).

Meanwhile, Williams and Lepeyre (2017) analysing the 2015 EWCS and employing multivariate analysis conclude that those in dependent self-employment suffer significantly poorer working conditions compared with the rest of the workforce only as far as their social environment is concerned. The same conclusion that the dependent self-employed experience less favourable social environments than other categories of worker (e.g. short- and long-term temporary workers, the genuine self-employed, permanent workers) was reached by Eurofound (2018b). However, a study analysing five sectors, namely construction, transport, accountancy, insurance and creative sector, concludes that the level of precarity depends on the sector, and that the working conditions of the dependent self-employed are not always precarious (Eichhorst et al. 2013). For example, dependent self-employment has less harmful effects in the accountancy and insurance sectors compared with transport and construction (Eichhorst et al. 2013).

Methods and Data

Few, if any, surveys collect data on how many workers are dependent self-employed. The one exception is the EWCS. The sample used in the EWCS is representative of those aged 15 and over living in private households and in employment who did at least one hour of work for pay or profit during the week preceding the interview. The sample in each country is stratified by region (NUTS 2 or equivalent) and degree of urbanisation. The sixth edition of the EWCS undertaken in 2015 comprised 43,850 interviews in the 28 EU member states, as well as Norway, Switzerland, Albania, the Former Yugoslav Republic of Macedonia, Montenegro, Serbia and Turkey. Of these, 35,765 interviews were conducted in the EU28 member states.

To evaluate the extent of dependent self-employment, three questions were asked to estimate whether the 'self-employed without employees' are genuinely self-employed or are dependent self-employed (Eurofound 2013). These are that:

- a self-employed person without employees should have more than one client to be considered really self-employed;
- a self-employed person without employees should be able to hire employees if necessary;
- a self-employed person without employees should be able to make the most important decisions about how to run their business.

A self-employed person without employees who complies with fewer than two of these three criteria is deemed to be dependent self-employed. Conversely, those complying with two or more of these criteria are considered 'genuine' self-employed without employees. Those self-employed without employees considered to be dependent self-employed are thus those: (1) who have only one client, (2) have no authority to hire staff, and/or (3) have no authority to make important strategic decisions. In addition to this, and as Eurofound (2016b) pointed out, there is an important grey zone of about 30% of the self-employed without employees comprising the self-employed without employees who only complied with two criteria out of three. Indeed, this grey zone was accounted for in some subsequent studies (Williams and Horodnic 2018; Williams and Lapeyre 2017). Akin to these studies, we account for the grey zone and, as such, we include under the umbrella of dependent self-employment all the self-employees without employees which fails to meet at least one criteria out of three (e.g. if they do not have more than one client).

To analyse the prevalence and the distribution of dependent self-employment and to compare the working conditions of workers in dependent self-employment with other categories of worker, we have classified those in employment into seven categories, namely: self-employed without employees (broken down into dependent self-employed or genuine self-employed); self-employed with employees, and employees (broken down into those with indefinite contracts, with fixed-term and temporary employment agency contracts, with other types of contract and with no written contract). In order to do so, we analysed the following questions: (1) whether they work as an employee or as self-employed; (2)

whether they have the authority to hire or dismiss employees; whether they have employees working for them; whether they have in general more than one client; whether they have the authority to make the most important decisions about how their business is ran (for self-employed) and (3) what type of contract they have: contract of unlimited duration, contract of limited duration, a temporary employment agency contract, an apprenticeship or other training scheme, no contract, other (for employees). However, it is important to interpret the results with caution because the subsample of dependent self-employed persons is relatively small. Indeed, when using a similar approach for the 2010 EWCS, Eurofound (2013) warns that the small differences in the outcomes might represent the differences generated by the sampling procedure and not the real differences in outcomes. However, given the lack of alternative multinational databases on dependent self-employment, the EWCS is here analysed.

For the descriptive statistics reported below, a weighting scheme is used as recommended in the EWCS 2015 technical report. Country-level post-stratification weighting has been used for carrying out the analysis. We analysed all cases available for each analysed variable (don't know and refusal were excluded).

To understand the working conditions of those in employment, this chapter uses six indices of job quality (and their sub-indices) developed by Eurofound (2016b) to analyse the EWCS. These six main indices comprise: the physical working environment index, the work intensity index, the working time quality index, the social environment index, the skills and discretion index and the prospects index. The six job quality indices are measured on a scale from 0 to 100, and they cover manly the same dimensions as the Eurofound overview report (2016b). Only in the case of *the social environment index*, the *management quality dimension* is excluded due to the lack of availability for self-employment, and in the case of *prospects index*, the *employment status* dimension is excluded because we take the employment status into account for obtaining the groups (e.g. dependent self-employment, genuine self-employment and all workforce). With the exception of *work intensity*, the higher the index score, the better the job quality. The variables are normalised and rescaled with value 0 for the lowest level of the variable (the worse condition for the worker) and gradually increased to 100, the highest level of the variable (the best condition for the worker), with the exception of work intensity. For *work intensity*, the values were set in the opposite fashion. Each of the job quality indices comprises some sub-dimensions. The same weight was used when calculating the job quality indices mean on all indicators and sub-dimensions.

Findings

Prevalence and Distribution by Country of the Dependent Self-Employment

Table 1 displays the variations in the prevalence of dependent self-employment. The first column depicts the share of all self-employed without employees who are dependent self-employed, the second column the share of all self-employed (with or without employees) who are dependent self-employed and the third column the share of all employment that is dependent self-employment. This reveals that in 2015, 4% of total employment in the European Union member states was dependent self-employment, failing to meet at least one of the three criteria described above. The dependent self-employed are 31% of all the self-employed and 47% of those in self-employment without employees. This, therefore, is not some minor form of employment relationship. Similar results on the magnitude of dependent self-employment have been obtained by other studies analysing the EWCS (Williams and Horodnic 2018; Williams and Lapeyre 2017).

There are, nevertheless, cross-national variations in the prevalence of dependent self-employment. As the third column in Table 1 reveals, dependent self-employment ranges from 9% of total employment in Portugal, and 8% in Italy, Greece and Romania, to 1% of total employment in Denmark and Sweden, and 2% in Belgium, Estonia, France and Germany. Turning to dependent self-employment as a share of all self-employment or all the self-employed without employees, it is again the case that stark variations exist cross-nationally. Dependent self-employment as a share of all self-employment ranges from 63% of all self-employment in Romania, 52% in Slovakia, 43% in the UK and Austria and 42% in Lithuania and Poland, to at the lower end 18% of all self-employment in Germany and Belgium, 12% in Sweden and 11% in Denmark. Similarly, as a share of all the self-employed without employees, dependent self-employment ranges from 16% in Sweden to 64% in Austria and Latvia, 67% in Slovakia and 80% in Romania.

Table 1 Prevalence of dependent self-employment by country, socio-economic and firm characteristics (EU28 2015)

	Prevalence of dependent self-employment percent of		
	Self-employment without employees	*All self-employment*	*All employment*
All EU28	*47*	*31*	*4*
Country			
Austria	64	43	5
Belgium	34	18	2
Bulgaria	40	26	4
Croatia	58	39	4
Cyprus	38	26	5
Czech Republic	58	37	5
Denmark	17	11	1
Estonia	55	24	2
Finland	44	29	5
France	45	26	2
Germany	35	18	2
Greece	30	21	8
Hungary	45	30	4
Ireland	44	28	5
Italy	45	32	8
Latvia	64	35	4
Lithuania	72	42	5
Luxembourg	49	34	3
Malta	47	35	4
Netherlands	32	23	3
Poland	61	42	5
Portugal	56	41	9
Romania	80	63	8
Slovakia	67	52	6
Slovenia	55	41	6
Spain	29	20	3
Sweden	16	12	1
UK	56	43	6
Gender			
Male	44	29	5
Female	50	36	4
Age (years)			
-35	54	41	3
35–49	42	27	4
50+	47	32	6

(continued)

Table 1 (continued)

	Prevalence of dependent self-employment percent of		
	Self-employment without employees	*All self-employment*	*All employment*
Education			
Less than primary and primary education	58	45	11
Lower/upper secondary and non-tertiary education	46	32	4
Tertiary education	44	28	4
Respondent and both parents born in the country of residence			
No	52	38	5
Yes	46	30	4
Household size (persons)			
One	48	36	5
Two	48	32	4
Three	45	30	4
Four	45	28	4
Five and more	46	32	4
Household ability to make ends meet			
Very easily/easily	43	24	4
Fairly easily	48	32	5
With some difficulty	48	35	4
With difficulty/great difficulty	50	44	7
Occupation			
Managers	33	13	4
Professionals	49	33	4
Technicians and associate professionals	36	27	3
Clerical support workers	55	33	1
Service and sales workers/armed forces	34	22	3
Skilled agricultural, forestry and fishery workers	68	51	30
Craft and related trades workers	38	27	5
Plant and machine operators, and assemblers	55	45	3

(continued)

Table 1 (continued)

	Prevalence of dependent self-employment percent of		
	Self-employment without employees	*All self-employment*	*All employment*
Elementary occupations	73	65	5
Economic activities, NACE Rev. 2			
Agriculture, forestry and fishing	69	51	27
Industry (except construction)	42	25	2
Construction	43	28	7
Wholesale and retail trade; repair of motors	30	18	3
Transportation and storage	57	44	4
Accommodation and food service activities	22	10	2
Information and communication	43	32	5
Financial and insurance/real estate activities	34	22	3
Professional, scientific, technical and administrative activities	39	26	5
Public administration, education, human health and social work	47	33	2
Arts, entertainment and recreation; other	53	42	11
Activities of households as employers	90	84	13
Sector			
The private sector	45	30	5
The public sector	59	37	1
A joint private-public organisation or company	58	32	2
The not-for-profit sector or an NGO/other	55	48	9

Source Own calculations based on EWCS 2015 and abridged from Williams and Horodnic (2018) and Williams and Lapeyre (2017)

Who Engages in Dependent Self-Employment? Socio-Demographic and Socio-Economic Characteristics

To evaluate whether certain socio-demographic and socio-economic groups are more likely to engage in dependent self-employment than others, Table 1 examines whether participation in dependent self-employment varies by gender. This reveals that 5% of all men and 4% of all women in employment are dependent self-employed. However, analysing the share of self-employment that is dependent self-employment, the finding is that 50% of self-employed women are dependent self-employed compared with 44% of self-employed men. Therefore, the results only partially support the assumption that women are more likely to be dependent self-employed, as previous studies argue (European Institute for Gender Equality 2015).

Participation in dependent self-employment also varies according to age. The proportion of the total workforce in dependent self-employment is 3% of the workforce under 35 years old, 4% of the workforce aged 35–49 years old and 6% of the workforce aged 50 and over. Therefore, the likelihood of being dependent self-employed increases with age, reinforcing previous results (Eurofound 2018b; Böheim and Mühlberger 2006). So too is it the case that a higher percentage of those with only primary level education are engaged in dependent self-employment (11%) compared with those with secondary or tertiary education (4%). Similarly, 58% of the self-employed without employees who have only primary level education are dependent self-employed, compared with 46% of those with lower or upper secondary and non-tertiary education, and 44% of those with tertiary education. This reinforces the results of Böheim and Mühlberger (2006) and Eurofound (2018b), and reveals that it is marginalised populations, in terms of educational level, who are more likely to engage in dependent self-employment.

Turning to nationality, Table 1 shows that 4% of workers who were born in the country they work in (including their parents) are dependent self-employed compared with 5% of workers who themselves and/or their parents were not born in the country they work in. Indeed, 52% of the self-employed without employees who were not born in the country they work in and/or their parents were not born in the country they work in, are dependent self-employed, compared with 46% of the self-employed without employees born in the country they work in. These results are in line with the findings of Spasova et al. (2017) who underline the high presence of dependent self-employment amongst migrant groups.

Those living in single-person households are also more likely to be dependent self-employed. Indeed, 5% of the workforce living in one-person households are dependent self-employed, 36% of those in self-employment and 48% of the self-employed without employees.

Similarly, dependent self-employment is more prevalent for those living in households who face difficulties making ends meet (i.e. a proxy indicator for deprived households). Indeed, 7% of the workforce living in households who have difficulty making ends meet are dependent self-employed. Some 50% of the self-employed without employees living in households who find it difficult to make ends meet are dependent self-employed, 48% of those living in households where there are some difficulties in making ends meet and 43% of those living in households where there are no difficulties. These findings suggest that dependent self-employment is more prevalent amongst self-employed persons living in single-person households and households who have difficulties making ends meet. This reinforces the results of Eurofound (2013).

Distribution Across Sectors, Organisations and Occupations

What types of sectors and occupations are more likely to use dependent self-employment? Table 1 reveals that 5% of all craft and related trade workers and those in elementary occupations, and 30% of all skilled agricultural, forestry and fisheries workers, are dependent self-employed. There are therefore marked variations between occupations. Analysing the self-employed without employees, the finding is that for some occupations, the share of the self-employed without employees that are dependent self-employed is more than a half; 55% of the self-employed without employees working in clerical support or working as plant and machine operators, and assemblers, are dependent self-employed. Similarly, 68% of skilled agricultural, forestry and fishery self-employed without employees are dependent self-employed, reinforcing the results of previous studies (Williams and Horodnic 2018; Williams and Lapeyre 2017).

Examining the sectors in which the dependent self-employed are found, Table 1 reveals that dependent self-employment is not confined to the private sector. Although 5% of all employment in the private sector is dependent self-employment, it is the not-for-profit sector in which this employment relationship is rife with 9% of all not-for-profit sector employment being dependent self-employment. Interestingly, however, when analysing the share of self-employed without employees that are dependent self-employed, the finding is that the largest share is to be found in public sector. Indeed, 59% of the self-employed without employees working in public sector are dependent self-employed.

A more detailed breakdown by sector of participation in dependent self-employment is provided in Table 1. The third column compounds the above finding regarding the concentration of dependent self-employment in occupations associated with agriculture, forestry and fishing. Some 27% of all employment in the agriculture, forestry and fishing sector is dependent self-employment. The next closest sector is the household services sector where 13% of all employment is dependent self-employment followed by the arts entertainment and recreation sector (11%). Examining the self-employed rather than total employment, however, it is the household services sector in which this employment relationship is rife. Some 84% of all the self-employed in the household services sector and some 90% of all self-employed without employees in this sector are dependent self-employed. Similar results regarding the high prevalence of the dependent self-employment in household services were obtained by Williams and Horodnic (2018).

Working Conditions of the Dependent Self-Employed

Table 2 evaluates the working conditions of the dependent self-employed. This provides a comparison between the dependent self-employed, genuine self-employed and all people in employment on six job quality indices, namely the physical working environment index, the work intensity index, the working time quality index, the social environment index, the skills and discretion index and the prospects index.

The physical environment index measures the exposure to vibrations, noise, low/high temperatures, tobacco smoke, smoke, fumes dust and vapours, chemical substances, and dangerous materials and substances (e.g. materials which could be infectious, such as waste, bodily fluids, laboratory materials), as well as whether the job involves tiring or painful positions, lifting or moving people, carrying or moving heavy loads and repetitive hand or arm movements. Is it the case, that the physical environment in which the dependent self-employed work is worse than that witnessed by others in employment or genuine self-employed? As Table 2

Table 2 Working conditions by employment status (EU28 2015)

Index/index dimension	*Dependent self-employed*	*Genuine self-employed (with and without employees)*	*All employment*
Mean index score:	*(0–100)*	*(0–100)*	*(0–100)*
Physical environment index	82	84	84
Work intensity index	28	33	36
Quantitative demands	32	37	39
Pace determinants and interdependency	26	32	39
Emotional demands	25	30	30
Working time quality index	75	69	76
Duration	69	51	76
Atypical working time	67	64	72
Working time arrangements	91	91	87
Flexibility	74	69	70
Social environment index	85	90	85
Adverse social behaviour	96	98	96
Social support	53	72	72
Skills and discretion index	56	68	55
Cognitive dimension	62	75	64
Decision latitude	78	91	62
Organisational participation	73	88	57
Training	13	20	36
Prospects index	54	60	57
Career prospects	45	56	48
Job security	70	79	74
Downsizing	49	49	50

Source Own calculations based on EWCS 2015 and abridged from Williams and Lapeyre (2017)

displays, dependent self-employed are more likely to be exposed for at least one-quarter of their working time to these physical hazards. In the Eurofound (2013) study, data from a previous wave of EWCS placed the dependent self-employment in between genuine self-employment and dependent employees as far as physical risk is concerned.

Examining work intensity, meanwhile, the finding is that the dependent self-employed are less likely to suffer high work intensity compared with the genuine self-employed or all people in employment. The work intensity index comprises three sub-indices: (1) quantitative demands measuring whether the work implies working at high speed, with tight deadlines, whether there is enough time for completing the work and whether frequent disruptive interruptions occurs; (2) pace determinants and interdependency measuring whether the work is dependent on colleagues' work, on the direct control of a boss, on the demands from customers, passengers, etc., or on the automatic speed of machine or moving of a product; and (3) emotional demands measuring whether the job involves hiding their feelings, emotionally disturbing situations or handling angry clients, customers, patients, etc. Those in dependent self-employment have better working conditions for all three sub-indices compared with both the genuine self-employed and all in employment. It must be concluded, therefore, that the self-employed, regardless of whether they are dependent or genuine self-employed, less commonly witness work intensity problems compared with all in employment. Previous findings suggest that the pace dependency of the dependent self-employed is more similar to that of dependent workers than of those in genuine self-employment (Eurofound 2013).

The working time quality index comprises 4 sub-indices, namely: (1) duration measuring the number of working hours during a week, whether a recovery period of at least 11 hours exists between two working days, and cases where the work takes 10 hours or more per day; (2) atypical working time measuring the night work, the work during the weekend and the shift work; (3) working time arrangements measuring who has the control over the working time arrangements (i.e. company, choice between different schedules, possibility of adapting the working hours, working time entirely determined by worker), how the change in working time arrangements can take place (i.e. no regular change, change in the same day, change the day before, change with several days before, change with several weeks in advance) and whether the worker is requested to come to work at short notice at least several times per month; and (4) flexibility measuring the ease to arrange taking time off during working hours in order to resolve personal or family issues and whether the workers have to work in their free time at least several times per month in order to meet work demands.

As can be seen in Table 2, working time quality is slightly lower for the dependent self-employed than for all in employment, suggesting that the working conditions on this issue are slightly worse for the dependent self-employed. However, compared with the genuine self-employed, those in dependent self-employment witness better working conditions as far as working time quality is concerned. This is not the case on all sub-indices however. Although on issues of duration and atypical working time, the dependent self-employed have worse working conditions than all in employment, on the issues of having control over working time arrangements and flexibility, they have better working conditions than all in employment. Compared with genuine self-employment, nevertheless, they have better or equal working conditions on working time quality. Overall, however, they more commonly suffer slightly worse working conditions than all in employment on the issue of work intensity.

Are the dependent self-employed more likely to suffer from a worse social environment when working compared with all others in employment and the genuine self-employed? As can be seen, the social environment is overall fairly similar for the dependent self-employed compared with all in employment but worse than the social environment of the genuine self-employed. However, there are marked differences in the two sub-indices. These indices measure the exposure to adverse social behaviour (i.e. exposure to verbal abuse, to unwanted sexual attention, sexual harassment, threats, humiliating behaviours, physical violence, bullying) and the help and support from colleagues. Although the likelihood of the dependent self-employed witnessing adverse social behaviour is very much on a par with all in employment but higher than for the genuine self-employed, the social support index manifested in terms of receiving help and support from colleagues is markedly lower than for all in employment or those in genuine self-employment. Only 53% of the dependent self-employed assert that they receive help and support from colleagues most/all of the time, compared with 72% of all others in employment or the genuine self-employed. Indeed, previous studies (Eurofound 2018a, b; Williams and Lepeyre 2017) similarly conclude that those in dependent self-employment experience a poorer social environment compared with the rest of the workforce.

Are the dependent self-employed also more likely to suffer from worse working conditions so far as the use of skills and discretion is concerned compared with all others in employment and with the genuine self-employed? As can be seen, the skills and discretion index for the dependent self-employed is overall slightly better compared with all in employment, but much lower than for the genuine self-employed. However, there are marked differences in the four sub-indices. Starting with the cognitive dimension of work (i.e. solving unforeseen problems, carrying out complex tasks, learning new things, working with computers, smartphones and laptops, ability to apply their own ideas at work), the finding is that those in dependent self-employment have a slightly lower working quality compared with all in employment and much lower than those in genuine self-employment. A very marked difference is observed for the training dimension (i.e. provided by the employer or themselves). Both the genuine and the dependent self-employed receive less training compared with all in employment. Indeed, the share of the dependent self-employed receiving training in the past 12 months is almost three times lower compared with all in employment, reinforcing the results of Williams and Lepeyre (2017) and Eurofound (2018a, b). However, on the decision latitude dimension (i.e. the ability to choose or change tasks, methods or speed/rate of work and having a say in choice of work colleagues) and organisation participation dimensions (i.e. to be consulted before objectives are set for their own work, to be involved in improving the work organisation and/or the work processes of their own department or organisation, and to have the ability to influence decisions that are important to their work), the dependent self-employed score markedly higher than all others in employment and yet markedly lower than genuine self-employed.

Finally, Table 2 displays that the dependent self-employed are more likely to perceive themselves as suffering from worse job and career prospects than all others in employment or the genuine self-employed. Indeed, this is the case across all three sub-indices related to career prospects, job security and the prospect of downsizing, reinforcing the results of Eurofound (2013) who conclude that the perceived job security and career prospects are at the lowest level for the dependent self-employed compared with the genuine self-employed and dependent employees.

Conclusions and Discussions

Reporting the 2015 EWCS, 4% of total employment in the European Union member states is found to be dependent self-employment, with a higher share of the total workforce in dependent self-employment in the Southern and Eastern European member states. Dependent self-employment is also more prevalent amongst those aged 50 years old or more, those with an education lower than primary education and those who live in households who have difficulties making ends meet. With respect to occupations and sectors, dependent self-employment is more likely to be found amongst skilled agricultural, forestry and fishery workers and in economic activities where households are employers. Workers in the public sector are less likely to be dependent self-employed than workers in the private sector or in the not-for-profit sector.

Examining the working conditions of the dependent self-employed compared with the rest of the workforce and those in genuine self-employment, the finding is that they have poorer working conditions as far as three out of six indices are concerned, namely the physical environment index, the working time quality and the prospects index. No difference is observed for the overall social environment index between the dependent self-employed and all in employment. However, in terms of work intensity issues, and skills and discretion, those in dependent self-employment face better conditions than the rest of the workforce. It is important to note that the dependent self-employed face poorer working conditions on four out of the six indices compared with those in genuine self-employment. Thus, they have a poorer physical environment, poorer social environment, poorer prospects for their career and poorer discretion and ability to use their skills than those in genuine self-employed. Nevertheless, marked differences are observed between sub-indices, with the poorest dimension represented by training where the dependent self-employed are far less likely to receive training than those in genuine self-employment or all those in employment.

These findings, therefore, suggest the need for a more nuanced and variegated understanding of the working conditions of the dependent self-employed. They do not universally have worse working conditions than the genuine self-employed and workers in general in all respects. Moreover, the aspects of their working conditions discussed above do not include every aspect of their working conditions. There are other important aspects that need to be noted. The dependent self-employed also suffer from the absence of labour law protection on issues such as minimum wage rates, dismissal, holiday pay and sick leave and are not covered by collective bargaining. It is not only due to these working conditions of the dependent self-employed, however, that there is a need to tackle this employment relationship.

Dependent self-employment also has negative implications for governments and the wider society, such as the loss of tax revenue which could be used for providing public goods and services (Eichhorst et al. 2013; Thörnqvist 2014). Legitimate businesses, moreover, suffer from unfair competition from businesses that disguise their employees under the status of self-employed to decrease their labour costs (Fehringer 2014; Seeley 2010; Thörnqvist 2014).

What can be done, therefore, to tackle dependent self-employment? Until now, several approaches have been employed. Many countries have maintained in their legislation the binary divide between dependent employment and self-employment, and their policy approach towards dependent self-employment has variously included: (i) presumptions that they are dependent employees and therefore they have been included in employment protection legislation (e.g. France, Greece, Luxembourg); (ii) reversal of the burden of proving employee status (e.g. Belgium); and (iii) developing criteria to classify such workers as either employees or self-employed (e.g. Austria, Belgium, Germany, Ireland). For other countries, however, a hybrid third legal category between dependent employment and self-employment has been created and legal rights attached to this hybrid third category that do not exist for the legal status of self-employment (e.g. Germany, Italy, Netherlands, Portugal), as is also proposed in the UK in the recent proposal for a 'dependent contractor' employment status (Taylor 2017). So far, nevertheless, rather less progress has been made on extending labour rights beyond dependent employees to all the self-employed, which is another way forward. An example of this happening can be found in Italy, where, under the new status of autonomous work (Law 81/2017), the social protection of the self-employed has been extended by ensuring that they are entitled to parental and sick leave as well as maternity allowances (Borghi et al. 2018).

What other initiatives can be pursued by governments to provide better working conditions for the dependent self-employed? A first step to answer this would be to identify the motives for using dependent self-employment. Different policies could then be implemented to tackle the various reasons for using dependent self-employment. This would entail an evaluation of whether this is purely a monetary cost/benefit calculation on the part of employers, and whether it is a choice or necessity for workers. Where the driving force is financial gain and the worker is involuntarily engaged in dependent self-employment, governments might increase the costs of misclassifying workers (i.e. ranging from requalification of the employment relationship into a dependent employment contract to criminal sanctions). They might alternatively equalise the financial costs of employers using dependent employment and self-employed persons. This has been implemented in Romania (Williams and Horodnic 2017) and proposed in the UK (Taylor 2017). Furthermore, incentives for employers could be used to put their affairs in order. For example, in Italy (Decree No. 81/2015), an amnesty was introduced for those employers who transformed existing self-employed contracts (i.e. suspected of being bogus self-employed) into a dependent employment contract (Eurofound 2016a, b).

As for those voluntarily in dependent self-employment, one option is recognition of a third hybrid category which has started to be adopted by some countries (e.g. Germany, Italy, Netherlands, Portugal). Other policy measures aiming to extend their limited rights can be also pursued. As a comparative study on self-employed professionals in Italy, Germany and UK concludes, there is a need for a more universal social protection system to reduce the gap between those in self-employment and those in dependent employment (Borghi et al. 2018).

This chapter, therefore, despite developing a more nuanced understanding of the prevalence and working conditions of the dependent self-employed, has limitations and caveats are required. Firstly, this survey examines some of the working conditions of the dependent self-employed, but does not analyse their wage rates, or their experiences in taking holidays and sick leave for example. For a fuller understanding of the working conditions of the dependent self-employed, not only is more in-depth qualitative understanding of workers' experiences in relation to these issues required but also further country-level and sector-specific studies. Secondly, there is also a need to evaluate whether the different policy approaches and measures for tackling dependent self-employment, such as creating a hybrid legal category, directly tackle those working conditions here shown to be significantly worse amongst the dependent self-employed (e.g. the greater emotional demands, exposure to adverse social behaviour, lower social support, less training). Until now, this has not been investigated.

In conclusion, this chapter has revealed the necessity for a more nuanced understanding of the precise working conditions which are worse for the dependent self-employed. If this chapter consequently stimulates research to further advance this finer-grained understanding, then it will have fulfilled one of its intentions. If it also encourages evaluation of which policy measures address the working conditions that are far worse for the dependent self-employed, then it will have fulfilled its wider intention.

References

Böheim, R., & Mühlberger, U. (2006). *Dependent Forms of Self-Employment in the UK: Identifying Workers on the Border Between Employment and Self-Employment* (Discussion Paper No. 1963). Bonn: IZA.

Borghi, P., Mori, A., & Semeza, R. (2018). Self-Employed Professionals in the European Labour Market: A Comparison Between Italy, Germany and the UK. *Transfer: European Review of Labour and Research*. https://doi.org/10.1177/1024258918761564.

Broughton, A., Green, M., Rickard, C., Swift, S., Eichhorst, W., Tobsch, V., et al. (2016). *Precarious Employment in Europe*. Brussels: European Parliament, Directorate-General for Internal Policies, Policy Department A: Economic and Scientific Policy.

Congregado, E., Esteve, V., & Golpe, A. A. (2012). *Job Creation and the Self-Employed Firm Size: Evidence from Spain* (Working Paper in Applied Economics). Valencia: Universitat de València.

Eichhorst, W., Braga, M., Famira-Mühlberger, U., Gerard, M., Horvath, T., Kahanec, M., et al. (2013). *Social Protection Rights of Economically Dependent Self-Employed Workers* (IZA Research Report No. 54). Bonn: IZA.

Eurofound. (2013). *Self-Employed or Not Self-Employed? Working Conditions of 'Economically Dependent Workers'*. Dublin: European Foundation for the Improvement of Living and Working Conditions.

Eurofound. (2016a). *Exploring the Fraudulent Contracting of Work in the European Union*. Luxembourg: Publications Office of the European Union.

Eurofound. (2016b). *Sixth European Working Conditions Survey—Overview Report*. Luxembourg: Publications Office of the European Union.

Eurofound. (2018a). *Does Employment Status Matter for Job Quality?* (Policy Brief). Luxembourg: Publications Office of the European Union.

Eurofound. (2018b). *Does Employment Status Matter for Job Quality?* (Working Paper). Luxembourg: Publications Office of the European Union.

European Commission. (2014). *Social Protection for the Self-Employed*. Brussels: European Commission.

European Commission. (2018). *Case Study: Gaps in Access to Social Protection for Economically Dependent Self-Employed in Spain*. Brussels: European Commission.

European Institute for Gender Equality. (2015). *Gender Equality and Economic Independence: Part-Time Work and Self-Employment*. Available from: https://eige.europa.eu/rdc/eige-publications/gender-equality-and-economic-independence-part-time-work-and-self-employment-report.

European Parliament. (2013). *Social Protection Rights of Economically Dependent Self-Employed Workers*. Directorate General for Internal Policies, Policy Department A: Employment Policy.

Fehringer, E. (2014). Tackling False (Bogus) Self-Employment. *Politics & Society, 32*(1), 7–39.

Fondeville, N., Ozdemir, E., Lelkes, O., Ward, T., & Zolyomi, E. (2015). *Recent Changes in Self-Employment and Entrepreneurship Across the EU* (Research Note 6/2015). Brussels: European Commission.

Harvey, M., & Behling, F. (2008). *The Evasion Economy: False Self-Employment in the UK Construction Industry*. London: Union of Construction, Allied Trades and Technicians (UCATT). Available from: http://ucatt.infobo.co.uk/files/publications/UCATT%20Report%Evasion%20Economy.pdf.

Hatfield, I. (2015). *Self-Employment in Europe*. London: Institute for Public Policy Research.

ILO. (2015, February 16–19). *Non-Standard Forms of Employment*. Report for Discussion at the Meeting of Experts on Non-Standard Forms of Employment (Geneva)/Conditions of Work and Equality Department. Geneva: International Labour Office.

ILO. (2016). *Non-Standard Employment Around the World: Understanding Challenges, Shaping Prospects*. Geneva: International Labour Office.

Jorens, Y. (2008). *Self-Employment and Bogus Self-Employment in the European Construction Industry—Part 1: Summary of a Comparative Study of 11 Member States*. EFBWW, FIEC, European Commission.

Kautonen, T., Down, S., Welter, F., Vainio, P., Palmroos, J., Althoff, K., et al. (2010). 'Involuntary Self-Employment' as a Public Policy Issue: A Cross-Country European Review. *International Journal of Entrepreneurial Behavior and Research, 16*(1), 112–129.

Kautonen, T., Palmroos, J., & Vainio, P. (2009). Involuntary Self-Employment in Finland: A Bleak Future? *International Journal of Public Policy, 4*(4), 533–548.

Mandrone, E., Marocco, M., & Radicchia, D. (2014). *Is Decline in Employment the Outcome or Cause of Crisis in Italy?* (Working Paper No. 7/2014). Roma: ASTRIL—Associazione Studie Ricerche Interdisciplinari sul Lavoro.

McKay, S., Jefferys, S., Paraksevopoulou, A., & Keles, J. (2012). *Study on Precarious Work and Social Rights*. London: Working Lives Research Institute, Faculty of Social Sciences and Humanities, London Metropolitan University.

Millán, A., Millán, J. M., & Román, C. (2018). Are False Own Account Workers Less Job Satisfied than True Ones? *Applied Economics Letters, 25*(13), 945–950.

Moore, S., & Newsome, K. J. (2018). Paying for Free Delivery: Dependent Self-Employment as a Measure of Precarity in Parcel Delivery. *Work, Employment & Society, 32*(3), 475–492.

Mühlberger, U., & Bertolini, S. (2008). The Organizational Governance of Work Relationships Between Employment and Self-Employment. *Socio-Economic Review, 6*(3), 449–472.

OECD. (2014). *Employment Outlook 2014. Non-Regular Employment, Job Security and the Labour Market Divide*. Paris: OECD. http://dx.doi.org/10.1787/empl_outlook-2014-7-en.

OECD. (2018). *Job Creation and Local Economic Development 2018: Preparing for the Future of Work*. Paris: OECD Publishing. https://doi.org/10.1787/9789264305342-en.

Pedersini, R., & Coletto, D. (2010). *Self-Employed Workers: Industrial Relations and Working Conditions*. Dublin: Eurofound.

Pulignano, V., Ortíz Gervasi, L., & de Franceschi, F. (2016). Union Responses to Precarious Workers: Italy and Spain Compared. *European Journal of Industrial Relations, 22*(1), 39–55.

Seeley, A. (2010). *Self-Employment in the Construction Industry*. Great Britain, Parliament House of Commons Library, Issuing Body. Standard Note: SN/BT/196.

Social Security Advisory Committee. (2014). *Social Security Provision and the Self-Employed* (Occasional Paper No. 13). London: Social Security Advisory Committee.

Spasova, S., Bouget, D., Ghailani, D., & Vanhercke, B. (2017). *Access to Social Protection for People Working on Non-Standard Contracts and as Self-Employed in Europe: A Study of National Policies*. European Social Policy Network (ESPN). Brussels: European Commission.

Suárez Corujo, B. (2017). The 'Gig' Economy and Its Impact on Social Security: The Spanish Example. *European Journal of Social Security, 19*(4), 293–312.

Taylor, M. (2017). *Good Work: The Taylor Review of Modern Working Practices*. London: Department for Business, Energy and Industrial Strategy.

Thörnqvist, C. (2014, September 1–3). *Bogus Self-Employment in the European Union*, Paper for the UACES Panel Vulnerabilities of Regular Labour Migration in the EU, Cork, Ireland.

Walby, K. (2009). Joint Review: Ulrike Mühlberger *Dependent Self-Employment: Workers on the Border Between Employment and Self-Employment*. Basingstoke: Palgrave Macmillan, 2007. Stella Vettori, *The Employment Contract and the Changed World of Work*. Aldershot: Ashgate, 2007. *Work, Employment and Society, 23*(2), 377–380.

Williams, C. C., & Horodnic, I. A. (2017). Tackling Bogus Self-Employment: Some Lessons from Romania. *Journal of Developmental Entrepreneurship, 22*(2), 1750011.

Williams, C. C., & Horodnic, I. A. (2018). Evaluating the Prevalence and Distribution of Dependent Self-Employment: Some Lessons from the European Working Conditions Survey. *Industrial Relations Journal, 49*(2), 109–127.

Williams, C. C., & Lapeyre, F. (2017). *Dependent Self-Employment: Trends, Challenges and Policy Responses in the EU* (Employment Policy Department, Employment Working Paper No. 228). Geneva: ILO.

Political Economy, Inward Foreign Direct Investment and EU Accession of the Western Balkans

John Marangos, Eirini Triarchi and Themis Anthrakidis

Introduction

The Western Balkans (WB) is a term used by the institutions of the European Union (EU) to describe the countries of the Balkan area that are not yet accomplished EU membership. This non-EU Balkan area consists of five sovereign countries, but six economies: Albania, Bosnia and Herzegovina, the Former Yugoslav Republic of Macedonia (FYROM), Montenegro, Serbia and the partially recognized Kosovo. Kosovo has declared independence unilaterally in 2008, pending its recognition by the entire international community (Adebahr 2018). For the purposes of the chapter, it is acknowledged that Kosovo located in

J. Marangos (✉) · E. Triarchi · T. Anthrakidis
University of Macedonia, Thessaloniki, Greece

J. Marangos
Hellenic Open University, Patras, Greece

E. Triarchi
University of Ioannina, Ioannina, Greece

V. Vlachos and A. Bitzenis (eds.), *European Union*,
https://doi.org/10.1007/978-3-030-18103-1_8

the WB, a subregion of South Eastern Europe (SEE) and is a relatively separate economic entity.

After the fall of the Berlin Wall, the WB ended as a strongly fragmented European subregion reaching recently a total population of 18 million (fewer than the 20 million of Romania, which joined the EU in 2007) and a GDP of almost €80 billion (Sanfey and Milatovic 2018, p. 3). Nonetheless, holding a significant geopolitical interest due to its strategic location, at the heart of Europe and surrounded by EU member countries. People of the region and of the EU have a common heritage, route in history and anchor their future on shared opportunities and challenges. EU is their largest trading partner, the main source of foreign direct investment (FDI) and main target country for outward migration. The region is serving as the shortest transit route between the South–East area of the EU (Greece, Bulgaria and Romania) and central European countries (Hungary, Croatia, Slovenia and Austria) which its importance came in front fore during the 2015–2016 refugee crisis (Dabrowski and Muachenkova 2018).

The EU has strong interests in the WB countries and supports their integration since 2003. After 15 years, the countries remain in the EU's waiting list, due to unresolved legacies of the 1990s, the slow pace of implementation of the required reforms according to the Copenhagen Accession Criteria, and the outburst of the financial and European debt crises. The delayed WB-EU enlargement creates a geopolitical vacuum that generates fears of destabilization of the region which in turn can cross onto the EU. Already, outside players such as Russia, China and Turkey exploit the opportunity to establish their presence in the region, to attain their economic and geopolitical goals and grasp part of the EU's share of influence.

The status of WB-EU accession process is: FYROM has been a candidate since 2005 (but frozen by Greece's reservations over the country's name); Montenegro since 2010; Serbia since 2012; and Albania since 2014. Montenegro started membership negotiations in 2012. Bosnia applied to join in 2016 and still holds the potential candidate status, while Kosovo's Stabilization and Association Agreement (SAA) with the EU was activated the same year. EU officials reiterate that WB countries membership to the Union by the target date necessitates acceleration in the adoption and implementation of the EU accession reforms.

The purpose of the chapter is to determine using a political economy approach the impact of inward FDI to the EU accession of the Western

Balkans. To our knowledge, such an approach in linking inward FDI to progress of EU accession using a political economy approach has not been endeavored. Scholars and students of Balkan studies and in general international studies would benefit from this novel approach in assessing the impact inward FDI on EU accession in the WB.

The chapter is structured as follows: First, the political economy issues of the EU accession of the WB are provided; second, the impact of the inward FDI on the EU accessions discussed with subsections; and finally, concluding remarks are given.

Political Economy Issues and EU Accession of the Western Balkans

Political and Economic Transformation of the Western Balkans in the Post-socialist Period

The WB transformation represents a complicated process in economic and political terms. The region experienced disintegration and an incomplete transition to democracy and the market economy. In fact, in WB there is still an interplay between nation- and state-building processes (Džankić et al. 2019, p. 3). Since 1990, the WB countries have undertaken a transformative process moving away from "Balkanization" and adopting the Europeanization paradigm. However, they still face multiple transition challenges (Radovanovik 2012, p. 207).

During the 1990s, the transition of Eastern European countries to democracy and market economy was peaceful, but in the same period, many WB countries confronted the devastating consequences of war. This regional conflict put the WB's economic transformation on hold during that decade. Since then, however, the WB has experienced a remarkable economic transformation and made considerable steps toward rebuilding their war-torn economies. In particular, the countries of the area have been notably transitioned toward a market-based economic system, developed modern banking systems, enhanced their economic openness and privatized a number of state-owned enterprises. Following this transformation, the WB achieved a substantial catch-up in living standards. However, the income convergence and the pace of economic transition still lags behind other Eastern European countries. In fact, the economic transition efforts were undermined by the deceleration of the structural transformation process, since the mid-2000, due to reform fatigue, resistance from powerful vested interests, weak political support and tough economic conditions. Overall, despite the advance of the economic transformation of the WB the inadequate reforms over the last decade is holding back economic growth (Murgasova et al. 2015, pp. 11–15).

Indeed, the six WB economies deal with a convergence challenge. It is argued that the region will need decades for catching-up the living standards of Europe. Sustained economic development requires a boost to productivity and investment across the region. Besides, the key impediment that holds back the WB's economic growth is low productivity. The weak economic performance of the WB, accompanied by the political instability, does not allow the region to realize its potentials. Narrowing the gap in terms of prosperity and living standards require the enhancement of comprehensive reforms that are needed for establishing sustainable market economies and promoting a dynamic private sector along with a growth-enabling public sector. In practice, the establishment of sustainable market economies in the WB depends on several key impediments that must be overcome. These obstacles include among others weak rule of law, limited access to finance, unfair competition, corruption, tax administration difficulties, chronic under-investment, weak institutions, corporate over-indebtedness, inadequate transport and telecommunications networks (Sanfey and Milatovic 2018).

The political and economic transformation of the WB in the post-socialist period is better understood within the concept of Europeanization. In particular, this concept is being described as a "process of a) construction, b) diffusion and c) institutionalization of formal and informal rules, procedures, policy paradigms, styles, 'ways of doing things', and shared beliefs and norms which are first defined and consolidated in the making of EU public policy and politics and then incorporated in the logic of domestic discourse, identities, political structures and public policies" (Radaelli 2003, p. 30). Besides, the EU is one of the key drivers for political and economic transformation of the region owing to the prospect of the EU membership. In this context, the EU is actively involved in state-building that these countries carry out since the end of the conflicts in the 1990s. Therefore, the Europeanization process encourages far-reaching shifts in the political and economic structures. However, the WB countries are still making efforts to consolidate and strengthen democratic and state structures. In fact, their sovereignty is still contested, while the establishment of efficient governance institutions remains a challenging issue. So, state-building is crucial for the transformation of the WB. As long as, the countries of the region are unable to perform basic state functions, establish a basic level of social welfare, launch democratic political institutions and procedures and ensure internal and external security their ability to comply with the European requirements will be limited (Keil 2013, p. 334). In this context, taking into account the challenging starting conditions of the WB countries they have made a considerable progress in state-building since the 2000s, however, currently these countries appear to be more or less stuck in transition (Borzel and Grimm 2018, p. 118).

The Stabilization and Association Process

The involvement of the EU in WB was initially placing emphasis on peace and stability across the region. At that period, the EU did not promote any coherent policy for the region; hence, it lacked the required legitimacy and authority to exert any influence. More importantly, the absence of an accession prospect for the WB countries or any other contractual relations undermined the image of the EU. However, as long as the WB was still struggling for their viability and survival, the need for a European perspective was vital. In this context, at the end of the 1990s, EU demonstrated its readiness to support the Europeanization of the WB through a number of initiatives and policies such as the Stability Pact for South Eastern Europe (SEE), the Stabilization and Association Process (SAP) and the Zagreb Summit Declaration (Demetropoulou 2002, pp. 93–4).

The SAP was established by the EU in 1999 in order to encourage and facilitate WB to implement various reforms. The rationale of SAP was to offer a realistic perspective to WB countries concerning their conditional accession to the EU. The process of the regional integration through SAP would take place in three phases. The first phase was preparatory, setting the path for the initial reforms and preparing each of the WB countries for signing the agreement with the EU. The second phase included the negotiation of the agreement and its adoption by the counterparts involved. The third phase would launch the enactment of the agreement and the implementation of the required reforms (Schenker 2008, pp. 1–2).

In fact, the SAP had a dual objective, namely regional stability and integration. In this context, the idea of enhancing cooperation between the WB states and the EU was built upon the Regional Approach, which was comprising all SEE countries without association agreements with the EU. The idea of enforcing conditionality for EU membership was built upon the experiences of the EU enlargement in Central and Eastern European Countries (CEECs). The SAP however was innovative in comparison with the Regional Approach and the enlargement process in CEECs. The SAP was a comprehensive framework that would motivate reforms in WB, not only through the prospect of potential membership in the EU, but also through various instruments. These instruments were designed to enhance economic relations, increase the existing financial assistance, support governance and develop dialogue across the region. The key instruments of the SAP framework were a package of autonomous trade preferences that were offering access to the EU market, and the Community Assistance for Reconstruction, Development and Stabilization (CARDS) program that was allocating funds across the region. It is important that these key instruments were aiding, having explicit conditions. This conditionality was crucial for reinforcing the SAP. The most important instrument of the SAP though was the bilateral Stabilization and Association Agreements (SAAs), which constituted the key framework of the relations between the EU and the WB states concerning SAP implementation (Elbasani 2008, pp. 8–9).

The SAP has been designed in a way that facilitates reforms and assists each of the WB countries to meet the EU accession criteria and especially the political conditionality, which was seen as the "cement" of the SAP (Tatham 2009, p. 165). The political conditionality is an incentives-based instrument that had successfully contributed to the transformation processes of the CEECs. It is acknowledged that conditionality foster reforms, if the expected political costs of compliance with EU criteria do not exceed the benefits of the membership. Thus, the EU has been heavily relied on strict conditionality in order to enforce the WB countries to comply with its accession political, economic and institutional criteria (Freyburg and Richter 2010, p. 264). However, it should be noticed that the SAP is not an undifferentiated pre-accession mechanism. In fact, the SAP is a tailor-made instrument that places emphasis on a step-by-step progress. In this context, each WB country progress toward the EU membership is in accordance with its individual capacities and specific conditions. Therefore, the progress of these countries is based on their own performance. In this framework, European Commission assesses the SAP process and monitors WB countries' progress annually (Schwarzinger and Sajdik 2009, p. 314).

Overall, the SAP can be understood as a tool of Europeanization that facilitates the process of reforms in WB by reinforcing the aim of EU membership. Indeed, the SAP is seen as the EU's flagship policy in the region, which effectively contributed to the post-conflict stabilization of the WB states and facilitates their post-socialist transition and gradual integration into the EU. Contrary to the failed EU's efforts for ad hoc conflict management in the Former Yugoslavia in the 1990s, the SAP is a post-conflict instrument, whose efficacy though has been questioned (Gordon 2009, p. 327).

In fact, the EU dealt with conflicting objectives in the WB. On the one hand, it was primarily concerned about security and stability that called for integration, and on the other hand, it was interested in a cautious enlargement that took into account democratization (Richter 2012, p. 507). Actually, the progress of the integration of the WB into the EU structures has been slowed down owing to an enlargement "fatigue". The success story of the Eastern Enlargement has been intended to be replicated to WB through the SAP. The EU initially promoted this intense Europeanization strategy in order to progressively transform this fragile part of Europe. However, during this process the EU had to face severe economic and political crisis, which had a detrimental impact on the EU enlargement in the WB.

The EU' s commitment to the EU perspective of the WB countries has been eroded and Europeanization has remained largely shallow in the region (O'Brennan 2014, p. 222). As a result, the inclusion of WB countries in European institutions is currently in strife. Nevertheless, all countries in the region have made a progress according to SAP. However, the speed and depth of the political and economic reforms of all WB states fall behind the EU's expectations. In fact, the "pull" of the EU has been gradually weakened given that its commitment to the enlargement to the WB has been more and more questionable. As long as the EU is unable to project a credible vision and strategy to the WB countries their efforts for compliance with the EU requirements have been withered (Belloni and Brunazzo 2017, pp. 25–27). It should be underlined though that recently, in 2018, the European Commission adopted a strategy for "a credible enlargement perspective for and enhanced EU engagement with the Western Balkans" which reaffirms that if WB candidate countries implement the necessary reforms, the EU will respond by promoting their membership (Vachudova 2019, p. 64). This regenerated enlargement process points out that the EU membership for the WB is in the EU's political and economic interest. In this context, the EU, launching this new strategy, re-commits itself to the WB European perspective, demanding in turn from the countries of the region to fulfill their own commitments and meet membership conditions (European Commission 2018).

Geopolitical Tensions in the Western Balkans

WB, being geographically located at the crossroad between East and West, were always playing a significant geopolitical role. As a result, throughout the history of this region, WB always was drawing the interest of major regional and global state actors, such as the EU, US, Russia and Turkey.

In this context, the EU had always shown a vital interest to pursue a coherent strategy to stabilize the volatile WB countries at its backyard. Following its failure to avoid the dissolution of Yugoslavia and prevent the atrocities of ethnic conflicts in Bosnia and Kosovo, the EU contributed to peace- and state-building in the region. Today, however, the EU deals with new threats in WB, which does not correspond to traditional security issues. In fact, the EU interests can be directly and indirectly undermined by non-traditional security threats, which mainly refer to networks of organized crime, terrorism and radicalization and uncontrolled illegal immigration. Overall, these non-traditional issues export instability and pose a security threat to the EU countries (Agir et al. 2016, pp. 45–47). Indeed, the focus of the EU in WB has shifted from peace- and state-building to the establishment of accountable state institutions that would accommodate EU's internal security concerns, such as terrorism and organized crime. Thus, the rationale of the EU external policy toward WB is, on the one hand, to promote political and economic reforms and safeguard security and stability transforming these post-conflict counties to full-fledged EU member states, and on the other hand, to achieve the EU internal security objectives (Ioannides and Collantes-Celador 2011, pp. 416–417). In this context, the enlargement of the EU to the WB countries implies significant geopolitical benefits in terms of stability and security which eventually reinforce the commitment of the EU to the enlargement process (Vachudova 2019, pp. 68–69). Besides, the ongoing integration of the WB into European economic and political structures is advancing and at the same time the mutual interdependencies are deepening. However, the required reforms in the WB states for achieving EU membership are progressing slower than anticipated, while in the same time the EU deals with internal challenges such as the Eurozone crisis, migration flows and Brexit (Hänsel and Feyerabend 2018, p. 4).

USA played a key role in WB in the past, given the active American military and diplomatic presence in the region providing a certain level of stability, which pushed forward economic and political reforms. In the course of the years, some of the WB countries joined NATO (Albania, Montenegro, Slovenia, Croatia) whereas other countries are still pursuing NATO membership (FYROM, Bosnia and Herzegovina). Nevertheless, the WB remains a tenuous region and there are concerns that any decrease in the presence of the US interference could create a regional vacuum. This vacuum can potentially allow rival state actors to enhance their economic and political role in WB and deepen existing problems of economic stagnation, radicalization, terrorism organized crime (Morelli and Garding 2018, p. 2). Indeed, USA's interests in the region seem to be diminished owing to its continuing shift of geostrategic focus. The USA is still interested in maintaining stability in WB and integrating the countries into Euro-Atlantic security structures, however, its commitment tends to be inconsistent (Hänsel and Feyerabend 2018).

Russia, in the beginning of the post-Cold War era, had lost a considerable part of its military, economic, political, ideological and power. Since, the 2000s though Russia made efforts to restore its hegemonic role in Eurasia, including Balkans, and to re-establish its status as a superpower. As a result, Russia has been engaged in geopolitical struggle against other major actors along its borders and within its sphere of influence (Petrillo 2013, pp. 1–2). Indeed, for Russian geopolitical concerns the WB is an area of significant interest. Owing to the presence of cultural, historical and political affiliations, the WB remains a link between Russia and Europe. The active engagement of other actors in the WB though has limited the ability of Moscow to re-establish stronger pro-Russian relationships in the region. However, the economic and political cooperation between Russian and the WB remains inspired by the common Slavic heritage (Mulalic and Karic 2014, pp. 93–95). Nevertheless, the WB is not a top priority in the foreign policy agenda of Moscow. For Russia, the WB is a key region of continuing rivalry, although with a diminishing strategic value for conducting its energy policy. Despite the Russian dominance in the energy sector and its strong economic engagement in the region, Moscow has not seriously challenged the EU aspirations, nevertheless, it has actively contested the NATO expansion in WB countries (Bieri 2015, p. 2). Overall, Russia does not pursue a solid strategy in WB apart from obstructing NATO's expansion in the region. In fact, Moscow lacks the prerequisites to establish itself as a regional hegemon in WB, which are deeply dependent on the EU (Bechev 2018, p. 3).

Turkey since the 2000s has reoriented its foreign policy and adopted a multidimensional approach, which implies a deeper involvement of Ankara in politics in the neighboring regions. This new era of Turkish foreign policy signals a crucial shift from Kemalism to neo-Ottomanism, namely from isolationism to a vision of Turkey as a leader of Muslim and Turkic worlds and a regional key actor in Eurasia. This new doctrine stresses the importance of the strategic depth of Turkey, which is described in geographical and historical terms. Turkey leveraging the historical legacy of the Ottoman Empire projected its power and engaged in many geopolitical areas or spheres of influence, including Balkans (Murinson 2006, p. 952). In this context, the Turkish engagement in the WB is attributed to numerous factors including the long-standing common history of Turkey with this region, the Turkish minorities and Muslim communities that live in WB, the geopolitical importance of the region as a buffer-zone for Turkey and the increasing Turkish economic interests in the area (Türbedar 2011, pp. 140–142). Overall, the revitalization of Ankara's interest in the WB and its active engagement is an attempt of a neo-Ottoman influence in the region. However, Turkey's assertive engagement in the WB has not established yet any permanent political and economic stronghold. Even though the relations between Ankara and the WB countries had never been tighter, Turkey cannot play the role as a regional hegemon. In fact, its influence is limited to the Muslim population in the WB. Turkey, without any doubt, has become a regional actor in this region, but realistically its capabilities cannot meet its neo-Ottoman aspirations (Petrović and Reljić 2011, pp. 161–162).

Inward FDI and EU Accession of the Western Balkans

The Evolution of Inward FDI in Western Balkans

Although the literature on FDI issues is voluminous and even the number of studies referring to transition economies is remarkable, due to the lack of reliable data studies concerning the WB are scarce.

In the time followed the fall of the Berlin Wall, the SEE region lost valuable time due to political, ethnic and national conflicts that vanished FDI inflows, despite the perceptions for economic opportunities. WB countries have been associated with the trouble image of wars and conflicts experienced through the 1990s. Their "notorious" past limited any potential for FDI growth vital for the region due to their limited domestic savings (Estrin and Uvalic 2016a, b). Most of all, FDI enables recipient countries to increase their domestic savings and investment concurrently with the transfer of technology, knowledge management, business culture and accessing foreign markets (Dabour 2000, p. 48). The breakup of the Yugoslav Federation in mid-1991 into smaller independent states perplexed the transition process to market economy since each newly established state inheriting different dynamics, followed diverging routes in implementing political, economic and social reforms. Most of the new states are small by any standard, which inhibits FDI inflows relative to countries that can offer a large domestic market. In addition, at the time, embargos were imposed on the Federal Republic of Yugoslavia consisting of Serbia, Kosovo and Montenegro by the UN and EU and in the case of the FYROM by Greece (Uvalic 2010, p. 3). These blockades restricted the prospects of political and economic stability and inward FDI.

Until the sign of Dayton Peace Accords in 1995 that put an end to the almost three and a half years of war, no remarkable sign of FDI inflows was recorded in the examined WB transition economies. The Dayton Accords peace agreements were a positive development to reduce political instability, to stabilize economies and to boost privatization (Brada et al. 2006, p. 675) enabling the transition to the market economy. Nevertheless, the Kosovo conflict at late 1990s (1998–1999) postponed any progress and caused delays in the implementation of any major reforms that would rescue these suffering economies. Any prospects for FDI growth were not realized, proving that the costs of instability in terms of foregone FDI inflows are quite high. In this vein, other transition countries in SEE less affected by conflicts such as Bulgaria and Croatia experienced a rise in the FDI inflows, in particular in telecommunications due to the starting one-off privatization policy in this sector. The FYROM also recorded increase in FDI inflows directed to the oil refinery sector (UNCTAD 2000, p. 66).

From 2000 onwards, the large-scale privatizations in the banking sector, telecommunications companies and the sale of mining concessions,

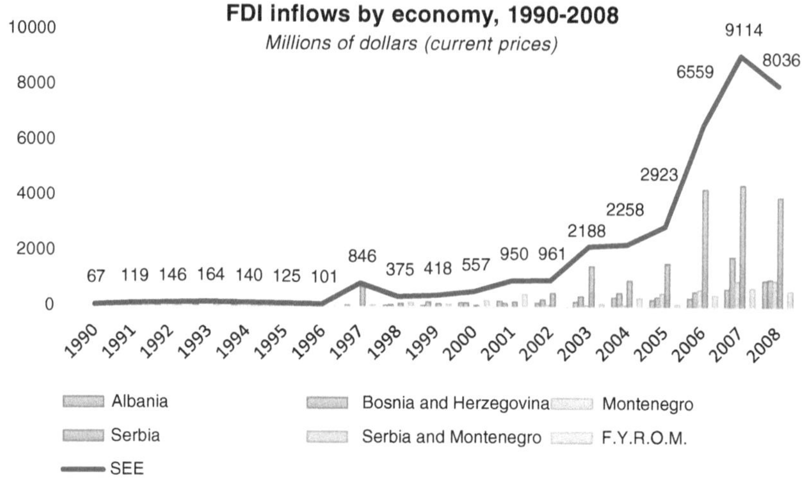

Fig. 1 FDI Inflows by economy in non-EU SEEC during the period 1990–2008 (*Source* Adopted from UNCTAD [2018a], FDI inflows by region and economy, 1990–2017 FDI/MNC database [www.unctad.org/fdistatistics])

resulted to an upward trend in FDI inflows in WB. As Fig. 1 shows, the booming of inward FDI in the region took place during the years 2002–2003, recording an increase of 127.7% from \$961 to \$2188 million. The second largest increase (124.4%) recorded during 2005–2006, whereas the highest value on FDI inflows was in 2007.

FDI inflows in the region are mainly directed to the non-tradable sectors, suggesting the strengthening of domestic demand and the rise of imports. This stimulates a higher trade deficit than having flows to the tradable sector and inhibits the efficient restructuring of key industries (Kinoshita 2011; Uvalic 2010). The EU enlargement of 2004 included eight countries of Central and Eastern Europe (CEE) and acted as a catalyst to Serbia and Montenegro to speed up reforms, aimed at achieving the admission criteria. UNCTAD (2004, p. 75) reports that "Serbia and Montenegro permitted the free transfer of financial and other resources related to foreign investment, lifted previous limitations on the establishment of wholly owned foreign affiliates in the telecom and public information industries and lifted approval requirements for establishing foreign affiliates or for the acquisition of domestic companies (Foreign Direct Investment Law of 2003)." Since 2005, WB intensified their reform policies—aimed also at judicial independence, accountability, tackling of corruption and organized crime, protection against expropriation, introduction of flat tax rate and fighting tax evasion—in line with their ambition to join the EU. Albania, Bosnia and Herzegovina, Croatia (withdrew in July 2013 after joining the EU), the FYROM, Moldova, Montenegro, Serbia and the United Nations Interim Administration Mission in Kosovo (UNMIK) on behalf of Kosovo, signed an regional trade agreement, the CEFTA in 2006, that enabled intra-regional investment, as well as, trade flows (Cefta.int 2019; OECD 2011, p. 20). Further, the six Western Balkans states accelerated the privatization rate of public assets, especially those in telecommunication and energy (UNCTAD 2007, pp. 65–66; 2008, p. 70).

The State of Inward FDI in the Western Balkans

The global economic crisis in the WB economies generated weak and unstable economic growth, high rate of unemployment, rise of poverty and reverse in the pre-crisis investment climate (Sanfey and Zeh 2012, p. 2). WB countries being depended mostly on EU market for trade and investments were affected strongly by the Eurozone sovereign debt crisis. From the largest global investors countries that are located in Europe, Germany, Switzerland and the Netherlands are the main FDI source countries for Kosovo and FYROM. For the remaining examined countries received flows from Italy and from smaller economies like Austria, Greece, Hungary and Slovenia (Kalotay 2013, p. 254).

The recovery and integration into the global economy deemed too difficult since the region lacked export-oriented projects involved in international productions networks that have proved to stimulate growth. As well, FDI inflows have been concentrated on the sectors mostly exposed to crisis those of finance and retail (UNCTAD 2011, 2013). However, in the mid-2000s the development of the financial sector has facilitated access to funds for firms and households and boosted inward FDI (IMF 2014, p. 6). The sector of manufacturing regarded as a channel of efficiency, in the sense of transfer of technology, organization of the firm and superior managerial skills, still underperforms in the region with the exceptions of Serbia and the FYROM (Kalotay 2013; Malovic et al. 2018, p. 8).

From 2009 onwards, as Fig. 2 demonstrates, FDI inflows in the region of WB fluctuated, recording only recently a better performance

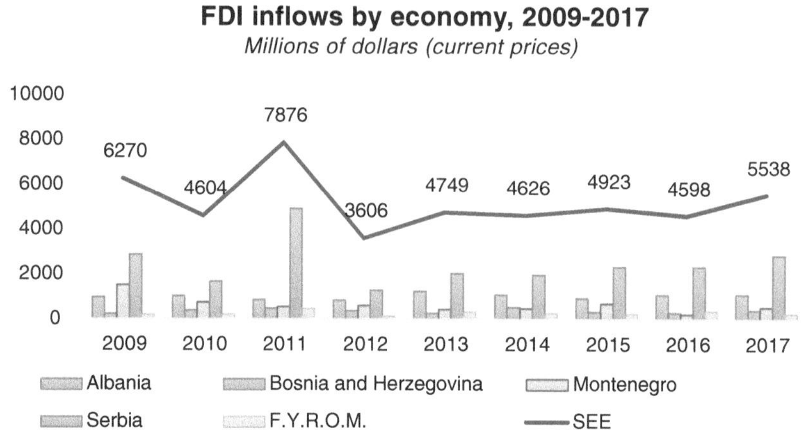

Fig. 2 FDI inflows by economy in WB during the period 2009–2017 (*Source* Adjusted from UNCTAD [2018a], FDI inflows by region and economy, 1990–2017 FDI/MNC database [www.unctad.org/fdistatistics])

but not reaching the pre-crisis period. Reporting the current state of inward FDI in the WB, Serbia is the largest economy of the region and the most important FDI target. In 2011, the country reached its peak FDI flows, as it received $4.9 billion, thus 62.6% of the total inward FDI in the region. In 2017, FDI in Serbia grew by 22%, however, much of this growth was due to reinvested earnings in and intracompany loans to foreign affiliates (UNCTAD 2018b). Since 2010, Albania has received the second largest amount of FDI inflows due to the implementation of FDI projects on energy sector (Trans Adriatic Pipeline and the Devolli hydropower plant projects) and mining. As these projects in 2017 are near to completion, as such the established foreign investors initiated investments in renewable energy projects pushing FDI to grow marginally by 2% (UNCTAD 2018b). During 2016–2017, the FYROM had a reduction of 31.5% in inward FDI, due to mounting political uncertainty.

Since 2009, Montenegro holds the highest FDI intensity reaching the 116.31% of inward FDI stock as a percentage of GDP in 2017 due to Azerbaijan and Russian real estate investments (Hunya and Schwarzhappel 2016; UNCTAD 2018b). Serbia has the second largest in 2017 (85.6% of inward FDI stock as a percentage of GDP) while Albania the third (51.9% of inward FDI stock as a percentage of GDP)

(UNCTAD 2018c). Bosnia and Herzegovina have increased its percentage from 39.4% of inward FDI stock in 2009 to 45.8% in 2017 as a percentage of GDP (UNCTAD 2018c) due to a doubling of reinvested earnings. The key comparative advantages that still hold foreign interest to invest in the WB countries beyond being considered as a natural gateway to Europe are flexibility in labor policies, low labor costs combined with a relatively educated population, favorable taxation and the perspective of EU membership. The main difference from the pre-crisis period is that although the bulk of FDI inflows are still originating from European countries, China has emerged as an important source of FDI investing in finance, aviation and tourism. Prospects for further Chinese involvement seriously exist on the basis of the completion of the ambitious "Belt and Road Initiative" (BRI) to connect Asia with Africa and Europe via land and maritime networks along with six corridors (Sanfey and Milatovic 2018; UNCTAD 2018b). This program is aiming in regional integration, increasing trade and stimulating economic growth. The budget is expected to reach the amount of $1 trillion. BRI includes up to now 70 countries, including WB, from Beijing to Athens and connecting with Belgrade, Sarajevo, Skopje, Budapest, Tirana and other capitals (Bennett 2017; EBRD 2019).

In the aftermath of the global and Eurozone crises, WB countries continue to have fiscal and competitiveness issues and face external vulnerabilities. This background prevails in the region, while it is still positioned as the last "land of opportunity" in Europe, repeating the success of CEEC in achieving a satisfactory level of economic prosperity and political freedom (Fullani and Tanku 2013). Crisis reminds to all the main disincentives for engaging in FDI in the region, such as the small size of the domestic market with low per capita income, natural resources lacking strategic importance (only exception the Serbian lithium) and the high external debts and/or budget deficits fueled by cross-border non-performing loans. To continue, the high risk of the region being vulnerable to social and political instability, the retarded pace in structural reforms, the high unemployment rate and the low productivity in the private sector lagging well behind EU standards. Finally, the existence of the weak public infrastructure, the high level of corruption in economy, the low institutional and administrative capacity reflecting the institutional and political deficiencies are characteristics of the WB. In addition, the lower quality of bureaucracy and the weak capacity of policymaking elites have been dominated in the region, since the Ottoman rule and reproduced through the education system and the legacy of bureaucratic malpractices (The Economist Intelligence Unit 2018, p. 12). In this context, WB countries cannot be considered as functioning competitive market economies and hold a satisfactory level of stock of FDI inflows, compared to EU28 and Commonwealth of Independent States (CIS), according to data presented in Table 1. Despite the slight increase of 24% in 2017, WB has a poor performance in terms of inward FDI stock. The European Commission (2018) concludes that WB countries should raise investments through the building of a strong economic governance and the implementation of efficient structural reforms that target increases of competitiveness.

The Role of Inward FDI in Western Balkan During the EU Accession Process

Although market-oriented reforms of the past, provided to all of the Yugoslav successor countries a substantial advantage in contradistinction to former socialist countries, however, at the end of the transition process, their performance was judged unsatisfactory (Uvalic 2010). In 2003, EU-WB Summit of Thessaloniki, the EU underlined the prospect of EU membership and presented best practices for WB to move toward European integration. Following the Summit, WB countries stepped up the pace of required political and economic reforms and even managed to partially converge in income levels with the EU. Experience confirms that reforms and growth go hand-in-hand in transition countries (Sanfey and Zeh 2012). This rate of progress stopped in the outbreak of the 2008 global financial crisis. Yet, the EU did not turn its back to the WB despite the delays in reforms and released in 2015 "The new European Commission Enlargement Strategy" ensuring in the long run all WB countries' European future. This latest strategy proceeded in changes in the methodology for the assessment of the candidate WB country progress. The key areas still to be improved are (1) the rule of law, the functioning of the judiciary, fight against corruption and fight against organized crime, (2) public administration reform and (3) key economic criteria in the presence of a functioning market economy and the capacity to cope with competitive pressures of market forces within the EU (Sanfey et al. 2016, p. 10). In 2018, the EC formally reenergized enlargement process by setting a new deadline of 2025 for the admission of at least two of the best WB candidates, Serbia and Montenegro (Dabrowski and Muachenkova 2018). These are economies

Table 1 FDI inward stock by region during the period 2009–2017

FDI inward stock, by region, 2009–2017 (Millions of dollars)

Region/economy	*2009*	*2010*	*2011*	*2012*	*2013*	*2014*	*2015*	*2016*	*2017*
EU-28	7,484,772	7,357,407	7,682,088	7,919,288	8,228,780	7,936,558	7,933,003	8,028,100	9,123,982
SEE	17,010	21,179	23,423	24,767	58,167	54,457	53,254	55,181	68,369
CIS	522,747	646,340	633,297	690,341	739,020	559,083	536,391	686,992	753,946

Source Adjusted from UNCTAD (2018d), FDI inward stock by region and economy, 1990–2017 FDI/MNC database (www.unctad.org/fdistatistics)

distinguished in their FDI performance since Serbia is the biggest recipient of FDI in aggregate terms (Fig. 2) and Montenegro in inward FDI stock per capita. It appears that the FDI precession performance of Serbia and Montenegro enhances growth potential in the region and achieves the overarching goal of EU membership.

One of the main obstacles that retarded EU enlargement in WB was the low growth rates. Optimism was created during the last decade as the FDI inflows acted as a channel of growth, enhancing prospects of EU accession. But the lack of national and subnational FDI strategies to address the main challenges within WB states became evident in the long-term. The current economic situation in the region seems to be improved, yet not to the level achieved by the countries in the previous accession rounds. The structural issues these states face are significant, concerning regulatory issues and infrastructure deficiencies. WB must overcome these challenges to achieve sustainable comparative advantages and strengthen its position in the competitive EU market.

Concluding Remarks

All the WB countries, except Albania, were part of Yugoslavia, a socialist country but relatively open to the world in terms of trade and freedom to travel. After the fall of the Berlin Wall, the transition was initiated from an authoritarian collective economy in Yugoslavia (firms where owned by the workers and coordination was based on market relations), while in Albania a centrally administered economy, toward a democratic free-market economy. In the 1990's the Socialist Federal Republic of Yugoslavia dismantled, and the successor states battered by Yugoslav wars, experienced the downfall of their economy, poverty, human suffering, refugee flows, sanctions, crime and corruption.

Concerns of re-emergence of intra-regional conflicts between Kosovo and Serbia and the threat of instability in Bosnia still exist (Grieveson et al. 2018). European policymakers seems to realize the danger of losing WB that traditionally belong in Europe and in this context the European Commission (EC) President Jean-Claude Juncker stated that if EU invests in the stability and prosperity of the WB, then it invests in the security and future of the EU (Nawaz and Rafique 2018). In 2018, under the pressure of Brexit, the EC announced a new strategy for WB accession with a target date of 2025.

The WB countries are lagging behind to their peers in the EU11 (East European EU member states: Bulgaria, Croatia, The Czech Republic,

Estonia, Hungary, Latvia, Lithuania, Poland, Romania, Slovakia and Slovenia) and the other emerging-market regions, in attracting FDI. FDI is considered to be a fueling channel of competitiveness and economic development to recipient countries, which are a requisite in meeting the economic membership conditions as defined in the Copenhagen Criteria (Füle 2013).

To this end, EU provides substantial funding through the Instrument for Pre-Accession Assistance (IPA) (Sanfey et al. 2016). This regional IPA may be the starting point for change in WB's investments policy. IPA's focus is on developing investment opportunities, where economies can provide comparative advantages through their value chains (UNCTAD 2017, p. 57). The prospects of region's EU accession are once again an opportunity for restoring investors' confidence and supporting the building of a strong image as an investment destination. The higher the FDI flows region receives, the greater the export capacity and the upraise of the value chain. In turn, this would enhance the per capita income convergence with EU member states (Stehrer and Holzner 2018). The crucial point for the WB countries is to get rid of their previous differences and to cooperate supplementing each other. This policy will mitigate the complexities and risks of investing in the region, will create a larger integrated market and improve region's visibility. At the 2017, Western Balkans Trieste Summit, the six WB economies committed to work together for promoting economic cooperation and regional integration. The Multi-Annual Action Plan for Regional Economic Area in the Western Balkans (MAP REA) was established to support this commitment. If the WB countries follow the MAP REA reform agenda, then they will be aligned with EU and international best practices and standards. In consequence, the region will be developed as an attractive destination for investment and commerce, and succeed convergence with EU (CEFTA 2018, p. 2).

References

Adebahr, C. (2018). Is Kosovo a Country, or a Cause—And for What? *Global Policy*. Available at https://www.globalpolicyjournal.com/blog/19/06/2018/kosovo-country-or-cause-and-what. Accessed 4 January 2019.

Agir, B. S., Gürsoy, B., & Arman, M. N. (2016). European Perspective of Human Security and the Western Balkans. *Revista de Stiinte Politice, 50*(50), 41–54.

Bechev, D. (2018). *Understanding Russia's Influence in the Western Balkans*. Helsinki: Hybrid CoE.

Belloni, R., & Brunazzo, M. (2017). After Brexit: The Western Balkans in the European Waiting Room. *European Review of International Studies, 1*(1), 21–38.

Bennett, V. (2017). *What China's 'Belt and Road Initiative' Means for the Western Balkans.*

Bieri, M. (2015, March). *The Western Balkans Between Europe and Russia* (CSS Analyses in Security Policy, No. 170, pp. 1–4).

Borzel, T., & Grimm, S. (2018). Building Good (Enough) Governance in Postconflict Societies & Areas of Limited Statehood: The European Union & the Western Balkans. *Daedalus, 147*(1), 116–127.

Brada, J. C., Kutan, A. M., & Yigit, T. M. (2006). The Effects of Transition and Political Instability on Foreign Direct Investment Inflows: Central Europe and the Balkans. *Economics of Transition, 14*(4), 649–680.

CEFTA. (2018). *Regional Investment Reform Agenda for the Western Balkans Six.* CEFTA.

Cefta.int. (2019). CEFTA Parties.

Dabour, N. M. (2000). The Role of Foireign Direct Investment (FDI) in Development and Growth in OIC Member Countries. *Journal of Economic Cooperation, 21*(3), 27–55.

Dabrowski, M., & Muachenkova, Y. (2018). *The Western Balkans on the Road to the European Union, Policy Contribution* (Vol. 38). https://doi.org/10.1002/mmnd.18940380315.

Demetropoulou, L. (2002). Europe and the Balkans: Membership Aspiration, EU Involvement and Europeanization Capacity in South Eastern Europe. *Southeast European Politics, 3*(2–3), 87–106.

Džankić, J., Keil, S., & Kmezić, M. (2019). Introduction: The Europeanisation of the Western Balkans. In J. Džankić, S. Keil, & M. Kmezić (Eds.), *The Europeanisation of the Western Balkans. New Perspectives on South-East Europe* (pp. 1–14). Cham: Palgrave Macmillan.

EBRD. (2019). *Belt and Road Initiative (BRI).* Available at https://www.ebrd.com/what-we-do/belt-androad/overview.html. Accessed 3 January 2019.

Elbasani, A. (2008). *The Stabilisation and Association Process in the Balkans: Overloaded Agenda and Weak Incentives?* (Vol. 3) (EUI Working Paper SPS).

Estrin, S., & Uvalic, M. (2016a). Foreign Direct Investment in the Western Balkans: What Role Has It Played During Transition? *Comparative Economic Studies, 58*(3), 455–483.

Estrin, S., & Uvalic, M. (2016b). Are Foreign Direct Investments in the Balkans Different? In *Contemporary Issues in Development Economics* (pp. 178–193). London: Palgrave Macmillan.

European Commission. (2018). *A Credible Enlargement Perspective for and Enhanced EU Engagement with the Western Balkans.* Strasbourg: European Commission.

Freyburg, T., & Richter, S. (2010). National Identity Matters: The Limited Impact of EU Political Conditionality in the Western Balkans. *Journal of European Public Policy, 17*(2), 263–281.

Füle, S. (2013). Copenhagen Criteria—The Backbone of EU Enlargement. In *The Copenhagen Criteria and the Enlargement of the European Union.* (Conference Report, 9–11).

Fullani, A., & Tanku, A. (2013). Defining a New Reform Agenda Paths to Sustainable Convergence in South East Europe. In O. Anastasakis, P. Sanfey, & M. Watson (Eds.), *Defining a New Reform Agenda Paths to Sustainable Convergence in South East Europe* (p. 117). Oxford: SEESOX.

Gordon, C. (2009). The Stabilization and Association Process in the Western Balkans: An Effective Instrument of Post-conflict Management? *Ethnopolitics, 8*(3–4), 325–340.

Grieveson, R., Grübler, J., & Holzner, M. (2018). *Western Balkans EU Accession: Is the 2025 Target Date Realistic?* No. 20. Available at https://wiiw.ac.at/western-balkans-eu-accession-is-the-2025-target-date-realistic--dlp-4526.pdf. Accessed 28 November 2018.

Hänsel, L., & Feyerabend, F. (2018). The Role of External Actors in the Western Balkans. In L. Hänsel & F. Feyerabend (Eds.), *The Influence of External Actors in the Western Balkans: A Map of Geopolitical Players* (p. 41). Konrad-Adenauer-Stiftung.

Hunya, G., & Schwarzhappel, M. (2016). *FDI Report FDI in Central, East and Southeast Europe: Slump despite Global Upturn.* Vienna: The Vienna Institute for International Economic Studies.

IMF. (2014). *25 Years of Transition Post-communist Europe and the IMF.* Washington, DC: IMF.

Ioannides, I., & Collantes-Celador, G. (2011). The Internal-External Security Nexus and EU Police/Rule of Law Missions in the Western Balkans. *Conflict, Security and Development, 11*(4), 415–445.

Kalotay, K. (2013). Inward FDI in the Western Balkans in the Wake of Croatia's EU Accession. *The Journal of World Investment & Trade, 14*(2), 241–263.

Keil, S. (2013). Europeanization, State-Building and Democratization in the Western Balkans. *Nationalities Papers, 41*(3), 343–353.

Kinoshita, Y. (2011). *Sectoral Composition of Foreign Direct Investment and External Vulnerability in Eastern Europe* (Vol. 11, p. 1) (IMF Working Papers, No. 123).

Malovic, M., Özer, M., & Zdravkovic, A. (2018). Misunderstanding of FDI in the Western Balkans: Cart Before the Horse and Wheels Without Suspension. *Journal of Balkan and Near Eastern Studies*, 1–16.

Morelli, V., & Garding, S. (2018). *Serbia: Background and U.S. Relations* (Congressional Research Service Report).

Mulalic, M., & Karic, M. (2014). The Western Balkans Geopolitics and Russian Energy Politics. *Epiphany, 7*(1), 87–108.

Murgasova, Z., Ilahi, N., Miniane, J., Scott, A., & Vladkova-Hollar, I. (2015). *The Western Balkans 15 Years of Economic Transition* (International Monetary Fund Special Report).

Murinson, A. (2006). The Strategic Depth Doctrine of Turkish Foreign Policy. *Middle Eastern Studies, 42*(6), 945–964.

Nawaz, S., & Rafique, N. (2018). *EU'S Western Balkan's Policy Put to Test.* Islamabad: Institute of Strategic Studies.

O'Brennan, J. (2014). 'On the Slow Train to Nowhere?' The European Union, 'Enlargement Fatigue' and the Western Balkans. *European Foreign Affairs Review, 19*(2), 221–242.

OECD. (2011). *OECD Investment Compact for South East Europe: A Decade of Partnership for Prosperity and Stability.* Paris: OECD.

Petrillo, E. R. (2013). Russian Foreign Policy Towards the Balkans: Which Perspective? *Istituto Per Gli Studi Di Politica Internazionale, 169,* 1–7.

Petrović, Ž., & Reljić, D. (2011). Turkish Interests and Involvement in the Western Balkans: A Score-Card. *Insight Turkey, 13*(3), 159–172.

Radaelli, C. (2003). The Europeanization of Public Policy. In K. Featherstone & C. Radaelli (Eds.), *The Politics of Europeanization* (pp. 27–56). Oxford: Oxford University Press.

Radovanovik, T. (2012). From 'Balkanization' to 'Europeanization' of the the Western Balkan Countries. *American International Journal of Contemporary Research, 2*(4), 207–214.

Richter, S. (2012). Two at One Blow? The EU and Its Quest for Security and Democracy by Political Conditionality in the Western Balkans. *Democratization, 19*(3), 507–534.

Sanfey, P., & Milatovic, J. (2018). *The Western Balkans in Transition: Diagnosing the Constraints on the Path to a Sustainable Market Economy.* London: EBRD.

Sanfey, P., Milatovic, J., & Kresic, A. (2016). *How the Western Balkans Can Catch Up, European Bank for Reconstruction and Development (EBRD).* https://doi.org/10.2139/ssrn.3119685.

Sanfey, P., & Zeh, S. (2012). *Making Sense of Competitiveness Indicators in South-Eastern Europe* (EBRD Working Paper, No. 145).

Schenker, H. (2008). The Stabilization and Association Process: An Engine of European Integration in Need of Tuning. *Jemie, 7*(1), 1–19.

Schwarzinger, M., & Sajdik, M. (2009). *European Union Enlargement: Background, Developments, Facts.* New Brunswick and London: Transcation.

Stehrer, R., & Holzner, M. (2018). *Western Balkan Countries Knocking on EU's Door.* Wiiw. Available at https://wiiw.ac.at/western-balkan-countries-knocking-on-eu-s-door-n-282.html.

Tatham, A. (2009). *Enlargement of the European Union.* Alphen Aan Den Rijn: Kluwer Law International.

The Economist Intelligence Unit. (2018). *Western Balkans to 2025 A Brighter Future or Permanent Marginalisation?* London: The Economist Intelligence Unit.

Türbedar, E. (2011). Turkey's New Activism in the Western Balkans: Ambitions and Obstacles. *Insight Turkey, 13*(3), 139–158.
UNCTAD. (2000). *World Investment Report 2000: Cross-Border Mergers and Acquisitions and Development, United Nations.* New York and Geneva: UNCTAD.
UNCTAD. (2004). *World Investment Report 2004: The Shift Towards Services.* New York and Geneva. https://doi.org/10.1109/IPDPS.2011.205.
UNCTAD. (2007). *World Investment Report 2007: Transnational Corporations, Extractive Industries and Development.* New York and Geneva. https://doi.org/10.1590/S0101-31572008000300011.
UNCTAD. (2008). *World Investment Report 2008: Transnational Corporations and the Infrastructure Challenge, United Nations Conference on Trade and Development.* New York and Geneva: UNCTAD.
UNCTAD. (2011). *World Investment Report 2011: Non-equity Modes of International Production and Development, United Nations Conference on Trade and Development.* New York and Geneva: UNCTAD.
UNCTAD. (2013). *World Investment Report 2013. Global Value Chains: Investment and Trade for Development, United Nations Conference on Trade and Development, United Nations.* New York and Geneva. ISBN: 978-92-1-112868-0.
UNCTAD. (2017). *Investment Policy Review of South-East Europe.* Available at https://unctad.org/en/PublicationsLibrary/diaepcb2017d6_en.pdf. Accessed 16 November 2018.
UNCTAD. (2018a). *FDI Inflows by Region and Economy, 1990–2017, FDI/MNC Database: United Nations Conference on Trade and Development.* Available at https://www.unctad.org/fdistatistics.
UNCTAD. (2018b). *World Investment Report 2018: Investment and New Industrial Policies, United Nations Conference on Trade and Development.* New York and Geneva. https://doi.org/10.1016/j.tws.2017.07.006.
UNCTAD. (2018c). *Foreign Direct Investment: Inward and Outward Flows and Stock, Annual.* New York and Geneva: UNCTAD.
UNCTAD. (2018d). *FDI Inward Stock by Region and Economy, 1990–2017, FDI/MNC Database.* New York and Geneva: UNCTAD.
Uvalic, M. (2010). *Transition in Southeast Europe: Understanding Economic Development and Institutional Change* (No. 2010/41). Helsinki: World Institute for Development Economics Research.
Vachudova, M. A. (2019). EU Enlargement and State Capture in the Western Balkans. In J. Džankić, S. Keil, & M. Kmezić (Eds.), *The Europeanisation of the Western Balkans. New Perspectives on South-East Europe* (pp. 63–85). Cham: Palgrave Macmillan.

Greece as a Bridge to the Most Vibrant Region of the Next Decades

Karl Aiginger

Introduction

Greece has recovered from its largest economic crisis and new confidence is setting in. But development will not be smooth if the high debt burden is not reduced. This can be done if Greece presents a vision for its position in the globalizing world as of 2030. Any path chosen by Greece will be easier if the peace and integration process in the Western Balkans continue and Europe commits to a strategy of reconnecting with its citizens after the elections in May 2019.

Greece has the historic chance to become the bridge between Europe, Asia and Africa. Countries east of Europe, in the Middle East and in North Africa, are potentially vibrant, with a predicted growth rate of more than 5% p.a. as compared to at best 2% in Europe. But the neighbourhood is politically unstable today, and potential new "hegemons" like Russia, Turkey or Iran are eager to dominate the region.

K. Aiginger (✉)
Policy Crossover Center: Vienna-Europe, Vienna, Austria
e-mail: karl.aiginger@querdenkereuropa.at

Vienna University of Economics, Vienna, Austria

V. Vlachos and A. Bitzenis (eds.), *European Union*,
https://doi.org/10.1007/978-3-030-18103-1_9

To take advantage of the opportunities, Greece must make use of the existing qualifications of young Greeks, but also those of migrants. It must switch from an inward-looking policy to better relations with its close neighbours. Greece should furthermore try to attract new foreign capital, not the least with the assistance of its large and successful diaspora, and it should incentivize the return of untaxed capital hidden in tax shelters. Finally, Greece could become a hotspot for renewable energy, the regional technology leader. This would save such a large amount of imports for oil and gas for Greece that the balance of payment of Greece would turn deeply into the positive, without an overly restrictive fiscal policy in the future.

Europe as a Success Model Lacking a Strategy

The EU is, seen in the long term, a success model (Sachs 2008). It now has 28 members and has developed from a free trade agreement (starting with coal and steel) to a common market. The majority of the EU members have a common currency, which, despite short-term crises, is now stronger than at its start and challenging the dominance of the US dollar. Europe is an area in which no military conflict has taken place over the last seventy years, and it is spreading rule of law and conflict management to countries applying for membership. The former socialist countries were integrated in a shorter period than any other transformations in history—for this, the EU has been called an integration machine by the World Bank (Gill and Raiser 2012).

But Europe is now stuck in a midlife crisis. Economic dynamics are low, inequality is rising, and youth unemployment is high. Development is not even across countries and over time, and if progress is reached, it is not interpreted as a European achievement. Reforms in southern Europe were not fast enough, as a part of production was transferred to low-wage countries without clusters of new firms or more sophisticated industries substituting the loss. Smaller crises were always met with higher public expenditures, without a focus on innovation and training—activities that would foster future competitiveness. Now, East–West as well as North–South splits are endangering the consensus among countries. Europe lacks a new narrative, since peace is taken—erroneously—as a given and support of citizens for "ever deeper integration" no longer exists, even if global challenges are on the rise. As outside challenges, the

US administration wants to weaken Europe and Vladimir Putin seeks to regain political dominance in Central and Eastern Europe and the Western Balkans.

The Crossroads for Europe

Connecting with Neighbours vs. Losing Global Leverage

Europe is currently the largest economic region in the world and enjoys the highest standard of living (defined by economic, social and ecological goals), and life expectancy is increasing in contrast to the USA. But to remain an important international player, Europe must start ambitious internal reforms and engage in a new partnership with its dynamic neighbourhood. The alternative would be to become an isolated region of less than 10% of world output and 5% of population up to the end of this century, lower than the shares of India and South Africa. A small, ageing and shrinking Europe would be surrounded by a "ring of fire" and countries longing for "past glory"—which never existed or requires border changes—and new hegemonial powers supported by autocratic regimes (from Russia to Turkey or Iran) (Table 1).

Populist Calls for Protection vs. Future-Oriented Reforms

Populist movements, such as that which led to Brexit, would like their countries to exit from the European project (see France or Hungary). They favour illiberal democracies without the checks and balances needed for a balanced governance, and they recall past glory. They are fuelled by rising inequality within countries, as well as regions with high brain drain and a consequently decreasing workforce. The catching up of lagging regions is being achieved, but often not as fast as expected by low-income countries and new members. Inward migration is needed in general due to ageing, but it is not managed and coordinated, and is therefore often rejected by electorates or governments.

High vs. Low Road

On a low road, path wages are cut, and social and ecological standards are neglected. A high-road strategy focusses on innovation and skills, raising productivity and fostering new firms and technologies.

Table 1 Development of real GDP and population

	Real GDP		*Population*	
	2000/2017	*2017/2022*	*2000/2017*	*2017/2050*
	Average percentage change p.a.			
World	3.8	3.7	1.2	0.8
Advanced economies	1.7	1.8	0.5	0.2
Emerging and developing countries	5.7	5.0	1.3	0.9
China	9.3	6.1	0.6	−0.1
EU 28	1.5	1.8	0.3	0.0
Central and Eastern Europe	3.3	2.9	−0.3	−0.5
Black Sea Region	4.7	3.5	−0.2	0.3
CIS	3.9	2.2	0.2	0.0
Middle East and North Africa	4.4	3.3	2.0	1.3
Sub-Saharan Africa	5.1	3.6	2.8	2.4
European Neighbourhood (ENB)	4.5	3.1	2.0	1.8
ENB + EU 28	2.3	2.2	1.5	1.4

Notes European Neighbourhood: CIS, Turkey, Middle East and North Africa, Sub-Saharan Africa
Source IMF, World Bank, UNO. GDP: 2017 until 2022 IMF forecast; population: 2017 until 2050 UNO forecast

Looking Inward vs. Connecting with Neighbours

An inward-looking strategy calls for protection and military border control. An outward strategy invests into a new partnership with Europe's dynamic however unstable neighbourhood. The European neighbourhood (the former Soviet Union, Black Sea, Arab countries, Africa) could be a turbine for European exports. A new partnership policy could fight the root causes of migration (poverty and increasing desertification; Aiginger and Handler 2018).

More vs. Less Europe

Global challenges call for common European solutions, but most members and citizens tend to reject intervention by "Brussels". The solution is that the EU sets common goals and empowers member countries to choose better solutions. Europe should try to define targets it wants to achieve but not intervene in detail (Aiginger 2017). If climate goals are set, each country can decide which instruments to use, and which innovations to accelerate. If there are tax transparency and a common tax base, each member can fix its individual rates. If the financial system is stable and short-run speculation is taxed, each country and firm will invest more. More Europe on the goal-level combined with less micro-management is the best solution.

Summary

If Europe can solve its internal problems, it will be able to shape globalization according to its values and priorities (for limits of globalization as it happens today, see Rodrik 2016). Europe could remain—together with its neighbours and on par with China—the largest economic power. A sound financial sector has to serve the real economy. Europe is becoming a region with high and increasing well-being, as well as the largest choices, and is enjoying the diversity and skills provided by migration and openness. In short, it is becoming a role model for a high-income region with social and ecological responsibility (Aiginger 2016, 2018) (Table 2).

The Need for a Vision for Greece

Greece has made some striking policy changes and achieved remarkable progress, e.g. in cutting public expenditures as well as external deficits. However, public debt and youth unemployment are still high, and the improvements depend on tourist seasons and a favourable business climate in Europe. The recovery is not built on new strengths, innovation and clusters of new firms so far. A vision is needed for a dynamic Greece in the globalizing world with new power structures and future technologies.

This vision could be based on unique location. Greece has a specific geographical position compared to all other European countries. It is closest to the Black Sea region, the Middle East and North Africa. Its distance to Cairo is 1.2 km and to Kiev 1.5 km. This is much less than the distance to Berlin, Paris or Brussels (all more than 3000 flight kilometres away). Historically, this location between Asia, Europe and Africa was the reason why civilization took hold early in this region; Greek merchants took the lead in trade and Greek ideas enriched philosophy and science.

Table 2 Distribution of GDP and population

	Real GDP/capita		*Nominal GDP*			*Population*		
	2017		*2000*	*2017*	*2022*	*2000*	*2017*	*2050*
	USD	*World = 100*	*Percentage shares*					
World	11,167	100	100.0	100.0	100.0	100.0	100.0	100.0
Advanced economies	46,320	415	79.2	60.5	56.1	15.7	14.0	11.5
Emerging and developing countries	4955	44	20.8	39.5	43.9	83.6	85.3	87.8
China	7163	64	3.6	15.1	17.8	20.9	18.7	14.0
EU 28	36,946	331	26.4	21.6	20.3	7.9	6.7	5.1
Central and Eastern Europe	16,359	146	1.2	1.7	1.8	1.6	1.2	0.8
Black Sea Region	16,801	150	0.9	1.3	1.3	1.4	1.1	0.9
CIS	8354	75	1.1	2.5	2.5	4.6	3.8	3.0
Middle East and North Africa	6765	61	3.2	3.7	3.8	5.6	6.4	7.7
Sub-Saharan Africa	1727	15	0.7	1.5	1.7	9.8	12.8	21.4
European Neighbourhood (ENB)	4805	43	6.4	9.4	9.7	20.6	23.4	32.3
ENB + EU 28	11,822	106	32.8	31.0	30.0	28.5	30.1	37.5

Notes European Neighbourhood: CIS, Turkey, Middle East and North Africa, Sub-Saharan Africa
Source IMF, World Bank, UNO. GDP: 2017 until 2022 IMF forecast; population: 2017 until 2050 UNO forecast

But today Greece is not on good terms with any of its neighbours. It is at odds with Turkey with respect to Cyprus and other islands. Greece is preventing Macedonia (the Former Yugoslav Republic of Macedonia [FYROM]) from becoming a member of the EU, because Macedonia claims Alexander the Great as Macedonian. It does not consider Bulgaria and Albany as countries on equal terms, but mainly as source countries for construction workers and service personnel. Consequently, trade with its neighbours amounts less for Greece than for any other European countries. Greece does not trade intensively or invest in North Africa, nor with all the countries on the other side of "mare nostrum". It is accustomed to a large and privileged military sector, which requires more tax receipts than universities and childcare institutions together.

The central idea of the vision is that Greece can become a hub for production, exports and trade in a dynamic geographical region. The Greek neighbour countries are growing fast, whenever there is peace. This holds for Turkey, the Arab countries, North Africa and even more for sub-Saharan Africa (to a lesser degree for former Soviet Union countries and the Western Balkans, see Table 1). Greece has a well-educated population, knowledge in ICT and entrepreneurial spirit demonstrated by entrepreneurs all over the world, and it could use this potential to take the lead in technological development in Southern Europe. Deindustrialization that took place in the past two decades should be stopped by new firms, start-ups and economic zones along the highways and around ports.

Game-Changers on the New Road

Reform zones could attract international firms, which do not currently invest in Greece because of burdensome procedures and the length of legal disputes. Start-up centres could supply computer facilities, office space, meeting rooms and joint secretarial services for business start-ups. Rent, electricity costs and taxes could be waived for young firms in such centres for one year.

Youth Reform Boards

A competition for the best ideas on how to increase opportunities for young people should be initiated. It can be organized via social networks, and the best proposals could be presented in a televised event. Young people, including the winners of the contest, could then build an advisory reform board to government (e.g. providing a "youth test" for all reforms).

Greece is still dominated by "old boy" networks, large government, an expensive military sector and tax-free shipowners. Young people have excellent command of ICT technology, but do not find work today, and if they do, it is not adequately paid. They are underrepresented in the political process and especially young women.

Private Funds Managed by the Diaspora

Government money for reforms will be limited for a considerable time, but private funding is in principle abundant, given the uneven distribution of incomes and property, the success of expatriates in the world and the money sequestered abroad tax-free in other European countries or tax havens. This foreign capital should be incentivized to be returned; a lump sum payment of 25% could be combined with tax amnesty. On the other hand, if foreign accounts are not reported within a year, the full penalties by law should be applied. Funds from expatriates or wealthy Greeks at home, as well as the money returned, should together be invested in a Greek Future Fund managed by expatriates and the ECB.

Making Use of the Qualifications of Migrants

Quasi-governmental institutions could be set up to foster the integration of migrants into the Greek economy and their children into schools and preschool care. Greece needs migration and migration helps to connect with neighbours. Practical skills and the entrepreneurial spirit of migrants are definitely needed in Greece.

Regional Leader in Decarbonization

Greece is a relatively energy- and resource-intensive society with high input of coal, oil, gas and nuclear energy. Imports of fossil energy are large and have negatively shifted the trade balance. Large subsidies for fossil energy are maintained and prevent energy-saving technologies and the inroads of alternative energy. They also present a heavy burden on public budgets.

Greece should try to become the first decarbonized society in Europe. Energy saving and renewable energy using the wind and the sun should be the top priority. Cars using combustion technology should be forbidden step by step up to 2025. Efficient loading infrastructure has to be provided in all homes and offices—traditionally gasoline stations and public buildings. As a first decarbonized society, Greek could improve technologies and then export them to neighbour countries in the Black Sea, the Western Balkans and North Africa.

Cutting Debt in Three Stages

Greek debt can be cut if Greece develops a vision and sticks to it. This could be done in three stages: one third should be cut directly through decisions made by the EU and its members, the second third should be paid back but at a very low interest rate, subsidized by institutions connected with the EIB, and the third part can be paid back through repatriation of Greek capital currently stored in foreign banks and tax shelters.

To summarize, we have provided a menu of game-changers for Greece, which could shift attention away from problems and failures to future possibilities, and away from measures demanded by the troika to issues improving the chances of Greece being able to gain an adequate and excellent position in the globalized world of 2030. Greek citizens, Greek youth and a Greek diaspora committed to its home base should all be in the driver's seat of the reforms.

Conclusions

Greece could use its unique geographical position to become the bridge between Europe and Asia, as well as the Middle East and North Africa. This region is growing by more than 5% per year but is also replete with dormant or actual conflicts. Russia, Turkey and Iran want to dominate this region. China builds Silk Roads to establish logistic centres in this region as to regain its position as leading world economy, and it invests in Africa as to get access to raw materials and a market for cheap products. The USA is retreating from multilateralism and will lose importance in this region.

Greece will recover if Europe performs better. This depends on a coherent European strategy, which needs to be developed after the parliamentary elections in May 2019. Europe should strive to become the region with the highest and fastest growing standard of living, with lower inequality and more ambitious environmental standards than any other regions in the world. Together with its neighbours, Europe may still be the largest region in 2050, on par with China and larger than the USA combined with Canada and Mexico. As the EU and most of its current member countries have a shrinking population, and in the European neighbourhood the population is increasing, migration could become a win–win situation for both. But this process has to be managed, and migration should be circular, with migrants returning and disseminating knowledge and technologies at home, creating new firms and reforming the administration.

Europe has to invest in the ENB, with a focus on practical qualifications and vocational training, and migrants at least to some extent should return to their country of origin to prevent brain drain and foster cultural dialog and understanding. At the same time, the EU needs to negotiate with China, with a view to make the Silk Road and China's investment in European firms and infrastructure a win–win situation respecting the goals and values of the partners. Both Putin's and Trump's ambitions to destroy the EU by destabilizing the Western Balkans will be pre-empted if Europe cooperates with China as well as its vibrant neighbourhood in partnerships on equal terms.

But Greece has also to develop an own vision about its position in the globalizing world. A Greek strategy could follow the vision of bridging Europe, Asia and Africa. This will help Greece to grasp the chances of its vibrant neighbourhoods. Greece could become the regional technology leader in renewable energy and invite its successful diaspora to invest in new firms and technologies. The Greek society must give young people and females a greater role in reshaping the society, to limit the current influence of old boys' networks, lobbies and the large and inefficient bureaucracy, which dominates Greece today. Following the vision of a bridge to the dynamic neighbourhood should enable also to cut a large part of Greek's current debt.

References

Aiginger, K. (2016). *New Dynamics for Europe: Reaping the Benefits of Socio-ecological Transition*. Part I: Synthesis (WWW for Europe Synthesis Report). Vienna-Brussels.

Aiginger, K. (2017). *How a Strong Europe Could Create More National Scope of Action* (Policy Crossover Flash Paper No. 1).

Aiginger, K. (2018). Harnessing Competitiveness for Social and Ecological Goals. In P. Chiocchetti & F. Allemand (Eds.), *Competitiveness and Solidarity in the European Union: Interdisciplinary Perspectives*. Abingdon: Routledge.

Aiginger, K., & Handler, H. (2018). Fostering a Dynamic and Stable Neighborhood for Europe. *Review of Economics & Finance, 4*, 39–54.

Gill, I., & Raiser, M. (2012). *Golden Growth: Restoring the Lustre of the European Economic Model*. Washington, DC: The World Bank.

Rodrik, D. (2016, October 4). There Is No Need to Fret About Deglobalisation. *Financial Times*.

Sachs, J. D. (2008, August 19). Europe as a Soft Power. *Financial Times*.

The Third Hellenic Economic Adjustment Program

Success Story of Macroeconomic Stabilization or Failed Story of Economic Growth Restoration?

Konstantinos J. Hazakis

Introduction

Disastrous negotiations on national public debt issues between Greece and official creditors (January 2015–June 2015) led Greece near exit from the eurozone in July 2015.

After a short period of turbulence and economic uncertainty, Greece made an official request for support in the form of a government loan from the European Stability Mechanism (ESM) on July 8, 2015. The ESM Board of Governors asked from the European Commission to evaluate, the existence of risks to the financial stability of the eurozone, the debt sustainability of Greece and the country's financing needs and soon after the European Commission together with the ECB issued on July 10, 2015, the country's assessment. The ESM Board of Governors

K. J. Hazakis (✉)
Democritus University of Thrace, Komotini, Greece
e-mail: kmhazaki@otenet.gr

V. Vlachos and A. Bitzenis (eds.), *European Union*,
https://doi.org/10.1007/978-3-030-18103-1_10

underlined the necessity of a new financial assistance program and Greece signed on August 2015 the third economic adjustment program (EAP) which among others linked the support of the official creditors to Greece to a memorandum of understanding (MoU).

The MoU policies were categorized into four pillars, namely restoring fiscal sustainability, safeguarding financial stability, achieving growth, competitiveness and investment, and creating a modern state-public administration. The financial assistance was considerable during the third EAP (August 19, 2015–August 20, 2018) and Greece received 61.9 billion Euros of financial assistance by the ESM (out of a total scheduled program of €86 billion). Following the Eurogroup meeting of June 21, 2018 (Eurogroup 2018b), the President of the Eurogroup stated that Greece adopted over 450 policy actions during the ESM program and underlined that over 240 billion Euros were disbursed at low interest rates during the three fully fledged programs. The Eurogroup further underlined that Greece is committed to preserve its program achievements, by completing the reforms that were enacted under the program with the target of increasing its growth potential. Following regulation EU 472/2013, Greece is integrated in the surveillance framework for euro area states after August 2018 and is obliged to apply the euro semester provisions.

The end of the program was followed by intense academic debate over the effects of the third program, reflecting different assessment methodologies and political priorities. Some studies argue that fiscal and structural adjustments have been realized to the detriment of growth and social welfare and they also failed to restore public debt sustainability and long-term economic stability (Hazakis 2018). Accordingly, it is suggested that the third consolidation program was based on reduction of fiscal deficits, internal devaluation of wages, higher direct/indirect taxes, downplaying the development—investment gap, which undermines the reorganization of Greece's economic—productive structures. The program further ignored that the economic effect of any stabilization effort is highly contextual and is depended on the specific political/institutional setting and economic conditions of Greece.

As a result after August 20, 2018, economic policy uncertainty remains, banks are not able to face severe liquidity problems due to bad loans and business confidence is not restored to pre-crisis levels. Equally important, it becomes evident that fiscal consolidation attains primary surpluses while it leaves public debt at non-sustainable levels. Lastly, the terms of the economic consolidation program in Greece (incorporated in MoU) do not favor structural and real convergence to euro area average but mainly target nominal convergence with eurozone economies. Thus, an anti-growth tetralogy had been imposed during the third program, which consisted of excessive direct and indirect taxation, internal devaluation of incomes, institutional inertia on critical growth issues, and public investment contraction.

Other reports (Ministry of Finance of Greece 2018a, b, c) argue the opposite. They insist that the third adjustment program raised business expectations, and it acts as a signal that the country is pursuing sound macroeconomic policies. Moreover, the successful end of program marks a return to macroeconomic normality and an autonomous access to capital markets, creating enough fiscal space to restore economic/social inequalities without putting into danger macroeconomic stabilization.

The article uses a "before-after" methodology comparing five major issue areas before and after the implementation of the third program, stated in the initial agreement between Greece and the "institutions" (the official creditors which participated in the program and have been called during the previous two programs "troika").

It is a result-oriented critical study, an effort to perceive if the program met its stated objectives and at which cost, presenting an ex post-economic evaluation of the program design, implementation, and outcomes. Indeed, whatever criterion is being chosen to reach conclusions, "problem-solvency effectiveness" (Young 1989) is vital to see whether the program really addressed the initial targets/expectations.

Taking into consideration the content and results of the first two adjustment programs (European Commission 2010, 2014; IMF 2013, 2016), the evaluation includes among others, debt sustainability, restoration of positive economic growth rates, and financial sustainability. The article also suggests that there is an alternative adjustment path involving a completely different identification of problems, hierarchy of issue areas and policy priorities. Such an alternative strategy should equally target from the beginning structural and fiscal consolidation and enforcement of local productive networks, taking into consideration the necessity to protect the most vulnerable social groups.

The article is structured as follows. Section two evaluates the performance of the third program in selected issue areas while section three presents the major tenets of an alternative adjustment strategy. Finally, section four concludes and provides useful policy implications.

The Assessment of the Third Adjustment Program in Greece

Although there is an impressive literature on the context and assessment of fiscal adjustment programs (European Parliament 2014; Bi et al. 2013), no consensus has been reached on a unified explanatory model.

Studies often link fiscal adjustment success to expenditure cuts (Alesina and Ardagna 2012), to the content traits of adjustment (Gros and Alcidi 2013; Karger 2014; Blanchard and Leigh 2013), to the time period and size of consolidation (Aiginger and Schratzenstaller 2011; Anderson et al. 2014; Sapir et al. 2014; Larch et al. 2014), to public debt (Sapir 2018) or to institutional and political factors (Hazakis 2015, 2018; Bitzenis et al. 2013).

In any case, it is difficult to evaluate the effects of an intense and long-term fiscal adjustment strategy as it usually takes time before they can be observed (Carnot 2014; Fernandez and Paulet 2014). In the same manner, it is hard to prove the existence of a clear cause and effect relationship in EAPs (Kotios et al. 2018). Even more, economic agents' expectations and perceptions of the impact of consolidation measures on economy are critical to the success or failure of the program and this explains why expectations attach different degrees of risk and uncertainty to different fiscal strategies. As a result, arguments in favor of expansionary fiscal austerity (Alesina and Ardagna 1998) or Keynesian intervention in countries following adjustment programs (Botta 2015; De Grauwe and Ji 2013; Stuckler and Basu 2013) deal differently with the expectations of households and firms.

The focus of the article is on specific major areas, namely fiscal sustainability, debt sustainability, financial sector resilience, national GDP growth, national competitiveness, structural reforms, and social inequalities.

Restoring Sustainable Public Finances

The 2017 primary surplus reached 3.9% of GDP (it was 0.3% in 2014, −2.1% in 2015, and 3.7% in 2016), thus over performing significantly the fiscal target of the ESM program. Although the Greek government insists that high surpluses create enough fiscal space, no real analysis is taking place on the impact of sustained tax originating surpluses on debt.

Indeed, the performance in primary fiscal surplus is linked to high direct/indirect taxation, public investment underspending, horizontal cuts in social expenditure, and it is totally pro-cyclical undermining growth drivers. This is why even European Commission stated soon after the debt agreement in summer 2018, that "there is uncertainty surrounding the capacity of the Greek government to sustain high surpluses."

Thus, serious doubts remain on the potential to achieve the nominal targets of high primary fiscal surpluses in the following years for several reasons.

First, rulings of the Council of State in Greece, which have already been finalized create financial liabilities for the Greek government of around 0.4% of GDP in net terms that will need to be cleared in 2019 (mainly stemming from wage cuts in the public sector). Further, there are rulings related to pension reforms applied in 2012, 2015, and 2016 as well as to measures of 2012 to abolish the 13th and 14th on the wage of employees in Greek public sector. If all of them are realized, how the Greek government will counterbalance the derived fiscal expenditure?

Second, there is pressure and wide consensus on the necessity to apply a reduction in the personal income tax credit in 2020. Third, irrespective of programmed and politically inelastic obligations, one should always remember that high fiscal surpluses over the next years are considered from the institutions conditio sine qua non for the implementation of the debt relief measures and for the safety net offered during the post-surveillance period by the eurozone.

Fourth, based on the policy projections it is suggested that privatization revenues from bank and nonbank assets will reach 14 billion Euros between 2018 and 2060 (11.5 billion Euros from the privatization of nonbank assets) based on agreed sales and concessions. Furthermore, it is assumed that more than three-quarters of the funds used for bank recapitalization in 2015 can be recovered from the privatization of bank assets (4.5 billion Euros). Thus, it is argued that there will be no recapitalization needs from the Greek banks despite high ratios of nonperforming loans (NPLs) to total loans of households/firms. Finally, one should also mention that the stock of arrears continues its rising trajectory and stood at 3.2 billion Euros in August 2018.

In sum, while the third EAP succeeded to achieve the nominal targets, it did not add significantly to fiscal credibility since it undermines the growth drivers, it has negative repercussions on projected economic growth, it is based on over taxation and it delivers anti-growth surpluses in a stagnated economy. Apparently, the problem is not horizontal expenditure reductions but focused cuts, rationalization of expenditures and reduction of tax invasion, especially VAT revenues. To make a long story short, a persistent "tax based high surplus regime" irrespective of the economic cycle, of the specificities of national productive economic structure and of the national transmission channels/multipliers undermines growth drivers in the medium and long term (Table 1).

Restoring Debt Sustainability

The second major issue in the third program is debt sustainability. There are many studies on the factors that influence the debt-growth interaction as well as many analyses on the critical thresholds of debt to GDP (e.g., Reinhart and Rogoff 2014), and on the critical variables affecting debt dynamics and debt sustainability in the long term (Sapir 2018). The article underlines two basic indicators, namely the ratio between the total general government debt and the GDP (debt to GDP ratio) and the ratio between the debt repayment obligations (interests plus amortization payments) and its GDP (gross financing needs to GDP or GFN to GDP).

The target of the Eurogroup is to ensure through medium- and long-term debt measures that the agreed GFN are met. Moreover, the Eurogroup has also agreed on a debt relief package to safeguard Greece's debt sustainability which includes a number of important actions. First, a 10-year extension on European financial stability fund (EFSF) loans and a 10-year deferral on interest and amortization had been decided so as to allow Greece to return to market financing. Second, Greece will be able to retrieve the interest accumulated by the Eurosystem on Greek government bonds, by semiannual payments until 2022 under the condition of full application of reforms adopted under the ESM program. Third, IMF will participate in the monitoring of the post-memorandum period. Fourth, the Eurogroup has mandated the ESM to disburse 15 billion Euros to Greece as the last program tranche, subject to the completion of national procedures. Overall, Greece left the program with a cash buffer of 24.1 billion Euros covering the sovereign financial needs until August 2020.

Analyzing the debt profile of Greece in 2018, it is crystal clear that the key target of debt sustainability was missed. This is why even the

Table 1 Selected indicators for Greece 2010–2018 (*Source* Eurostat, November 2018)

	2010	*2014*	*2015*	*2016*	*2017*	*2018*
Pillar 1: Restoring fiscal sustainability						
Net lending (+)/net borrowing (−) as % of GDP		−3.6	−5.6	0.5	0.8	0.6*
General gross government debt (as a percentage of GDP)	146.2	178.9	175.9	178.5	176.1	182.5*
Pillar 2: Safeguarding financial stability						
Private sector debt consolidated, November 2018 (% GDP)	128.1	129.2	126.7	124.0	116.4	
NPLs (bank non-performing loans to total gross loans,%, World Bank)	9.1	33.8	36.6	36.3	45.6	
Pillar 3: Growth, competitiveness and investment						
Gross domestic product (market prices)	226,031	178,656	177,258	176,487	180,217	
Gross domestic expenditure on R and D (% of GDP)	0.60	0.83	0.96	0.99	1.13	–
Real effective exchange rate (Index 2010=100) Euro area trading partners	100.00	94.76	93.68	93.49	93.14	
Current account balance (% GDP)	−11.4	−1.6	−0.2	−1.3	−1.0	
Exports of high technology products (as a share of total exports of the country)	5.6	3.7	4.6	5.0	4.3	
Gross fixed capital formation (% of GDP)	17.6	11.5	11.6	12.1	12.9	
Pillar 4: Social inequalities						
People at risk of poverty	27.7	36.0	35.7	35.6	34.8	
Severely materially deprived people	11.6	21.5	22.2	22.4	21.1	
Unemployment rates (number of unemployed as % of total labor force)	12.7	26.5	24.9	23.6	21.5	

*Projections

Eurogroup (June 2018) agreed "*that it will review at the end of the EFSF grace period in 2032, whether additional debt measures are needed to ensure the respect of the agreed GFN targets … and take appropriate actions, if needed. It also stated that it recalled the May 2016 agreement on a contingency mechanism on debt which could be activated in the case of an unexpectedly more adverse scenario. If activated by the Eurogroup, it could entail measures such as a further re-profiling and capping and deferral of interest payments of the EFSF to the extent needed to meet the GFN benchmarks defined above*" (Eurogroup 2018a, b).

The government insists that the third program secured funds required to cover Greece financing needs but the question remains how and at which cost. Greece's general government gross debt is 317.407 billion Euros after the end of the program (Eurostat, September 18, 2018) larger than in 2015 (311.724 billion Euros) and the debt to GDP ratio stands at 178.6% of GDP (2017). If one considers that IMF target for debt sustainability (2013) was 124% of GDP in 2020 and 110% of GDP in 2022, Greece third program marks a clear failure concerning the debt target. Perhaps this is why both the Greek government and the "institutions" changed the way of debt assessment and insist that GFN to GDP should be the main criterion as it is liquidation and servicing of debt that matter. This could have a point if capital to pay debt derived from GDP growth rates but unfortunately, it is derived from high taxation downplaying growth drivers. Further, many issues raise significant doubts on the Greek debt sustainability.

First, debt sustainability scenarios do not take into serious consideration possible bank recapitalization needs of the four systemic banks (when all studies agree that NPLs are a serious problem not adequately addressed) and consider a rapid recover of funds used for bank recapitalization from the privatization of bank assets (when assets prices hit a historical low in 2018). Second, debt sustainability is based on an extremely optimistic tax-fueled primary surplus of 3.5% until 2022 and 2.2% of GDP after when IMF and several studies underline that sustaining high primary surpluses without an export-based GDP growth and without significantly settling debt obligations is infeasible (IMF 2018).

Third, GFN to GDP levels are extremely high to be considered viable. GFN is forecast at 21.8% of GDP in 2018 (ESM Compliance Report 2018) before decreasing to 9.6% in 2020 (under the condition of robust growth rates) and it is projected to increase from 2020 onwards reaching 28.1% in 2060. However, even if one considers that any ratio above 10%

is viable, one cannot ignore the effects on state revenues over the next decades from factors such as ageing population and increased pension expenditure in Greece.

Fourth, the "institutions" liquidity safety net is provided under strong conditions making the debt relief difficult to be applied in the medium term. It is no coincidence that the Eurogroup agreed in 2018 to review at the end of the EFSF grace period in 2032, whether additional measures are needed to ensure the accomplishment of the agreed GFN targets. So, any assistance and appropriate action are linked once again to compliance of Greece with rigid fiscal and structural provisions. This is why critics of the third program insist that in post-surveillance period there is still a program (because of conditionality and long-term obligation for high primary fiscal surpluses until 2060) but no secured and low interest financing (as Greece will have financial help only when and if it is needed).

Fifth, the ten-year government bond yields remain high (4.37% in October 2018) which makes Greece autonomous access in the international markets too costly (the ten-year bond yields are 1.01 for Ireland, 1.60 for Spain, and 1.96 for Portugal). One should also remember that international markets are characterized by high fluctuations and thus they behave nervously to unilateral fiscal actions not embedded in the usual EU economic decision-making process. Higher and unsustainable interest rates in the long term will deteriorate the debt profile, posing the necessity for a new haircut on bonds held by private investors (as OSI or official sector involvement is out of question) or a ESM driven adjustment program perhaps with the contribution of a newly created European monetary fund. Equally important, Greece's credit ratings are better than in the disastrous summer of 2015, but are still below investment grade taking into consideration unsustainable medium- and long-term debt position but also short term unstable and volatile conditions in regional capital market.

Evidently, the Eurogroup measures of June 22, 2018, were not enough to control debt dynamics and uncertainty, meaning that the capacity of Greek government to sustain liquidation over debt needs is limited, calling for debt restructuring. It is also apparent that the four critical issues for debt sustainability (growth-based primary surpluses, sustainable growth rates, low interest rates, low levels of accumulated debt as % of GDP) have not been addressed cultivating further economic uncertainty. IMF itself states in several cases that the prospects of debt sustainability remain uncertain (IMF 2018).

Instead, what Greek economy should follow is a triple policy recipe, namely primary fiscal surplus below 1%, low interest rates linked only to implementation of structural reforms and export growth strategy supported by the eurozone states with positive balance of payments. As Eurogroup denies the prospect of any face value debt relief, a generous debt re-profiling and a reduction in GFN (meaning also lower taxation), could bring positive growth results in the short and medium term. In sum, the debt problem is still subject to a "wait and see policy" in the medium term and a catastrophic "no change policy" in the short term, which undermines macroeconomic certainty and sustainability of debt in the long term.

Restoring Sustainable Growth Rates

Concerning GDP, recovery emerged in 2014 but was reversed in January 2015 due to a confrontation attitude of the Greek coalition government toward any economic adjustment mechanism until June 2015. The contracted Greek economy with a cumulative 26% of GDP loss during 2010–2015, experienced a short period of high economic turbulence and uncertainty which led to the imposition of capital controls in summer 2015. Despite Eurozone continuous upward trend in GDP since 2013, Greek progress in GDP terms is anemic.

Thus, the Greek economy succeeded for a second time during adjustment (the first was in 2014), to restore the road to economic normality but it still faces four key challenges. First, the growth drivers of the Greek economy are anemic. Exports rose from 20% of GDP in early 2009 (45.1 billion Euros) to 30% of GDP in 2017 (59.5 billion Euros) but are still below EU average (46%) and are based on specific activities of services sector. Even in tourism where the number of visitors rose significantly, there is decrease of the average duration per trip for non-residents from 7.7 nights in 2014 to 6.9 nights in 2016 while the mix of visitors tends to be more low spenders coming from Balkan states. Moreover, the share of the total gross value added of tradable sectors rose from 40% in 2013 to 43% in 2017 which demonstrates inability to animate and enforce export-oriented activities so as to achieve the positive Balassa–Samuelson effects on the tradables sector. Again, it becomes apparent that the anti-development mix of high cost of bank credit, high taxes, high energy prices, and high non-wage costs put obstacles to enforcement of Greek exports.

Second, the contribution of investment expenditure to GDP remains low underling the difficulty to shift critical resources from the non-tradables to the tradables sector of the economy. The gross fixed capital formation remains far below its 2008 level, investment in dwellings continued to decline in 2017, and investment in machinery and equipment is low (annual fixed investment fell by 65% between 2007 and 2017). One should again note that the problem of underinvestment is further aggravated due to NPLs of the four Greek systemic banks, depriving crucial capital from private sector.

Third, private investment which was the engine of growth until 2008 is at low levels due to internal devaluation strategy, high taxation and low expectations of firms/households. Concerning the latter, despite a positive trend in indicators such as the economic sentiment indicator (98.50 in October 2017, 101.30 in September 2018, lower than in other Eurozone countries), uncertainty prevails and private consumption is anemic.

Finally, public investment and especially what OECD calls productive investment (i.e., high-quality infrastructure investment, education, and skills investment) is low due to decline of the public investment program during 2015–2018. In sum, the four major growth drivers (public consumption, private consumption, investment, net exports) are still underperforming. Even worse, there is no comprehensive national plan of economic restructuring and thus no national ownership of growth-oriented reforms. This is why the Eurogroup stated already on January 22, 2018 (Eurogroup 2018c), that "the Eurogroup reconfirms the importance of an ambitious comprehensive growth strategy with strong ownership from the Greek authorities. The authorities are invited to finalize it in cooperation with the institutions well before the end of the program." Such a program should take into account not only uncertainties stemming from domestic environment (i.e., structural reforms, privatizations, deregulation of product markets) but also uncontrollable uncertainties of the international environment (i.e., energy prices fluctuations, trade protectionism, Euroscepticism in 2019, refugee crisis).

Restoring Competitiveness in Greek Economy

Unit labor costs have not converged in the euro area and the common currency has not led to a convergence of member states' trade and production structures, but rather to real divergence (Kyrkilis and Hazakis

2014). As the German economy focuses more in high-value-added sectors and states of eurozone periphery focus in lower-technology non-tradable sectors the productivity gap becomes larger. The third program has focused to unit labor cost and not to non-wage structural competitiveness factors which can provide a solid export-led growth trajectory.

It is evident that Greek economy is characterized by a high fiscal multiplier, and thus a fiscal adjustment does impact severely on output as it is not counterbalanced by an increase in other components of demand, such as exports or investment. The effect of fiscal consolidation on output is highly influenced by the marginal propensity to save and the degree of openness to trade. In the Greek case, the fiscal multiplier was larger than expected, the savings rate was low, the degree of trade openness was low, and the exports did not counterbalance low domestic demand. Moreover, individuals are credit constrained and monetary policy is less able to be accommodative, delaying consolidation efforts.

Greek exports price competitiveness has not changed as expected and as much as its cost/wage competitiveness and as the Greek goods are mainly exports in low- and medium-technology products for which price competitiveness matters, the performance has been low.

Lastly, despite slight improvements in specific sectors of World Bank ease of doing business index, the overall index of Greece felt further for a third consecutive year marking the lack of a sustainable and comprehensive national competitiveness strategy and structural weaknesses concerning enforcing of contracts and registering property rights. Deterioration in the competitiveness position of Greece is also recorded in the global competitiveness index of the world economic forum, and thus Greece is ranked in the 57th place in competitiveness below other states in the area such as Bulgaria and Romania.

Restoring Financial Resilience

European anxiety over the contagion of crisis in the banking sector is clearly marked by the rising interest of the European Banking Authority which realized on January 31, 2018, EU-wide stress tests, on a sample of bank institutions that had a minimum of 30 billion Euros in assets and covered about 70% of the banking sector in the EU.

The four systemic Greek banks (Alpha Bank, National Bank of Greece, Piraeus Bank, and Eurobank) had similar stress tests which had been published on May 5, 2018. The results clearly indicate an average capital depletion of the four banks in the adverse scenario of around nine percentage points in terms of Common Equity Tier 1 (CET1) capital (15.5 billion Euros), driven by credit risk and net interest income. The CET1 ratios of the four banks were projected to be 9.7% (Alpha Bank), 6.8% (Eurobank), 6.9% (National bank) and 5.9% (Piraeus Bank) under the adverse scenario.

However, the tests show that the Greek banks have the highest ratio of NPLs in euro area and that their NPL ratio is several times larger than that of other European banks reflecting the structural weaknesses of the Greek systemic banks. It is no coincidence that capital controls have been partially removed in the end of September 2018 and they are expected to be fully abolished within 2019. Indeed, the reform of the financial sector in Greece had three main objectives, namely normalizing liquidity and payment conditions after the disastrous implementation of capital controls in 2015, addressing the high level of nonperforming exposures (NPEs) on banks' balance sheets, and enforcing corporate governance in banks and in the Hellenic financial stability fund.

Indeed, the reduction of the NPEs ratio in the next decade is a key challenge for macroeconomic stabilization in Greece. In June 2018, the stock of NPEs stood at 88.6 billion Euros or 48.0% of total exposures, excluding off-balance sheet exposures (in September 2017 the NPE ratio was 42% against 14% in Portugal and 10% in Italy). Taking into consideration that a large percentage of NPEs consists of loans toward small- and medium-sized firms as well as toward residential mortgages, one can easily perceive the negative impact not only on bank lending ability and on financial system resilience but broadly on the national economic system. The debt to disposable income ratio of households follows an upward path over passing 140%, exposing further the Greek banking system to greater credit risk (consolidated private sector debt was 210,856 billion Euros in 2017). Additionally, bank deposits are still almost 50% down than in 2009 and slow progress has been made to recapture deposits which left the banking system after the disastrous capital controls in summer 2015.

Overall, the banks do not play their traditional role as intermediaries between deposits and investment and thus they cannot lend the capital required to restart domestic investment. Apart from the inadequate volume of credit supply, impaired balance sheets do impact on lending cost with loan rates being higher in Greece compared to other euro area states. Significant differences continue to exist between Greek banks and banks in other euro area states concerning asset quality, CET1 ratios, quality of capital, NPEs ratio (Greek government expects it to be reduced in 20% by 2021), loan to deposit ratio (78.4% in the second-quarter of 2018), and access of firms to loans. Unavoidably, the challenge is to reshuffle NPEs and to strengthen bank's governance so as to impose stringent risk controls and to attain high credit scoring.

One should also underline that one of the basic indexes concerning companies which is the Athens composite share price index is also far below its early crisis levels. More specifically, the price of the index on 30th November of 2018 was only 630.23 relative to 1459.81 in November 24, 2010 (the price of the index was 740.20 on November 30, 2017). This downward trend has direct negative results not only on capitalization of the companies but also on taxation revenues and on the ability of Greek companies to find capital in international markets at low interest rates.

Evaluating Progress in Structural Reforms

Structural reforms have been essential to all three adjustment programs in Greece. More open markets have been considered crucial for economic opportunities, curtailment of rent seeking, and oligopolistic behavior (Varga et al. 2013; Vogel 2014; Bourles et al. 2010; Canton et al. 2014). Reforms are also essential in the internal devaluation thesis that underlines the necessity of rationalization of both incomes and prices in an economy undergoing fiscal adjustment. However, in the first year of third adjustment program implementation, there was confusion over which structural conditions have been critical for growth drivers and which ones served only for macroeconomic stabilization. Structural reforms were not intertwined and had been applied disorderly and in an ad hoc way. Critical importance has not been attributed to the sequence or combination of structural reforms but rather to legislation.

However, how one combines reforms in different sectors is crucial for the growth drivers. For example, ad hoc privatization without adequate product/services deregulation or without significant reforms in the sector where privatization occurs does not reduce prices and does not extinguish the influence of vested interests. The third program achieved a nominal implementation of reforms with no real impact effects on economy. Despite the fact that all recommendations of reforms (i.e., OECD 366 recommendations) had been legislated there was small impact on product markets, competitiveness, and employment.

More specifically, at policy level the third program ignored the time lag between reforms adoption, reforms implementation, and reform results and thus it mistakenly supposed that reforms immediately increase flexibility of factors of production, lead to automatic transfer of resources from the non-tradables to the tradables sector, and orient firms to reduce price levels. Unfortunately, limited available private capital prefers a "wait and see" policy on investment issues and specialized labor force prefers to leave Greece for other European Union states or to choose part-time employment in the unofficial economy (or if lucky enough to be temporarily employed in eight-month contract in public sector). Balassa–Samuelson effects did not take place and exports rise was mainly due to ad hoc reorientation of local firms and did not derive from a long-term strategy to integrate local firms in global production/commercial networks.

Equally important, there was no strategy to counterbalance negative spillovers on production, demand, credit, and employment from structural reforms in the short term and no policy to create a pro-reform stance in Greek citizens. The lack of national ownership in the reform agenda promoted reforms as shock without learning or adaptation of involved economic agents, undermining the support of a reform strategy.

Drazen and Isard (2004) eloquently note that ownership is related not only to the willingness to carry out a program, but also to the technical capacity to implement the program and the political ability to do so. In their definition, the phrase "ownership is required for program implementation" is almost circular. All necessary changes served the dogma "reforms legislation for tranches of financial support" adding uncertainty to the post-surveillance period of adjustment, creating reform fatigue and reducing significantly the trust of citizens to the deliverability and effectiveness of reforms. Rather than targeting only to the non-tradables sector of the economy, rather than creating a cooperative pro-reform interaction with the citizens, the third program reform rationale left aside specific parts of the non-tradables sector, where vested interest are robust and chose conflictual interaction with sectors of the economy which were not part of the political clientele of the Greek coalition government.

Summing up, employment and investment had not been influenced by thousands of legislative reforms, barriers to entry in certain markets remain and oligopolies even in crucial daily products/services are strong. The insistence on legislative reforms and not on effective reforms is explained by the fact that so many rules, regulations have been applied but transaction cost, high prices and structural inelasticity are present in many sectors of the economy confirming that reforms had been speedy in bureaucratic-regulatory terms but inadequate in deliverability terms.

Moreover, reforms had a minimal effect on distributional/welfare terms, since high prices did not permit households and firms to improve their consumer or production status. In sum, losers from reforms had been left without a safety social net.

The data also support the ineffectiveness of structural reforms to alter the economy especially relating to property registration and the justice system. The World Bank doing business report underlines that it still takes many days to resolve a business dispute in Greek courts much longer than in any other European state. Equally important, the cadastral project does not cover all land and buildings in the country, which means not only small fiscal revenues from real estate tax but more importantly confusion in investment conditions, legal uncertainty over property rights (especially the incompleteness of forest maps) and contested property titles.

Assessing Social Inequalities

The third program did not address the social inequalities caused by the fiscal consolidation. Although there was a downward trend of unemployment, most of the new jobs were part-time and temporary ones compared to the full employment positions of the past. According to the latest data (November 2018) of the Greek labor confederation institute, 61% of the new labor contracts are part time and temporary outweighing the full-time ones (first eight months of 2018). Even more, many of the new temporary jobs have been created in the public sector (eight months duration) with no real value added to the economy and no skills enforcement of the employees. Unemployment rates remain high relative to euro area averages and employment rates are low (53.5% in 2017) relative to eurozone average (66.5%).

Unemployment persists in two categories, namely the young people reaching 37% for the age below 25 and the long-term unemployed reaching 72.1%. Wages and productivity remain at low levels and low-paid, low-skill positions tend to be the rule in the so-called new jobs. More specifically, 10% of employees in the private sector are paid less than 450 Euros, and only 10% with more than 1300 Euros. In sum, three-quarters of the people working in the private sector are paid with less than 1000 Euros. If the aforementioned fragile profile of new working places is combined with an ineffective social protection system, it becomes evident why poverty deteriorates and why the level of life of the most vulnerable groups in Greek economy (i.e., families with children, elderly people, long-term unemployed above 50) is aggravated. The effectiveness of social spending has been hampered by underfunding and overlapping responsibilities across ministries and between levels of government while weaknesses in administrative systems especially for in-kind benefits, raise administrative costs and lead to underperformance of social protection and healthcare indicators.

Is There an Alternative Adjustment Route?

The abovementioned analysis indicates the necessity for an alternative adjustment strategy. Figure 1 eloquently mentions the key issue areas for adjustment policy and looks at how the design and implementation of a program can contribute to the evolution of the Greek economy and the attainment of the growth objectives. It also examines the aspects of the program which cannot be quantified but may nevertheless be important (i.e., the institutional framework) to be considered.

Such an analysis facilitates a qualitative perception of different factors contribution to consolidation and reveals missing issues in the policy agenda. It also uncovers crucial issues concerning the scope of the program (i.e., the pillars of the EAP which should be analyzed) the mechanisms of the program and how they influence the behavior and values of the economic agents, the effects of the program on equity and growth, and the validity of different assessment criteria (i.e., distribution of costs/benefits of the program, national ownership, acceptability of reforms).

The relevance, appropriateness (efficiency), and effectiveness of a program inputs are assessed in terms of their contribution to the program intended results over the program period and their longer term impact on the economy of Greece. An alternative adjustment strategy takes into consideration that EAP trajectories differ with respect to

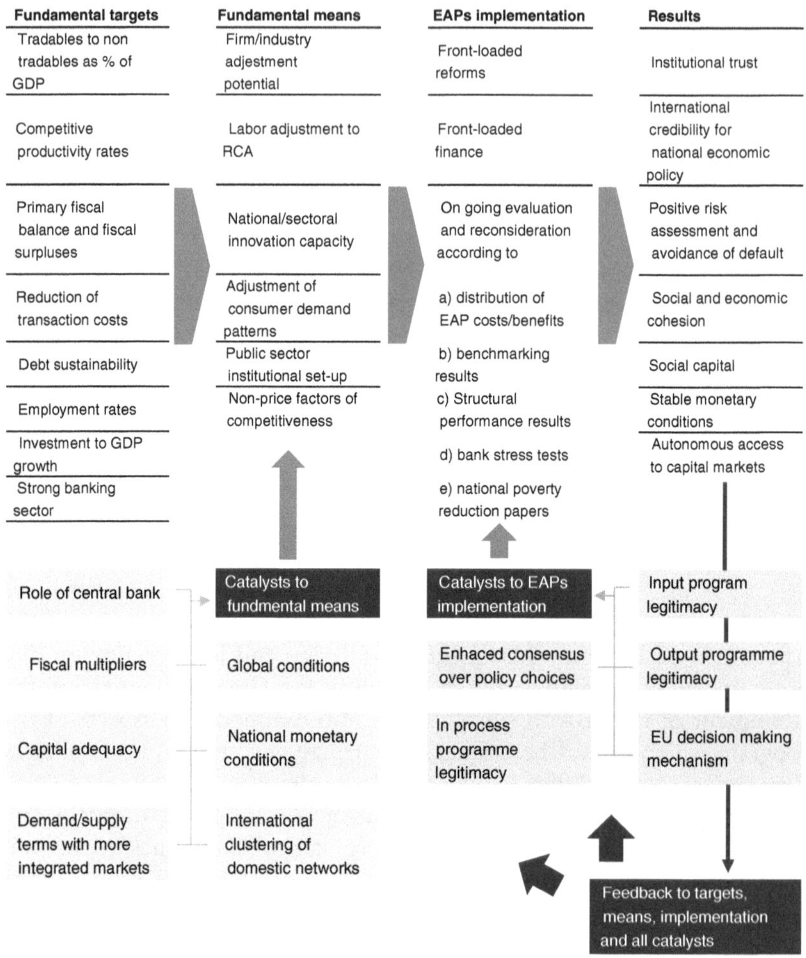

Fig. 1 An ideal type for economic adjustment programs in eurozone (*Source* Hazakis 2015, p. 834)

which organizational traits are involved in the adjustment process, how economic knowledge is diffused through EAP frameworks, which EAP cooperative patterns affect economic performance and how EAP institutions are modified and transformed in organizational terms or in policy terms. Moreover, to what degree EAP structures are proved efficient in the long-term policy learning depends on the efficiency of their structures, on the patterns of daily cooperative interaction among involved agents and on the ability of EAP processes to manage cooperation/conflict in regular meetings with the troika representatives (Hazakis 2018). Within such a policy framework, all EAP incentives can be seen as mechanisms of a regulatory regime creating opportunities for macroeconomic action.

Conclusions-Policy Implications

The article stressed the failures and successes of the third adjustment program in Greece. The answer to the inefficiency of the third program is not an easy one. Expenditure-based adjustments seem to be more successful than revenue-based ones but they underperform if based on horizontal rationale expenditure cuts and not on a thorough analysis of antigrowth expenditure. Valuable policy implications derive on fiscal/structural/welfare and institutional issues of the third adjustment program in Greece.

The targets of the program proved to be highly optimistic concerning the expected results from structural reforms, while institutional inertia in the public sector undermined the essence of effective reforms. It is apparent that the political economy of fiscal/structural adjustment is equally important for the success/failure of an adjustment program to standard economic fundamentals and that political economy variables contribute to persistence of fiscal distress. Further, high private and public indebtedness and a large stock of NPLs continue to weigh on domestic demand and growth.

It is evident that macroeconomic stabilization in nominal terms succeeded but to the detriment of growth drivers and social welfare involving asymmetrical social and welfare cost. Moreover, taxpaying capacity of Greece's productive forces has been exhausted and the increase in direct/indirect taxation had marginal effects despite exorbitant rise of tax rates.

Equally important, a sui generis internal devaluation insisting only to contraction of incomes and not to contraction of prices led to impoverishment of the population and left intact oligopolistic markets and economic rentiers in the Greek economy. Thus, reduction of incomes/state expenditure through internal devaluation coupled with high taxation rates had asymmetrical negative effects in different aspects of GDP and contributed negatively on investment, employment and consumption. Exports did not counterbalance fiscal contraction losses and private investment was anemic and did not cover state weakness to invest in projects with important multiplies and spillover effects.

At the policy level, the third program proved ineffective because of four failures: failures of policy mix, failures of economic policy cognitive framework, failures of implementation in key issue areas such as structural reforms and failure of strong political will to apply growth-oriented and market-friendly reforms, minimizing rent-seeking behavior.

It became also apparent that domestic institutions do influence the success of crisis management. Asymmetric information can contribute to serious delays in arriving at a negotiated settlement. This could happen because EAPs involve activities at multiple levels and any policy change overlaps with other policy situations so that activities in one initiative affect activities in another. Evidently, most policy situations are composed of multiple overlapping actions that are linked sequentially. They determine the extent to which people take initiatives, create economic activity, and thus generate taxable income. Strengthening ownership of programs is vital and successful implementation of reforms and the degree of national ownership is highly correlated. The reforms should be part and parcel of a national development plan but they should also be internalized and legitimized by the citizens.

The aforementioned suggestion means that effective governments should design and implement measures in a consensual way, through social coalition-building, legitimizing the stabilization policy. It follows then that incremental and processual economic adjustments are better pursued. Indeed, complex interplays of policy application and context that include factors such as timing of decision-making procedures, the nature/quality of national institutions and informal routines/practices of national macroeconomic policy influence significantly EAP performance.

An EAP should also improve the quality of institutions, the trust between the state and its citizens, the consistency of public policies, the public infrastructure, the access to finance for businesses, and the quality of public services so as to activate growth drivers.

According to article, EAPs are effective if they induce structural reforms with national ownership keeping positive and steady momentum in achieving fundamental macroeconomic and growth targets even if they fall short of or differ from full compliance to initial EAP targets.

Thus, the essence of compliance is not evaluated only in absolute targets set out initially but refers to the extent to which a state gathers reform momentum and conforms to the standards of euro area institutional framework taking into consideration usual design errors (i.e., multiplier impact).

As more open economies are less exposed to the trade off between austerity and growth, Greece needs to focus on the non-tradables sector problem but parallel the euro area states with trade surpluses need to incorporate and secure in the medium term the position of export-oriented Greek firms in their globalized productive/commercial networks.

Conclusively, it becomes evident that adjustment should equally target from the beginning structural and fiscal consolidation taking into consideration the necessity to protect the most vulnerable social groups and maintain programs with positive spillover effects in the economy (Hazakis 2018).

Bibliography

Aiginger, K., & Schratzenstaller, M. (2011, January). Consolidating the Budget Under Difficult Conditions—Ten Guidelines Viewed Against Europe's Beginning Consolidation Programmes. *Intereconomics, 46*(1), 36–42.

Alesina, A., & Ardagna, S. (1998, October). Fiscal Adjustments: Why They Can Be Expansionary. *Economic Policy, 13*, 488–545.

Alesina, A., & Ardagna, S. (2012). *The Design of Fiscal Adjustments* (NBER Working Paper Series, Working Paper No. 18423). Cambridge, MA: National Bureau for Economic Research. http://www.nber.org/papers/w18423. Accessed 10 November 2018.

Anderson, D., Hunt, B., & Snudden, S. (2014). Fiscal Consolidation in the Euro Area: How Much Pain Can Structural Reforms Ease? *Journal of Policy Modeling, 36*, 785–799.

Bi, R., Qu, H., & Roaf, J. (2013, June). *Assessing the Impact and Phasing of Multiyear Fiscal Adjustment: A General Framework* (IMF Working Paper No. 13/182). Washington DC: IMF.

Bitzenis, A., Papadopoulos, I., & Vlachos, V. (2013). *Reflections on the Greek Sovereign Debt Crisis: The EU Institutional Framework, Economic Adjustment in an Extensive Shadow Economy.* Cambridge, UK: Cambridge Scholars Publishing.

Blanchard, O., & Leigh, D. (2013). *Growth Forecasts Errors and Fiscal Multipliers* (IMF Working Paper No. 13/1). Washington, DC: IMF.

Botta, A. (2015). *The Theoretical Weaknesses of the Expansionary Austerity Doctrine* (Post Keynesian Economics Study Group, Working Paper No. 1511). Available at https://www.postkeynesian.net/downloads/working-papers/PKWP1511.pdf.

Bourles, R., Cette, G., Lopez, J., Mairesse, J., & Nicoletti, G. (2010). *Do Product Market Regulations in Upstream Sectors Curb Productivity Growth? Panel Data Evidence for OECD Countries* (National Bureau of Economic Research, Working Paper No. 16520). Washington, DC. Available at https://ideas.repec.org/a/tpr/restat/v95y2013i5p1750-1768.html.

Canton, E., Grilo, I., Monteagudo, J., Pierini, F., & Turrini, A. (2014, June 1–6). *The Role of Structural Reform for Adjustment and Growth, European Commission* (ECFIN Economic Brief, 34). Brussels.

Carnot, N. (2014, August). *Evaluating Fiscal Policy: A Rule of Thumb* (European Economy, Economic Paper No. 526) (pp. 1–41). Brussels.

De Grauwe, P., & Ji, Y. (2013, February 21). Panic-Driven Austerity in the Eurozone and Its Implications. *Vox EU*. Available at https://voxeu.org/article/panic-driven-austerity-eurozone-and-its-implications.

Drazen, A., & Isard, P. (2004). *Can Public Discussion Enhance Program Ownership?* (National Bureau of Economic Research, Working Paper No. 10927). Cambridge, MA: NBER.

ESM. (2018). *European Commission Directorate General Economic and Financial Affairs, Update 9 July, Compliance Report, ESM Stability Support Programme for Greece Fourth Review*. Available at https://ec.europa.eu/info/sites/info/files/economy-finance/compliance_report_4r_2018.06.20.docx.pdf.

Eurogroup. (2018a). *Remarks by M. Centeno Following the Eurogroup Meeting of 21 June 2018*. Available at https://www.consilium.europa.eu/en/press/press-releases/2018/06/22/remarks-by-m-centeno-following-the-eurogroup-meeting-of-21-june-2018/.

Eurogroup. (2018b). *President of the Euro Group, 21st June 2018*. Available at https://www.consilium.europa.eu/en/meetings/eurogroup/2018/06/21/.

Eurogroup. (2018c). *Statement on Greece, 22 January 2018*. https://www.consilium.europa.eu/el/press/press-releases/2018/01/22/eg-statement-on-greece/.

European Commission. (2010). *The Economic Adjustment Program for Greece* (European Economy, Occasional Paper No. 61). Brussels: DG Economic and Financial Affairs.

European Commission. (2014, April). *The Second Economic Adjustment Programme for Greece, Fourth Review* (Economic and Financial Affairs, Occasional Paper No. 192). Brussels.

European Commission. (2018a, Winter). *European Economic Forecast* (Directorate General for Economic and Financial Affairs, Issue, No. 1). Brussels.

European Commission. (2018b, Spring). *Statistical Annex to the European Economy*. Brussels: DG Economic and Financial Affairs.

European Parliament, Directorate General for Internal Policies. (2014, February). *State of Play in Implementing Macroeconomic Adjustment Programmes in Euro Area*. Study on the Request of the Economic and Monetary Affairs Committee. Strasbourg. http://www.europarl.europa.eu/document/activities/cont/201402/20140219ATT79589/20140219ATT79589EN.pdf. Accessed 10 November 2018.

Fernandez, S., & Paulet, T. (2014, May). Adjustment Programs in the Euro Area: Mission Accomplished? *Synthesis, 22*, 1–14.

Gros, D., & Alcidi, C. (2013, April). *Country Adjustment to a Sudden Stop: Does the Euro Make a Difference?* (European Economy, Economic Paper No. 492). Brussels.

Hazakis, K. (2015). The Political Economy of Economic Adjustment Programs in the Eurozone: A Detailed Policy Analysis. *Politics and Policy, 43*(6), 822–854.

Hazakis, K. (2018). *European Union Political Economy: Theory and Policy*. Lanham, MD: Lexington.

IMF. (2013). *Greece Ex Post Evaluation of Exceptional Access Under the 2010 Stand-By Arrangement*. Washington, DC: IMF.

IMF. (2016). *Greece Preliminary Sustainability Analysis-Updated Estimates and Further Considerations* (IMF Country Report No. 16/130). Available at http://www.imf.org/external/pubs/ft/scr/2016/cr16130.pdf. Accessed 29 May 2016.

IMF. (2018). *Greece, Article IV Consultation and Proposal for Post Program Monitoring* (Country Report No. 18/248). Washington, DC: IMF.

Karger, H. (2014). The Bitter Pill: Austerity, Debt, and the Attack on Europe's Welfare States. *Journal of Sociology and Social Welfare, 41*(2), 33–53.

Kotios, A., Galanos, G., & Poufinas, T. (2018). Assessment of the Effectiveness of Adjustment Programs at the Core of the Greek Economy. *Modern Economy, 9*(9), 1548–1591.

Kyrkilis, D., & Hazakis, K. (2014, April 4). *The Impact of Economic Adjustment Programs on Greek Competitiveness* (Working Paper No. 2). Volos: South and East European Development Center.

Larch, M., Magnusson, K., & Tatar, B. (2014, February). *Hard Work and More: How to Successfully Conduct Adjustment with Official Assistance* (European Economy, Economic Paper No. 514). Brussels.

Ministry of Finance. (2018a, August). Council of Advisors, Hellenic Republic. *Economic Bulletin*, issue 4, Athens.

Ministry of Finance. (2018b, September). Council of Advisors, Hellenic Republic. *Economic Bulletin*, issue 5, Athens.

Ministry of Finance. (2018c, November). Budget, Hellenic Republic. Athens.

Pisany-Ferry, J., Sapir, A., & Wolff, G. (2013). *EU-IMF Assistance to Euro Area Countries: An Early Assessment*. Brussels: Bruegel Institute.
Reinhart, C. M., & Rogoff, K. S. (2014). Recovery from Financial Crises: Evidence from 100 Episodes. *American Economic Review, 104*(5), 50–55.
Sapir, A. (2018). *High Public Debt in Euro Area Countries: Comparing Belgium and Italy, Policy Contribution* (Issue 15). Bruegel Institute.
Sapir, A., Wolff, G. B., Sousa, C., & Terzi, A. (2014). *The Troika and Financial Assistance in the Euro Area: Successes and Failures*. Study on the Request of the Economic and Monetary Affairs Committee. http://www.bruegel.org/publications/publication-detail/publication/815-the-troikaand-financial-assistance-in-the-euro-area-successes-and-failures/. Accessed 10 November 2018.
Stuckler, D., & Basu, S. (2013). *The Body Economic: Why Austerity Kills*. London: Allen Lane.
Varga, J., Roeger, W., & Veld, J. (2013, December). *Growth Effects of Structural Reforms in Southern Europe: The Case of Greece, Italy, Portugal and Spain* (European Economy, Economic Paper No. 511).
Vogel, L. (2014, November). *Structural Reforms at the Zero Bound* (European Economy, Economic Paper No. 537). Brussels.
World Bank. (2018). *World Bank Online Database*. Washington, DC: World Bank. http://data.worldbank.org/. Accessed 10 November 2018.
Young, O. (1989). *International Cooperation: Building Regimes for Natural Recourses and the Environment*. Ithaca: Cornell University Press.

The Quality of Domestic Institutions as a Driver for the Initiation of Firms' Exporting in the EU Post-crisis Period

Dimitris Manolopoulos

Introduction

At the end of the previous decade, the world economy had experienced its deepest decline in the post-World War II period (the so-called Great Recession), as a direct effect of the financial crisis that has significantly reshaped the context of business activity. Stemming from the collapse of the US real estate market and the subprime mortgage crisis, many advanced economies have unexpectedly slowed down and fallen into a persistent financial recession. As a result, a decrease in per capita gross domestic product (GDP) has been recorded, unemployment mounted at record high levels for many countries, industrial production has declined and the volume of international investment flows was shrinking worldwide (Reinhart and Rogoff 2009). In a similar vein with these investment patterns in the global economic scenery, the impact of crisis on EU trade volumes was also considerable. To be more specific, the decrease in

---

D. Manolopoulos (✉)
Athens University of Economics and Business, Athens, Greece
e-mail: dmanolop@aueb.gr

V. Vlachos and A. Bitzenis (eds.), *European Union*,
https://doi.org/10.1007/978-3-030-18103-1_11

EU exporting was unprecedented historically in terms of both its speed and magnitude, to a point that questions about the competitiveness of the region have been raised (Mauro et al. 2010). Fortunately enough, initial concerns of a devastating global protectionist war as a response to the recession did not materialize (UNCTAD 2010). Growth may be remained sluggish ever since, however, global trade experienced a remarkable recovery after the crisis.

The Great Recession constituted a major shock not only to economies, but also to most firms as well, since they were hit on their performance levels, market share, finances and sale volumes. How could they react to their profitability losses and decreased competitiveness? Many options were considered, yet, exporting emerged as a lucrative strategic response to overcome the malfunctions caused by the crisis. There exists a variety of reasons for that: Exporting increases sales' potential and subsequent profits, diversifies market segments, broadens firms' customer base compensating for decreased demand, assigns to the exporting firm knowledge and experience, introduces new products, extends the life cycle of the existing ones and exploits the advantages of technology sophistication and low transportation costs in foreign countries (Bernard and Jensen 2004; Higòn and Driffield 2011). In a nutshell, the initiation and strengthening of export activity appear an attractive strategic approach for both economies and firms in order to overcome recession phenomena in post-crisis periods.

While our interest in exporting has been revitalized in the recession and post-crisis era due to all the above considerations that positively link trade, growth, corporate sustainability and competitiveness, new theoretical and empirical challenges have aroused. Placing transaction costs at the core of export literature, the initial conceptual basis of firms' exporting was founded on the premises of transaction cost economics (TCE), assuming foreign entry as a 'transaction' (e.g., Anderson and Gatignon 1986). Mindful of TCE arguments, recent developments (e.g., Ngo et al. 2016) added an institutional perspective in export studies. Institutions that guide and affect trade are not only international organizations, such as the WTO, but mainly comprise 'the rules of the game' (North 1990), which affect market structures and social interactions in both home and export countries. To further explain, institutions (broadly defined and constructed) are often seen as a source of comparative advantage in trade and influence export decisions by impacting on financial markets, legal right enforcement, contracts, tariffs' reduction and the development of infrastructure that can lower costs in regional trade transactions. Thus, institutions have a direct effect on how well firms are able to formulate and implement their internationalization strategies (Meyer et al. 2009).

Despite the importance of institutions in understanding export dynamics, institutional arguments in firms' exporting are predominantly targeted on export counties, by investigating the effects of institutional distance (e.g., He et al. 2013; Yang et al. 2012), firm reputation abroad, the impact of global organizational structures on foreign expansion (e.g., Gimeno et al. 2005) and the influence of institutional changes (e.g., Peng 2003; Wu et al. 2007). While these studies have made substantial contributions to our understanding of the determinants of export decisions, an important gap in the empirical literature is the issue of how the *local* institutional quality influences firms' exporting (Manolopoulos et al. 2018; Stoian and Filippaios 2008). This area of investigation warrants further research, especially if we consider that in crisis periods the quality of home institutions becomes poorer, affecting their efficiency and impartiality, impacting on export growth. Since institutional impartiality is mainly reflected in governance quality (Rothstein and Teorell 2008), our study is propelled by the motivation to add empirical content to the impact of local governance quality on firms' decision to export. Such an investigation is significant, because it considers firms' dependency on their home environments for initiating internationalization activities. As already highlighted, successful firms' internationalization is pivotal for a country's national economic recovery. If internationalization activity is stifled by institutional voids, then an important determinant of national growth is limited in post-crisis periods.

To briefly foreshadow our findings, we produce evidence that may develop literature in several ways. First, we trace the background institutional context of Greece, an economy under an ongoing financial crisis and its effects on firms' export propensity. Since advancing extroversion is a prerequisite for stabilizing and achieving competitiveness of the EU countries affected by the economic recession, there is a firm believer among researchers that these growth prospects should be based on sustainable factors, such as exporting, rather than on consumption patterns fueled by external borrowing, and it is our objective to contribute in this direction. Second, conceptually, we advance our understanding of firms' internationalization by rediscovering the relationship between exporting and home governance quality after a period of neglect. Finally, we address some of the methodological shortcomings of previous institutional studies by providing *perceptual* evaluations of home governance effects on exporting, as compared to objective data demonstrated in secondary databases used by most researchers.

Theoretical Foundation and Development of Hypotheses

Institutions matter for export growth. Institutional theory is rooted back to an economic orientation emphasizing on efficiency (North 1990), sociological arguments related to cognition (Scott 1995) and political considerations that parallel institutional effects with political outcomes (Hall and Taylor 1996). Sociological, political and economic perspectives toward institutional arguments share similarities in their foundation and can be viewed as complementary (Peng and Heath 1996). Within these literatures, according to Bruton and associates (Bruton et al. 2010, p. 422), the term '*institution*' broadly refers to an interrelated system of behavioral and relationship patterns, including formal rules, i.e., laws and regulations (North 1990) and informal unwritten rules that shape incentives (North 1991) and shared interaction patterns, such as social norms and traditions (Jepperson 1991; Meyer and Rowan 1991). Following this line of argumentation, the World Bank categorizes institutions as *formal* and *informal*. Their purpose is to shape the actions of organizations and individuals and govern the interactions between them. Both types of institutions intertwine and their interplay shapes social patterns and business practices among society members and within the marketplace. Delving more deeply into institutions, Williamson (2000) proposed a four-level hierarchy (social, formal, regulatory and resource allocation), whereas Kostova (1997) introduced a three-dimensional taxonomy (cognitive, social and normative) to explain how policies, shared social knowledge and value systems impact on business activity. In a similar vein, Seyoum (2009, p. 166) argues that institutions consist of formal, normative and cognitive structures and activities that provide meaning and predictability to social interaction.

Institutional quality prevailing in a country affects all business transactions and in particular exporting, since it provides for a framework that directly influences resource allocations, reputation building, cost control and monitoring, market power and, subsequently, export potentials and performance. Thus, as domestic business activity gains an international orientation, an emerging strand of research had applied institutional ideas in international entrepreneurship studies (e.g., Estrin et al. 2013; Manolopoulos et al. 2018; Ngo et al. 2016). Whereas institutional perspectives have been detected as an influential determinant in foreign production research (e.g., Mudambi and Navarra 2002; Stoian and Filippaios 2008), international trade theory distances itself from institutional arguments. Yet, today there is an emerging macro- and micro-level literature on this area of investigation. At the macro-level analysis (e.g., Anderson and Marcouiller 2002; Berkowitz et al. 2006; Levchenko 2007), institutions promote economic reforms and boost international trade (Rodrik et al. 2004) and it is in the interest of any country to establish an institutional setting that '...will support the effective functioning of the market mechanism, such that firms can engage in transactions without incurring undue costs' (Meyer et al. 2009, p. 63). Institutional factors that have been investigated in this research stream include mutually beneficial transactions, government–market relations, development of factor markets (Lu et al. 2010), structural reforms (Cuervo-Cazurra and Dau 2009), market-based instruments (Yi et al. 2013) and the prospects of a country's investment climate as shaped by public policy, legislation and public policy (Khanna and Krishna 2000; LiPuma et al. 2013).

Micro-level studies (e.g., Estrin et al. 2013; Lee and Weng 2013; Mogos-Descotes et al. 2011) provide a broader empirical basis for also concluding in favor of institutional quality on the promotion of internationalization activity, by suggesting that strong institutions increase the survival rate of exporting firms (Araujo et al. 2016). In this direction, Huther and Shah (1996, p. 40) linked the notion of institutions with public governance, defining the latter as '...all aspects of the exercise of authority through formal and informal institutions in the management of the resource endowment of a state.' The positive association between institutions and governance quality is shaped by the degree to which the public sector achieves the objectives it is supposed to meet (Moore 2004). Arguably, qualitative institutions account for fairness, consistency, predictability, transition sequence, enforceability and the development of an impartial governance system which promotes transparency in business interactions, contributing to uncertainty diminishment and the avoidance of preferential treatment (LiPuma et al. 2013).

Conversely, institutional voids fail to ensure the functioning of effective markets and increase uncertainty and transaction costs, undermining the competitive position of an organization. In the extant literature, governance quality is reflected in a relatively benign bureaucracy, low levels of corruption and a modest regulatory system (e.g., Estrin et al. 2013; La Porta et al. 1998; Sofikitis and Manolopoulos 2012).

Corruption

Corruption is widely conceived as negatively associated with economic growth and one of the most severe barriers to firms' competitiveness and internationalization, since it undermines norms of governance and heightens uncertainty. It consists of an informal, slowly changed institutional layer, deeply embedded in the culture of a society, referring to situations where 'the administrative apparatus enjoys excessive and discretionary power' (Habib and Zurawicki 2002, p. 293). A culture of corruption—an environment where corruption is tolerated and accepted by firms as an inevitable feature of the conduct of business—leads public officials to value their own interests more than the state's priorities, facilitate unfairness and perpetuate inequality. All of these tend to have severe implications for firm growth strategies (Sofikitis and Manolopoulos 2012). The study of corruption in internationalization studies is important, mainly due to the fact that there is an increasing consensus among researchers that it affects firms' basis of further evolution and development, such as their decision to exploit foreign sourcing opportunities.

Literature suggests that there are two opposing predictions regarding the impact of corruption on exporting (Lee and Weng 2013). On the one hand, due to corruption, firms possess fewer resources at their disposal and allocate them away from productive activities, which makes it difficult for them to maintain their existing level of operation, let alone to expand abroad. In parallel, by addressing public misuse of entrusted power for private gains, firms are able to acquire preferential treatment, strengthening in that way their position in the home country (Martin et al. 2007). Firms with improved positions in the local market may not necessarily have an interest in exploring their potentials in foreign countries (Witt and Lewin 2007). In that sense, corruption at home may discourage international investments (e.g., Olken and Pande 2012).

An adverse reasoning though posits that corruption enhances predictability and efficiency by allowing firms to bypass regulations so as to fasten procedures (De Soto 1989), resist the harmful outcomes of uncertainty and acquire resources at lower prices (Rose-Ackerman 1999). Prior research has suggested that firms with greater efficiency may have advantageous positions within foreign sourcing (Bernard and Jensen 2004), since they are more effective in leveraging their home-based advantages in international locations (Gao et al. 2010). Here, we argue that with generally fewer resources at their disposal and greater reliance on external environments, the prevalence of corruption will reversely affect firms' initiation of exporting. Thus, we hypothesize:

Hypothesis 1 There will be a negative association between perceptions of a highly corrupted home market environment and firms' decision to internationalize through exports.

Regulatory Environment

Evidently, the regulatory framework of a country is part of a formal institutional setting. Williamson (2000) highlights its role in shaping business decisions. The regulatory dimension of governance quality refers to laws, regulations, contract enforcements and written rules that promote or restrict firm activity and competitiveness determinants. Heavily regulated environments can produce serious distortions in commercial markets. For exporting firms, this institutional dimension entails the laws, export regulations and those governmental policies that support or prevent exporting and facilitate or hamper their efforts to acquire resources to sustain internationalization (Mogos-Descotes et al. 2011, p. 1304). Institutional rules and regulations impact on foreign markets' entry (Stoian and Filippaios 2008), since regulatory weak domestic environments increase transaction costs and organizational uncertainty. For instance, imperfect enforcement of contracts can prevent mutually beneficial transactions that involve agents from different countries. As such, an ineffective home regulatory framework is seen as a core reason for poor internationalization performance and the several risks associated with the inconsistent enforcement of rules and ineffective legal frameworks may hinder firms' initiation of exporting (La Porta et al. 1998). Consequently, we expect that:

Hypothesis 2 There will be a positive association between perceptions of regulatory quality at home and firms' decision to internationalize through exports.

Bureaucracy

Likewise the regulatory framework, export bureaucracy is considered a major barrier that internationalizing firms have to face, since it is often associated with formalism and excessive delays in decision making, complicated procedures, cautiousness and inefficiency (De Korte and Van der Pijl 2009; Sofikitis and Manolopoulos 2012). As a result, it can be argued that cumbersome bureaucracy misallocates firm resources, restricts export potentials and limits export competitiveness. This argument parallels our earlier discussion of a complicated regulatory system, but rather than increasing costs and uncertainty, increased governmental intervention coupled with a number of exporting procedures which are particularly time-consuming and a lack of public effectiveness poses a more fundamental threat on exporting.

The study of the relationship between bureaucracy and exporting is largely under-investigated, yet there is evidence to support that excessive bureaucratic burden stifle exporting (e.g., Katsikeas and Morgan 1994; Naidu et al. 1997). On the contrary, the existence of an effective bureaucracy that facilitates the smooth transition between different governmental entities, codifies procedures and secures the continuity of the public sector increases the probability to internationalize (Stoian and Filippaios 2008). Thus, we suggest the following:

Hypothesis 3 There will be a negative association between perceptions of highly bureaucratic structures in the home market environment and firms' decision to internationalize through exports.

Interaction of Home Governance Dimensions

Since there is evidence to support that institutional facets impact on firms' decision to internationalize, we focus on the extent to which these dimensions of governance quality interact and influence firms' export decisions. A rigorous test of this relationship requires the investigation of the joint interaction of governance constructs with firms' exporting.

As mentioned, in general, domestic institutional voids make costly for firms to operate in the local context. To be more precise, the interaction of several costs associated with institutional susceptibility, especially those arising from complicated regulations, inconsistent enforcement of rules and ineffective legal frameworks (La Porta et al. 1998), government corruption and bribery (Doh et al. 2003) red tape, bureaucratic systems and preferential treatment in business relationships may hinder exporting. Also, to reverse the argument presented by Hessels and Terjesen (2010), firms based in countries with poor quality institutions are less able and willing to pursue foreign markets, since the margins on returns from exporting are reduced and this may act as a deterrent to export. Thus, despite some claims (e.g., Witt and Lewin 2007) arguing that when home markets are costly to operate in firms may consider expanding into foreign countries as they seek to compensate the weaknesses of their home environment, we posit:

Hypothesis 4 The interaction of governance quality dimensions is expected to impact on firms' decision to internationalize through exports. In particular, weak institutional environments will be negatively associated with firms' exporting.

Research Methodology

Sampling and Survey Instrument

The core objective of this study was to investigate the quality of domestic institutions as a driver for the initiation of firms' exporting in the EU post-crisis period. For this, our research was conducted within the context of Greece, a country of the EU periphery, where the consequences of all these years of economic hardship were severe. Many EU countries had recorded huge government debts, but Greece was worst affected, with an accompanying spiraling spending and current account deficit. As a result, Greece experienced an economic collapse that lasted longer than the other countries of the European south (and Ireland). According to official statistical reports provided by Eurostat, since 2010 its economy has shrunk by one-quarter and the disposable income of its citizens by almost one-third. The economic output of the country, in real terms, is still a quarter below that in 2007, and investments are approximately two-thirds lower. The crisis has also caused massive job losses in Greece. In 2013, the unemployment rate peaked at 27.5%, with almost 50% of young people being unemployed.

Eight years after seeking a bailout, Greece's final program has been completed. The economy is now growing, but rates lag behind compared to other euro zone countries. In the exporting field, trade balance recorded a deficit of €1.98 billion at the beginning of 2018, as exports rose at a significantly faster rate than imports (18.5% as opposed to 1.1%). In this vein, exports' growth consists of a solution for the recession. However, according to *Economist* (www.economist.com/), economists fear that, without further reforms to cut red tape, improve administration services, reduce bureaucracy and speed up its court's systems, the Greek economy will struggle to take off. Thus, the impact of domestic institutions on the post-crisis extroversion of economic activity and social recovery is determinant.

To test our hypotheses on the impact of the quality of the domestic institutional context on firms' exporting, we used data collected from the International Capital (ICAP) directory, a standard source of business information in the focal country, widely used by local researchers (e.g., Dimitratos et al. 2011; Manolopoulos et al. 2018). This research took place in the beginning of 2018 and our surveyed data were collected from the complete population of firms included in the ICAP database, via a stratified random sampling approach. The stratification was used to ensure that the size and inter-industry distribution of firms in the sample resembled that of the whole population. Among all firms included in the ICAP database, we finally selected 500.

To encourage participation, we first contacted firms' executives noting that this survey is part of a wider academic research project investigating the effects of local institutions in the economic development and extroversion of the country, with the overall purpose to provide feedback to policymakers in order to device guidelines to support exporting firms. Further, we have assured them anonymity and confidentiality: Neither the identities of the company nor the name of the respondents would be revealed. One hundred and seventy firms agreed to participate in the survey, rendering a response rate of 34%. Responding firms represented a wide range of industries, including both manufacturing and service sectors. Firm size ranged from 12 to 1.214 employees (average firm size is 72.5 employees). Most firms were domestically owned (74% among them had no foreign ownership involved) and were mostly manufacturing companies. Among these 170 firms, 49 (28.8%) have reported export activities.

Data for our survey were collected through the administration of a structured questionnaire. Questions were phrased in an indirect manner, so as to solicit genuine responses from firms. Our survey instrument was addressed to firms' top managers as these are considered the most appropriate informants on the impact of crucial aspects of the local context on their growth strategies. The questionnaire was pre-tested in three companies, not included in the final sample.

Variables Description

Dependent Variable: The decision to export is approached through firms' export propensity *(EXP)*. This is a binary, categorical variable indicating whether or not a firm exports (directly or indirectly). Therefore, our dependent variable (ψ) equals to 1 for exporting firms and 0 for the opposite case.

Institutional Constructs: The institutional dimensions used in this study reflecting governance quality (the prevalence of corruption, the extent of bureaucracy and regulation complexity) have been taken from the work of Sofikitis and Manolopoulos (2012), and their operationalization has been adopted from the research of Manolopoulos et al. (2018). Following the latter, we have used data from four survey questions to construct our measures for corruption (CORRUPT) and bureaucracy (BUREAU), whereas regulatory quality (REGUL) was measured with a five-item scale. In line with standard academic procedures, the subjective impact of each dimension of home governance quality on exporting has been measured by our respondents on seven-point Likert-type scales. It is argued that the use of this scaling reduces the frustration level of respondents and is considered as particularly valid with high discriminating power and reliability (Preston and Colman 2000). Each scale item used in the questionnaire was end-anchored with very poor indicators on the left (*1*) and very prevalent on the right (*7*). The indirect phrasing of institutional-related questions is consistent with the approach used by Svensson (2003).

Control Variables: Our study considers several, firm-level, controls. In line with prior work, apart from the institutional context, firms' decision to export is also affected by organizational 'profile' factors. Here, we have included in our analysis firm size and age, country of origin and the past experience in internationalization activities. Firm *size* (SIZE; absolute number of personnel) has been one of the most frequently researched constructs in the empirical literature on firms' exporting (Bonaccorsi 1992). While there is no consensus on the impact of firm size on exporting (Aaby and Slater 1989), the majority of studies support a positive relationship (e.g., Majocchi et al. 2005; Mittelstaedt et al. 2003). *Age* (YOPER; number of years since the firm's foundation) has also reached diverse conclusions in exporting. Some scholars have found that its impact is insignificant (e.g., Reid 1982), others have revealed a positive relationship (e.g., Abbas and Swiercz 1991), whereas some others have reported a negative effect (e.g., Ursic and Czinkota, 1984). Following Erramilli and Rao (1993), *prior experience* (EXPER) in international activity has been measured as the number of years of business experience outside the home country. Finally, to control for *country of origin* differences, a dummy variable was used (ORIG), where local firms were coded as 1 and subsidiaries of foreign operations as 0. Both our last two control variables have been detected as significant export predictors.

Method of Analysis

As our dependent variable (EXP) is dichotomous, we chose a basic logit regression model as our estimation technique, a method which is considered as relatively robust to the statistical assumptions that are made. The use of logit models has regained an increasing importance in empirical management research (Zelner 2009). Logit models ensure that the probabilities will be within the (0, 1) range. The equation employed in our research is given by the following formula:

$$P(y_i = 1/x_i) = \exp\left(x_i'\beta\right)/1 + \exp\left(x_i'\beta\right),$$

where β is the vector of coefficients to be estimated.

Results and Analysis

Table 1 reports the means, standard deviations and pairwise Pearson correlations between our dependent (ψ) and the core explanatory and control variables. According to the results reported, no substantive correlations (above $\pm$ 0.700) have been detected.

Table 1 Descriptive statistics and correlations

Variables	*Mnemonic*	*Mean*	*S.D.*	*Min*	*Max*	*1*	*2*	*3*	*4*	*5*	*6*	*7*	*8*
1. Firms' exporting	EXP	0.288	0.196	0	1	1							
2. Corruption	CORRUPT	5.56	1.18	1	7	−0.2345	1						
3. Bureaucracy	BUREAU	5.43	1.24	1	7	−0.2287	0.6247	1					
4. Regulatory context	REGUL	5.21	1.09	2	7	−0.3841	0.1985	0.5911	1				
5. Size of firm	SIZE	72.54	53.11	12	1.214	0.6186	0.2382	−0.2458	0.1058	1			
6. Years of operation	YOPER	24.08	18.75	2	67	0.0788	0.0124	0.0427	−0.3183	−0.0511	1		
7. Experience in internationali-zation activity	EXPER	11.87	9.28	1	32	0.5821	−0.1239	−0.1148	0.1087	0.2289	0.0224	1	
8. Country of orgin	ORIG	0.74	0.61	0	1	−0.3296	0.4982	0.2257	−0.0324	0.2651	−0.0369	0.1054	1

Notes
$n = 170$; corelations above 0.31 are significant at 0.001 and correlations above 0.24 are significant at 0.01

Table 2 Logistic regression results on firms' exporting

ψ (*EXP – firms' export propensity*)	*Model 1*	*Model 2*	*Model 3*	*Model 4*
Intercept	−3.137***	−1.521	−3.188**	−3.204**
	(1.419)	(2.142)	(1.647)	(1.5533)
CORRUPT		−0.238		
		(0.221)		
BUREAU		−0.305*		
		(0.188)		
REGUL		−0.358		
		(0.294)		
SIZE	0.021***	0.022***	0.031***	0.032***
	(0.004)	(0.005)	(0.006)	(0.006)
YOPER	0.022	0.028	0.027	0.172
	(0.018)	(0.021)	(0.022)	(0.293)
EXPER	0.018***	0.022***	0.019***	0.021***
	(0.004)	(0.006)	(0.005)	(0.003)
ORIG	0.428	0.580	0.534	0.574
	(0.397)	(0.454)	(0.488)	(0.490)
Corruption × bureaucracy[b]			−0.062*	
			(0.034)	
Corruption × regulatory framework[b]			−0.019	
			(0.038)	
Bureaucracy × regulatory framework[b]			0.016	
			(0.043)	
Corruption × bureaucracy × regulatory framework[b]				−0.18*
				(0.005)
Pseudo R square	0.05	0.26	0.25	0.24
F value[c]	65.32***	74.18***	72.25***	65.17***
Goodness of fit[d]	229.05***	344.2***	302.11***	289.98***

Notes
$n = 170$
Standard errors are in parentheses
* Significant at 0.05, ** Significant at 0.01, *** Significant at 0.001
[a]Logit regressions (cut-points omitted). Dependent variable: Firms' exporting. Robust standard errors in parentheses
[b]Institutional constructs have been mean-centered so as to limit the potential multicollinearity of the interaction terms
[c]LR χ^2
[d]Hosmer–Lemeshow test

Table 2 presents the logit regression results. We first estimated a baseline model (Model 1), reporting only the results of the controls on the dependent variable (EXP). Next, we introduced the terms testing the perceived impact of our institutional constructs (Model 2).

Model 2 represents an improvement over the respective baseline model (LR χ^2_{model2} 74.18, significant at the 0.001 level of significance and LR χ^2_{model1} 65.32 significant at the 0.001 level, respectively). Further, we investigated the paired interaction effects of the three governance quality dimensions (Model 3) and, finally, the joint interaction effect of all governance constructs employed in our survey (Model 4). Results in Model 1 are proven to be considerably inferior compared to those presented in Models 2, 3 and 4, which implies that the models including the governance quality dimensions and their interaction effects are statistically the preferred specifications. The Hosmer and Lemeshow tests indicate that all of our logistic models reach acceptable levels of fitness.

Results from the base model suggest that among our firm-level variables under investigation, *age* and *prior experience* in international markets emerge as very influential predictors of firms' decision to export, since both constructs are positively and statistically significantly related to exporting at the 0.001 level of significance. In addition, Table 2 further reveals that when our variables for the perceived impact of the home institutional quality on the dependent variable are added in specifications 2–4, the R^2 of the models increases significantly (from 0.05 to 0.26), reinforcing the high explanatory power of the quality of home institutional context in the initiation of export activity.

Coming to our hypothesized relationships, Model 2 provides support to our third hypothesis which has predicted a negative association ($p < 0.05$) between perceptions of highly bureaucratic structures in the home environment and firms' decision to internationalize through exports. The coefficient of bureaucracy in the home country suggests that a 1% increase in bureaucratic inefficiency in the home country lowers the probability to export by 0.30%. This is consistent with the idea that as the state sector intervenes in business transactions, the ineffective bureaucratization reduces firm incentives to exploit opportunities outside their geographical boundaries. Overall though, results from Model 2 indicate that when the governance quality dimensions are considered independently, they do not exert a severe impact on the initiation of firms' exporting. However, the interaction effects reported in Models 3 and 4 indicate that although institutions are separately established and comprise their own decision-making apparatuses, their effects on exporting cannot be studied independently if we seek for finer insights of their impact on firms' internationalization decisions. More specifically, in Model 3 the estimates of the paired regulatory interactions with the other institutional constructs are not significant. The paired interaction of corruption with bureaucracy decreases the probability that a firm exports ($\beta = -0.062$, $p < 0.05$). Finally, the results support our contention described in our last hypothesis that the joint interaction of institutional constructs is expected to impact on firms' decision to internationalize through exports. The negative and significant relationship ($p < 0.05$) between exporting and governance quality dimensions recorded in Model 4 suggests that firms' expansion strategies reflect, in part, the limitations defined by home institutions, in the sense that institutional pressures in the home country decrease the probability of exporting. Therefore, Hypothesis 4 is supported.

Psychometric Properties of the Measurement Scales and Sensitivity Analyses

A consideration of the research was the minimization of common method concerns. To correct for such effects, the following precautions were taken: First, the dependent variable was measured using secondary data, whereas our core explanatory variables were measured perceptually. Further, our control variables are archival, obviating any danger of common method bias with them. In addition, scale anchors in specific items of the questions related to the assessment of the local institutional context quality were reversed to reduce and compensate for the development of response patterns. Finally, in general, interaction effects are less vulnerable to common method bias. These precautions afford some confidence that any potential bias coming from our approach is likely to be minor.

The psychometric properties of our measurement scales were evaluated by following accepted practices in the literature in relation to the reliability of our measurement scales. The alpha reliability coefficient of all items reflecting governance quality dimensions used in this study is 0.78, well above the proposed 0.70 level. In relation to the three institutional constructs, our alpha values range between 0.76 and 0.80 (accepted level of reliability). Consequently, a large number of measures are free of random errors. We also estimated a series of alternative specifications to assess the robustness of our results. First, we have added to our models two measure of other firm-level characteristics that might plausibly affect exporting. First, to estimate the effect of innovation on exporting founded in product cycle work and technology theories of trade (Vernon 1966; Krugman 1979), we adopted the ideas provided by Higòn and Driffield (2011), including in our models a dummy variable indicating if the responding firm had introduced significantly a new product and/or process in the past 12 months. Also, we have included, as another control, the location of the firm (captured through a binary variable where 1 indicates those firms that are located in the capital of the country, and 0 in the periphery). However, since these variables were consistently insignificant in all models, and their inclusion or exclusion did not change the other parameter estimates, they were dropped from the analysis. Overall, we conclude that our results appear to be robust to different operationalizations and measurements of our variables.

Discussion and Conclusions

Traditionally, studies on exporting draw on the transaction cost theory, stressing the importance of cost considerations on export decisions. Since firms' exporting is also affected from both their domestic and foreign institutional environments, and managers scan opportunities and challenges in distant countries so as to devise growth responses in the contemporary, post-crisis, inter-connected globalized business landscape, a key motivation of our research was to offer insights on firms' internationalization decisions from an institutional perspective. We believe that addressing this issue is topical because the literature on the association between firms' internationalization and institutional theories may have proliferated (e.g., Bruton et al. 2010; Estrin et al. 2013); yet, more empirical evidence in this direction is required (Mogos-Descotes et al. 2011; Hessels and Terjesen 2010).

The context of this research may also extend its contribution. Studies on the relationship between institutional quality and exporting focus mainly on emerging economies, as well as economies under transition. Given the importance of exporting in the economic recovery of countries that have experienced a recession, literature should also be oriented toward more advanced economies that have suffered from an economic downturn. In this regard, we focus our research on Greece, an economy hardly hit by the crisis, which struggles to find its pathway back to development. An assessment of the impact of domestic institutions on firms' decision to export may entail useful policy recommendations that could facilitate the extroversion and competitiveness of the focal economy, since, in general, exporting firms contribute positively to growth by revenue generation, improvements in trade balance and increase in employment levels.

The core findings of this study are the following: First, exporting seems to be an attractive growth strategy, since exporters represent almost 30% of our randomly sampled firms. Otherwise stated, notwithstanding the disadvantages that the local firms have faced due to recession period, a considerable portion of them now pursue international markets to sell their goods and services and secure their development potentials. This further suggests that a focus on domestic markets only may not help firms maintain a sustainable competitive position in the long run. Second, the regressions establish the key result of our work: Domestic institutional quality is shown to be a highly significant factor in shaping firms' export decisions. Institutional dimensions coexist and increasingly exert influence on exporting. More specifically, whereas the isolated study of institutional dimensions was found to have a minor impact on export propensity, the interaction of institutional layers defines limitations for firms aiming to expand internationally. This evidence corroborates the notion that institutional pressures make market transactions costly and exporting activity less efficient, and that better developed institutions could reduce uncertainties, lower transaction search and costs and exploit more effectively firm resources in foreign locations (e.g., North 1990).

Our findings may have implications for policy and business support. According to the evidence recorded here, when a portion of firms faces institutional pressures in their home environment, they tend to be more active in internationalizing their operations. Since foreign markets may provide unique opportunities, such as access to new customers, acquisition of valuable resources and more optimal exploitation of competitive incentives, the remaining firms may bear a certain level of opportunity costs by focusing exclusively on domestic settings (Spencer and Gomez 2011). To the extent that exporting is considered as the initial step of entrance in the international market environment, it would be vital for non-exporters to comprehensively evaluate the limitations of focus on their home country only. Finally, our findings may entail interesting policy implications: Due to the fact that competition is increasingly global, local firms, as they seek to move beyond their home region, may face important challenges as they compete with other, more experienced in foreign markets, firms. Governance support targeted at this important transition point may well be of particular value. In addition, considering the importance of firm resources in international expansion strategies, governments could establish a favorable institutional infrastructure and prioritize policies that could provide incentives for local firms to engage in further capability building. In this vein, it can be also argued that despite the fact that Greece is still a surprisingly closed economy and its institutional context has severe pathogenies; it seems that reforms aiming at promoting entrepreneurship and competitiveness led to an improvement in governance quality dimensions, posing an important challenge to local firms to diversify their strategies and find out new markets for their existing competitive imperatives. It seems then sound to support that an improved institutional environment, capable of strengthening administrative systems, removing unnecessary regulations, reducing waiting times and minimizing corruption levels, will foster a better overall business environment, so that firms can become more competitive and more fully integrated into the global economy.

A number of potential limitations of the paper should be addressed by future research. First, firm resources are a very influential predictor of export activity and their impact on export propensity should be considered. In addition, by focusing our study on the institutional context, another limitation relates to a range of decision-makers' characteristics that can influence export propensity, such as demographic profiles and personality constructs. Further, while there are several dimensions shaping the institutional context, here we focus on governance quality. Other institutional measures, such as the level of economic freedom (Estrin et al. 2008) or the protection of property rights (Estrin et al. 2013), would provide us with additional insights on the impact of institutions on firms' exporting. Also, the single-country context of the study may limit the generalizability of its findings. Finally, in order to have a more complete assessment of the impact of institutions on post-crisis periods and adequately examine the proposed relationships, a longer time period may be required.

To sum up, drawing upon discussions on integrating diverse perspectives in exporting (e.g., Meyer and Peng 2005; Wheeler et al. 2008), our research develops and validates institutional arguments for understanding firms' internationalization decisions in our post-crisis era. In that sense, we develop a unique country-specific data set that allows broadening the framework of firms' export determinants in EU peripheral economies. Despite the study's limitations and until we see at least how the results of 2016 US presidential elections and the Brexit vote are imprinted in the globalization scenario and impact on the initiation of export activity, this study is one among the few to investigate the interaction effects of domestic institutional dimensions in export decisions.

References

Aaby, N. E., & Slater, S. F. (1989). Management Influences on Export Performance: A Review of the Empirical Literature 1978–88. *International Marketing Review, 6*(4), 7–26.

Abbas, A., & Swiercz, P. (1991). Firm Size and Export Behaviour: Lessons from the Midwest. *Journal of Small Business Management, 29*(2), 71–78.

Anderson, E., & Gatignon, H. (1986). Modes of Foreign Entry: A Transaction Cost Analysis and Propositions. *Journal of International Business Studies, 17*(3), 1–26.

Anderson, E. J., & Marcouiller, D. (2002). Insecurity and the Pattern of Trade: An Empirical Investigation. *Review of Economics and Statistics, 84*(2), 342–352.

Araujo, L., Mion, G., & Ornelas, E. (2016). Institutions and Export Dynamics. *Journal of International Economics, 98*, 2–20.

Berkowitz, D., Moenius, J., & Pistor, K. (2006). Trade, Law, and Product Complexity. *Review of Economics and Statistics, 88*(2), 363–373.

Bernard, A. B., & Jensen, J. B. (2004). Why Some Firms Export? *Review of Economics and Statistics, 86*(2), 561–569.

Bonaccorsi, A. (1992). On the Relationship Between Firm Size and Export Intensity. *Journal of International Business Studies, 23*(4), 605–636.

Bruton, G. D., Ahlstrom, D., and Li, H. L. (2010). Institutional Theory and Entrepreneurship: Where Are We Now and Where Do We Need to Move in the Future? *Entrepreneurship Theory and Practice, 34*(3), 421–440.

Cuervo-Cazurra, A., & Dau, L. A. (2009). Pro-market Reforms and Firm Profitability in Developing Countries. *Academy of Management Journal, 52*(6), 1348–1368.

De Korte, R., and Van der Pijl, G. (2009). Characteristics of a Central Change Programme Within a Governmental Bureaucracy: A Grounded Theory Study. *Journal of Management and Governance, 13*, 5–40.

De Soto, H. (1989). *The Other Path*. New York: Harper & Row.

Dimitratos, P., Petrou, A., Plakoyiannaki, E., & Johnson, J. E. (2011). Strategic Decision-Making Processes in Internationalization: Does National Culture of the Focal Firm Matter? *Journal of World Business, 46*(2), 194–204.

Doh, J., Rodriguez, P., Uhlenbruc, K., Collins, J., & Eden, L. (2003). Coping with Corruption in Foreign Markets. *Academy of Management Executive, 17*(3), 114–127.

Erramilli, M. K., & Rao, C. P. (1993). Service Firms' International Entry-Mode Choice: A Modified Transaction-Cost Analysis Approach. *Journal of Marketing, 57*(3), 19–38.

Estrin, S., Korosteleva, J., & Mickiewicz, T. (2013). Which Institutions Encourage Entrepreneurial Growth Aspirations? *Journal of Business Venturing, 28*, 564–580.

Estrin, S., Meyer, K. E., Wright, M., & Foliano, F. (2008). Export Propensity and Intensity of Subsidiaries in Emerging Economies. *International Business Review, 17*, 574–586.

Gao, G. Y., Murray, J. Y., Kotabe, M., & Lu, J. (2010). A "Strategy Tripod" Perspective on Export Behaviors: Evidence from Domestic and Foreign Firms Based in an Emerging Economy. *Journal of International Business Studies, 41*, 377–396.

Gimeno, J., Hoskisson, R. E., Beal, B. D., & Wan, W. P. (2005). Explaining the Clustering of International Expansion Moves: A Critical Test in the US Telecommunications Industry. *Academy of Management Journal, 48*(2), 297–319.

Habib, M., & Zurawicki, L. (2002). Corruption and Foreign Direct Investment. *Journal of International Business Studies, 33*(2), 291–307.

Hall, P. A., & Taylor, R. C. R. (1996). Political Science and the Three New Institutionalism. *Political Studies, 44*(5), 936–957.

He, X., Brouthers, K. D., & Filatotchev, I. (2013). Resource-Based and Institutional Perspectives on Export Channel Selection and Export Performance. *Journal of Management, 39*(1), 27–47.

Hessels, J., & Terjesen, J. (2010). Resource Dependency and Institutional Theory Perspectives on Direct and Indirect Export Choices. *Small Business Economics, 34*(2), 203–220.

Higòn, D. A., & Driffield, N. (2011). Exporting and Innovation Performance: Analysis of the Annual Small Business Survey in the UK. *International Small Business Journal, 29*(1), 4–24.

Huther, J., & Shah, A. (1996). *A Simple Measure of Simple Governance and Its Application to the Debate on the Appropriate Level of Fiscal Decentralization.* Washington, DC: World Bank.

Jepperson, R. (1991). Institutions, Institutional Effects, and Institutionalism. In W. W. Powell & P. J. DiMaggio (Eds.), *The New Institutionalism in Organizational Analysis* (pp. 143–163). Chicago: University of Chicago Press.

Katsikeas, C. S., & Morgan, R. E. (1994). Differences in Perceptions of Exporting Problems Based on Firm Size and Export Market Experience. *European Journal of Marketing, 28*(2), 17–35.

Khanna, T., & Krishna, P. (2000). The Future of Business Groups in Emerging Markets: Long-Run Evidence from Chile. *Academy of Management Journal, 43*, 268–285.

Kostova, T. (1997). Country Institutional Profiles: Concept and Measurement. *Proceedings Academy of Management* (Best Paper), 180–189.

Krugman, P. R. (1979). Increasing Returns, Monopolistic Competition and International Trade. *Journal of International Economics, 94*, 469–479.

La Porta, R., Lopez-de-Silanes, F., Shleifer, A., & Vishny, R. W. (1998). Law and Finance. *Journal of Political Economy, 106*(6), 1113–1155.

Lee, S. H., & Weng, D. H. (2013). Does Bribery in the Home Country Promote or Dampen Firm Exports? *Strategic Management Journal, 34*(12), 1472–1487.

Levchenko, A. (2007). Institutional Quality and International Trade. *Review of Economics and Statistics, 74*(3), 791–819.

LiPuma, J. A., Newbert, S. L., & Doh, J. P. (2013). The Effect of Institutional Quality on Firm Export Performance in Emerging Economies: A Contingency Model of Firm Age and Size. *Small Business Economics, 40*(4), 817–841.

Lu, J., Lu, Y., & Tao, Z. (2010). *Exporting Behavior in the Presence of Intermediaries: Theory and Evidence*. Mimeo, Peking University.

Majocchi, A., Bacchiocchi, E., & Mayrhofer, U. (2005). Firm Size, Business Experience and Export Intensity in SME's: A Longitudinal Approach to Complex Relationships. *International Business Review, 14*(6), 719–738.

Manolopoulos, D., Chatzopoulou, E., & Kottaridi, C. (2018). Resources, Home Institutional Context and SMEs' Exporting: Direct Relationships and Contingency Effects. *International Business Review, 27*(5), 993–1006.

Martin, K. D., Cullen, J. B., Johnson, J. L., & Parboteeah, K. P. (2007). Deciding to Bribe: A Cross-Level Analysis of Firm and Home Country Influences on Bribery Activity. *Academy of Management Journal, 50*(6), 1401–1422.

Mauro, F., Forster, K., & Lima, A. (2010). The Global Downturn and Its Impact on Euro Area Exporters and Competitiveness. European Central Bank Occasionally Paper Series 119. Available at: https://www.ecb.europa.eu/pub/pdf/scpops/ecbocp119.pdf.

Meyer, K. E., Estrin, S., Bhaumik, S. K., & Peng, M. W. (2009). Institutions, Resources, and Entry Strategies in Emerging Economies. *Strategic Management Journal, 30*(1), 61–80.

Meyer, K. E., & Peng, M. W. (2005). Probing Theoretically into Central and Eastern Europe: Transactions, Resources, and Institutions. *Journal of International Business Studies, 35*, 600–621.

Meyer, J. W., & Rowan, B. (1991). Institutionalized Organizations: Formal Structure as Myth and Ceremony. In W. W. Powell & P. J. DiMaggio (Eds.), *The New Institutionalism in Organizational Analysis* (pp. 41–62). Chicago: University of Chicago Press.

Mittelstaedt, J. D., Harben, G. N., & Ward, W. A. (2003). How Small Is Too Small? Firm Size as a Barrier to Exporting from the United States. *Journal of Small Business Management, 41*(1), 68–84.

Mogos-Descotes, R., Walliser, B., Holzmüller, H., & Guo, X. (2011). Capturing Institutional Home Country Conditions for Exporting Smes. *Journal of Business Research, 64*, 1303–1310.

Moore, M. (2004). Revenues, State Formation, and the Quality of Governance in Developing Countries. *International Political Science Review, 25*(3), 297–319.

Mudambi, R., & Navarra, P. (2002). Institutions and International Business: a Theoretical Overview. *International Business Review, 11*(6), 635–646.

Naidu, G. M., Cavusgil, S. T., Murthy, B. K., & Sarkar, M. (1997). An Export Promotion Model for India: Implications for Public Policy. *International Business Review, 6*(2), 113–125.

Ngo, V. D., Janssen, F., Leonidou, L., & Christodoulides, P. (2016). Domestic Institutional Attributes as Drivers of Export Performance in an Emerging and Transition Economy. *Journal of Business Research, 69*(8), 2911–2922.

North, D. C. (1990). *Institutions, Institutional Change and Economic Performance*. Cambridge: Cambridge University Press.

North, D. C. (1991). Institutions. *Journal of Economic Perspectives, 5*(1), 97–112.

Olken, B. A., & Pande, R. (2012). Corruption in Developing Countries. *Annual Review of Economics, 4*(1), 479–509.

Peng, M. W. (2003). Institutional Transitions and Strategic Choices. *Academy of Management Review, 28*(2), 275–296.

Peng, M. W., & Heath, P. S. (1996). The Growth of the Firm in Planned Economies in Transition: Institutions, Organizations, and Strategic Choice. *Academy of Management Review, 21*(2), 492–528.

Preston, C. C., & Colman, A. M. (2000). Optimal Number of Response Categories in Rating Scales: Reliability, Validity, Discriminating Power, and Respondent Preferences. *Acta Psychologica, 104*(1), 1–15.

Reid, S. D. (1982). The Impact of Size and Export Behaviour of Small Firms. In M. R. Czinkota & G. Tesar (Eds.), *Export Management: An International Context* (pp. 18–38). New York: Praeger Publishers.

Reinhart, C. M., & Rogoff, K. S. (2009). The Aftermath of Financial Crises. *American Economic Review, 99*(2), 466–472.

Rodrik, D., Subramanian, A., & Trebbi, F. (2004). Institutions Rule: The Primacy of Institutions Over Geography and Integration in Economic Development. *Journal of Economic Growth, 9*, 131–165.

Rose-Ackerman, S. (1999). *Corruption and Government: Causes, Consequences, and Reform*. Cambridge: Cambridge University Press.

Rothstein, B., & Teorell, J. (2008). What Is the Quality of Government? A Theory of Impartial Government Institutions. *Governance: An International Journal of Policy, Administration and Institutions, 21*(2), 165–190.

Scott, W. R. (1995). *Institutions and Organization*. Thousand Oaks: Sage.
Seyoum, B. (2009). Formal Institutions and Foreign Direct Investment. *Thunderbird International Business Review, 51*(2), 165–181.
Sofikitis, E., & Manolopoulos, D. (2012). Export Propensity During the Period of Economic Recession: The Impact of Home-Country Factors and Firm-Level Characteristics. In R. van Tulder, A. Verbeke, & L. Voinea (Eds.), *Progress in International Business Research: New Policy Challenges for European Multinationals* (pp. 367–392).
Spencer, J., & Gomez, C. B. (2011). MNEs and Corruption: The Impact of National Institutions and Subsidiary Strategy. *Strategic Management Journal, 32*(3), 280–300.
Stoian, C., & Filippaios, F. (2008). Dunning's Eclectic Paradigm: A Holistic, Yet Context Specific Framework for Analysing the Determinants of Outward FDI Evidence from International Greek Investments. *International Business Review, 17*, 349–367.
Svensson, J. (2003). Who Must Pay Bribes and How Much? Evidence from a Cross Section of Firms. *The Quarterly Journal of Economics, 118*(1), 207–230.
UNCTAD. (2010). *International Trade After the Economic Crisis: Challenges and New Opportunities*. Geneva: United Nation Publications.
Ursic, M., & Czinkota, M. (1984). An Experience Curve Explanation of Export Expansion. *Journal of Business Research, 12*(2), 159–168.
Vernon, R. (1966). International Investment and International Trade in the Product Cycle. *Quarterly Journal of Economics, 80*, 190–207.
Wheeler, C., Ibeh, K., & Dimitratos, P. (2008). UK Export Performance Research: Review and Implications. *International Small Business Journal, 26*(2), 207–239.
Williamson, O. (2000). New Institutional Economics. *Journal of Economic Literature, 38*, 595–613.
Witt, M. A., & Lewin, A. Y. (2007). Outward Foreign Direct Investment as Escape Response to Home Country Institutional Constraints. *Journal of International Business Studies, 38*, 579–594.
Wu, F., Sinkovics, R. R., Cavusgil, S. T., & Roath, A. S. (2007). Overcoming Export Manufacturers' Dilemma in International Expansion. *Journal of International Business Studies, 38*, 283–302.
Yang, Z., Su, C., & Fam, K. S. (2012). Dealing with Institutional Distances in International Marketing Channels: Governance Strategies that Engender Legitimacy and Efficiency. *Journal of Marketing, 76*(3), 41–55.
Yi, J., Wang, C., & Kafouros, M. (2013). The Effects of Innovative Capabilities on Exporting: Do Institutional Forces Matter? *International Business Review, 22*(2), 392–406.
Zelner, B. A. (2009). Using Simulation to Interpret Results from Logit, Probit and Other Nonlinear Models. *Strategic Management Journal, 30*(12), 1335–1348.

Labour Market Duality Under the Insider-Outsider Theory, Labour Division, Rent-Seeking, and Clientelism

The Case of a European Union Member Country

Achilleas Anagnostopoulos and Pyrros Papadimitriou

Introduction

This chapter gives an overview of a growing literature on the labour market duality and its persistence in a number of countries in continental Europe. We are more interested in Southern European countries because they share quite similar features of duality in their labour markets before and during the crisis. The effect of dualism on several labour market dimensions has been widely analysed in the literature but many of these issues have strongly re-emerged during the recent crisis due to the poor performance of countries subject to strong dualism (Dolado 2017). We mainly focus on Greece, since it is one of these countries, where labour

A. Anagnostopoulos (✉)
University of Thessaly, Larissa, Greece
e-mail: anagnos@uth.gr

P. Papadimitriou
University of Peloponnese, Korinthos, Greece

V. Vlachos and A. Bitzenis (eds.), *European Union*,
https://doi.org/10.1007/978-3-030-18103-1_12

market duality is not a recent phenomenon and that informal practices, economic depression (resulting to extremely high unemployment rates) and massive deregulation have altogether resulted into amplifying the phenomenon through official laws and regulations.

This chapter also provides a background to this study by discussing key issues of Greece's labour market. It describes the basic features of Greek labour market institutions and how these institutions are linked with the context of insider-outsider theory, where "insiders often enjoy more favorable employment opportunities than the outsiders" (Lindbeck and Snower 2001). Moreover, it discusses some of the main institutional changes that took place in the Greek labour marker during recession and how the fostered a dual labour market.

The Inside-Outside Model: Nature, Characteristics and Theoretical Considerations

Dual labour market theories have been developed in an attempt to explain the main argument; why workers, even if equally productive and "protected" from the labour regulation, finally are separated to those workers in the core "primary" sector and those in the "periphery" secondary sector or the excluded sector (vulnerable groups outside of the labour market) (Di Cintio and Grassi 2015). At the beginning, dual labour market theory has focused mainly on microeconomic factors such as discrimination, poverty, and public welfare (Saint-Paul 2004). Many researchers, from then, investigate the distinction between insiders and outsiders and its effects on employment, unemployment and other macroeconomic activities.

We describe below the nature of inside-outside divide, its characteristics, and its theoretical considerations. The argument of this theory is that the labour market consists of two tiers. Workers in the upper tier enjoy high wages, good benefits, and employment security, and they are often unionized. Workers in the lower tier experience low wages, high turnover, job insecurity, and little chance of promotion (Saint-Paul 2004). In other words, the main difference between these groups is that insiders have protected or "good" jobs while outsiders have temporary or "bad" positions in formal or informal employment or are unemployed (Anagnostopoulos 2011).

Botero et al. (2004) claim that nearly all governments intervene in their labour markets, since they are considered as imperfect, with an aim to protect workers from employers. The question of whether this state intervention "through labour regulation" is associated with the insider-outsider theory is vital; but this theory suggests that the state instead of helping outsiders (mainly unemployed or temporary workers), workers with permanent contracts and high job security use their insider market power and political influence to underbid the outsiders.

An issue which is of significant importance in the insider-outsider distinction has to deal with political economic implications. Saint-Paul (1996) notes that many of the rigidities are a direct result of the power political influences exerted by the people who have jobs. According to Elmeskov et al. (1998) argument, insiders may oppose reforms that lead to an increase in outsider employment. In other words, the incumbents are interested in raising labour rigidities in order to boost their bargaining power in wage negotiations. Consequently, insiders who benefit from strict employment protection legislation (EPL) may exert pressure for an administrative extension of wage agreements as a protection against the underbidding of their wages by outsiders. Consequently, unions (or protected workers) use the political power in order to have higher wages and better working conditions at the expense of the outsiders. The important issue here is to explain why the state did not pass any reforms in order to reduce the unemployment or to protect the outsiders. As Saint-Paul (2004) argues a number of European countries have failed to implement substantial labour market reforms because powerful constituencies of incumbent employees may seek to block labour market reforms.

Bertola (1999) and Hepple (1986) claim that—regulation and legislation aimed at protecting workers from—unfair labour market shock shave had a long history. This path started with the first steps of the European Community—and the signing of the European Social Charter in 1961—in order to achieve social and employment protection. Emerson (1988) and Di Cintio and Grassi (2015) mention that during the 1980s, European labour markets have been deeply shaped by the spread of fixed-term (also known as short-term or flexible) labour contracts. In the course of the 1990s—according to Visser (2000, p. 422)—the reassessment of the standards for social and employment protection in national labour markets and welfare states became the central element in a Europeanized employment and activation strategy temporary employment and unemployment particularly of the unskilled inevitably results.

In the late 1990s and early 2000s, a new "regulation wave" was introduced; this time the EU regulating labour framework was extended to non-regular forms of employment.[1] Furthermore, according to EIRO (2004), the overall thrust of EU regulation was to achieve equal treatment between "a typical" and "typical" workers, as far as this was possible. Following the 2008 crisis, triggered reforms took place in most policy domains in a large number of EU countries (mainly in Southern Europe). According to EC (2014), labour reforms divided into three phases. In a first phase, reforms were mostly aimed at cushioning the impact of the crisis on employment; in a second phase reforms aimed at increasing the adjustment capacity of labour markets (EPL, working time, wage setting) became more frequent, while reforms reducing the labour taxation or raising entitlements became less frequent, in the light of tightening budget constraints.

Thus, through the crisis, labour flexibility is increased on the whole; more particularly, Southern European countries (Spain, Italy, Greece, Portugal) which experienced similar labour market institutions in the past respectively adopted similar labour reforms during recession. For example, Garibaldi and Taddei (2013) argue that Italy is one of the most prominent examples of labour market dualism. Its reform process characterized marginal—in the sense that it applied only to new jobs, and asymmetric—in the sense that affected only a fraction of the population. In other words, the reform process acted mainly via the labour market flows (Boeri et al. 2012; Garibaldi and Taddei 2013). Based on Bentolila et al. (2011), the Spanish labour market stands out as an extreme case of a dual labour market in which the insider-outsider divide is very pronounced. They mainly focus on two peculiarities (a) the EPL, which gives rise to a very high incidence of fixed-term jobs (b) the automatic extension of collective bargaining agreements to all firms. Portugal, which also belongs to this Southern European countries group, indicates high rates of temporary employment; its labour market segmentation remains a significant challenge and need to be tackled (Eurofound 2017; OECD 2017).

To sum up, recession—which affect hardly these countries—"forced" the introduction of new measures: allowed dismissals in regular

[1]A number of EU Directives, based on social partner agreements regulated the following part-time work (1997/81/EC), fixed-term work (1999/70/EC), teleworking (2002—framework agreement), temporary and agent workers (proposed in 2002, and finally agreed in 2008/104/EC). Moreover, the working timedirective (updated in 2003/88/EC) also created minimum restrictions on the working hours per week, holidays and night work.

employment, decentralized the working conditions and wage bargaining and eased the working time arrangements to provide more "labour freedom" to employers. However, as a result, unemployment increased rapidly and youth unemployment rate is worsened which indicates that the youth-old age dualism is an essential component in the majority of Southern European countries. The rise of youth unemployed is also linked with the sharp increase in temporary and fixed-term contracts (Garibaldi and Taddei 2013). Thus, Spain and Portugal present high rates of temporary contracts especially in youth age. Greece shows lower rates of temporary contracts than other southern counterparts but it shows other peculiarities which we will discuss in more detail below.

Inside-Outside Model in Greece

The European labour regulation framework, as analysed above, affect Greece's labour market performance. In this section, we will try to investigate whether insider-outsider model fits the facts of Greek labour market. As a country which followed the French legal tradition (Botero et al. 2004), the Greek state introduced several labour laws which reflected the interests of unions or sectoral groups (e.g. in the public sector) without taking into consideration other demographic groups which suffered from unemployment. "Real" reforms did not take place over the past 30 years because the Greek politicians could not oppose the median voter (the insider). Spanou (2008) claims that Greek state has not comprehensive reform vision and labour flexibility has not increased because of systematic weaknesses and corporatism reactions by labour unions.

Greece, thus, was characterized as a "state capitalism" (Schmidt 2002; Zambarloukou 2015) or "Mediterranean style of capitalism" country (Amable 2003; Psychogios and Wood 2010; Anagnostopoulos and Siebert 2015; Koukiadaki and Kokkinou 2016), where the state has an extensive regulatory and interventionist role. State capitalism often reinforces corruption (*The Economist* 2012[2]); with regard to Greece, Katsios (2006) argues that public sector corruption affects all levels of government activities and fields of responsibility. Moreover, its socio-economic systems are characterized by organized interests which are traditionally

[2] http://www.economist.com/node/21542926.

able to procure privileges from the state (Molina and Rhodes 2007). This results in the inside-outside dichotomy[3] or in a dualistic labour market (Prosser 2016).

Kollintzas et al. (2018) argue that the Greek labour duality consists of "insiders" who enjoyed considerable market and/or political power. They consider as the main groups of insiders (a) civil servants, (b) employees of public sector corporations (DEKO), and (c) professionals of certain sectors, organized in powerful unions and professional associations, respectively. On the other hand, we have the "outsiders" who face many difficulties entering into the core of the labour market. These disadvantaged groups are mainly (a) first-time labour market entrants (mainly the young), (b) re-entrants (mainly women), (c) long-term unemployed which suffer more from unemployment (OECD 2007; Anagnostopoulos 2011), (d) immigrants (Labrianidis and Lyberaki 2001; Iosifidis 2001; Kouzis 2008), and (e) self-employed. In terms of employment status and job security (Tsakloglou and Cholezas 2005) consider as outsiders the low-skilled, self-employed or those employed in small firms, who receive low wages, work in unstable and precarious conditions, and face a highly competitive environment. Moreover, many scholars (Tatsios 2001; Lazaridis and Koumandraki 2003; Mihail 2004; Matsaganis 2007; Anagnostopoulos and Siebert 2015; Prosser 2016) believe that a large proportion of the latter category operates within the informal economy.

Kollintzas et al. (2018) categorize the rents of insiders based on the type of the market. In non-competitive (labour) markets, the employees in public sector/public corporation succeed in securing very high wages and incomes and enjoy far better working conditions. In competitive (product) markets, professional[4] associations' power is expressed through protection from competition by regulations and licensing requirements. These closed professions are typically unionized and enjoy special tax privileges that enable them to avoid taxes. Based on *The Economist* (2010), more than 150,000 Greeks are self-employed in about seventy closed-shop professions. That results in job barriers in the labour market, high prices for consumers—but a reliable living for insiders (*The New York Times* 2010).

[3] Many other scholars agree with the inside-outside dichotomy in Greece's labour market (Labrianidis and Lyberaki 2001; Iosifidis 2001; Matsaganis 2007; Kouzis 2008; Lyberaki 2009; Tsakloglou and Cholezas 2005; Zambarloukou 2015).

[4] For example, doctors, lawyers, notaries, engineers, pharmacists.

In addition, the high rent-related costs arise when there is a significant political connection between trade unions and the state (see more in Ioannou 2000; Zambarloukou 2006; Matsaganis 2007; Kouzis 2008). For example, Matsaganis (2007) considers that the most important determinant of most congress delegates' vote is party-political affiliation and that consequently, Greek unions are prone to defending the rights of insider over-protected employees. The particular situation seems to conform quite well with the political insider-outsider approach (e.g. see Lindvall and Rueda 2014) and several studies attribute the failure of successfully reforming the Greek labour market to aspects of the political economy of clientelism (Robinson and Verdier 2013). Several surveys of the literature on Greece's economic performance and studies on the capability to adapt and reform (e.g. see Featherstone et al. 2001; Pagoulatos 2003; Sotiropoulos 2004; Monastiriotis and Antoniadis 2009; Vlachos 2013) identify the failure of reforming the Greek labour and product markets due to: the lack of political will, the fragmentation of organized interests, the extent of rent-seeking and the absence of positive-sum exchanges between the interested parties. Other studies reaching similar conclusions are those focusing more on sociocultural and sociopolitical characteristics such as the history of clientelism, corruption and inefficient bureaucracy, and low social capital and informality (Lyberaki and Tsakalotos 2002; Lavdas 2005; Zambarloukou 2006; Bitzenis et al. 2016).

As expected, based on the above political and labour framework, Greece's labour market performed badly not only before the crisis but even in the prosperous years since its unemployment rate never fell below seven per cent during the last 25 years (Anagnostopoulos 2011). More specifically, Greece presented low employment and participation rates, and a high level of unemployment, particularly among long-term (56%), youth (25%) and women (14%) (OECD 2007). On the other hand, Greece indicates high rates of self-employment. Greeks traditionally prefer to turn to self-employment as their counterparts in Southern European countries (Spain and Italy) but with a greater extent. Greece has by far the highest rate of self-employed people in Europe (more than 34% according to OECD data), with almost one in three Greeks working for themselves. Self-employment can also represent a route out of unemployment in countries with poor labour market conditions (EEOR 2010).

Main Reforms in the Greek Dual Labour Market

The Greek state has implemented significant labour market reforms, but progress has been less on reducing oligopoly power, the regulatory burden and weaknesses in the public administration, due to administrative capacity constraints, little ownership of past reform programmes and vested interests (OECD 2016). Governmental policies intended to promote an institutional and legal framework with high labour flexibility even on regular employment. As a result, dismissal regulation is relaxed in order to narrow the inside-outside dichotomy (see more in Table 1). Thus, the Greek labour market, one of the most regulated and rigid markets in the EU, has been transformed to one of the most flexible labour markets of the EU (Karantinos 2013). Ioannides and Pissarides (2015) argue, in the same direction, that labour market reforms have been given greater priority in Greece than product market reforms, mistakenly in their view. They argue that successive Greek governments found it easier to reform labour markets than product markets.

It is worth considering here the main features which support the duality in the Greek labour market separating public form private-sector workers. To begin with, Tzannatos and Monogios (2013), provide useful employment data regarding the expansion of Greece's government sector. Thus, employment in the public sector increased from 264,000 in 1970 to 824,000 by 2009, equivalent to 3% per annum. On the other hand, at the same period, employment in the private sector increased by only 30%, from 3 million to 3.8 million—an annual growth of less than 1%. It is worth mentioning that the Greek private sector is represented by small and micro-enterprises employs 76% of Greek workers, generates 56% of total valued added of the private sector (EC 2016), and is quite difficult to regulate and engage in informal practices and atypical forms of employment. Following the sovereign debt crisis employment in the public sector has frozen; moreover, based on data (Eurofound 2016[5]), the number of public servants in Greece fell by 18% between 2009 and 2015 to just under 567,000, a condition of the country's IMF/EU/ECB memoranda On the other hand, almost 1.1 million jobs lost in the private sector during 2009–2013 (NBG

[5] https://www.eurofound.europa.eu/observatories/emcc-eurwork/articles/working-conditions-labour-market-industrial-relations/greece-reducing-the-number-of-public-servants-latest-developments.

Table 1 Main reforms of the Greek labour duality

Reforms	*Outcome*	*Pre-crisis*	*Post-crisis*
Regular employment			
Open-ended contracts—Individual dismissals	Extension in probation period	• 2-month probationary period Compensation was obligatory for employees who work at the same employer < 2 months	• 1-year probationary period There is no obligation of paying severance payment—in case of dismissal—for the first completed year
	Reduction of notice periods for white-collar workers	For 15 year tenure → 11-month pre-notification For 25 year tenure → 21-month pre-notification	For 15 year tenure → 6-month pre-notification For 25 year tenure → 6-month pre-notification
	Lowering of severance payment for white-collar workers	Notice period prior to dismissal reduces substantially the total severance payment for the salary earners (white collar)	
Minimum wages and Wage bargaining			
Collective agreements	Enterprise-level agreements are in power (Decentralization)	– Sectoral agreements dominate the Greek labour market – Enterprise level agreements may be enforced when a firm has over 50 employees	Enterprise-level agreements are eligible in firms with less than 50 employees and may be enforced when 3/5 of the company staff are given the right to the employer to enforce the agreement (Law 4024/2011)
Statutory minimum wages	Government legislate the minimum wages	Free Collective Agreement determined by the social partners (Law 1876/1990)	Establishing a base legislated minimum wage by the government (Law 4093/2012)

(continued)

Table 1 (continued)

Reforms	*Outcome*	*Pre-crisis*	*Post-crisis*
Reduction of minimum wages	Reduction of minimum wages	White-collar gross base monthly wage: 751€	White-collar gross base monthly wage: 586€ (reduction 22%)—(Law 4046/2012)
		Blue collar daily gross wage: 33,57€	Blue-collar gross daily wage: 26,18€
			Abolition two annual bonuses (13th and 14th monthly salaries in public sector)
	Sub minimum wages for young workers	–	Employees under 25 years old: 510€ (reduction 32%)
Wage allowances	Maturity allowance has frozen	– Maturity (tenure) allowances increased (every 3 years) by 10% – Marital status allowance/Children allowance	– Maturity allowances frozen (Law 4046/2012) – Other allowances are still valid
Reforms	Outcome	Pre-crisis	Post-crisis
Flexible contracts			
Part-time contracts	Part-time becomes more attractive	Increase salary if a part-timer (a) work less than 4 hours per day by 7.5% (b) works overtime by 10%	Abolished both entitlements
Temporary-time contracts	Fixed-term contracts – Increased the cumulated duration	Maximum cumulated duration 24 months	Maximum cumulated duration to 36 months
	Temporary work agency – Increased the cumulated duration	Maximum cumulated duration 18 months	Maximum cumulated duration to 36 months

Source Own research

2017); more specifically, 222,000 were lost in manufacturing, 219,000 in trade and 236,000 in construction (together a total of 68% of jobs lost) (Eurofound 2016).

Another issue which deserves attention is the pay gap between workers in the public and private sectors. Wages are of course an important determinant of employment. Tzannatos and Monogios (2013) mentioned that prior to the crisis and in terms of individual wages, average monthly earnings (adjusted differential[6]) of public-sector employees were 11% higher than those in the private sector. The reforms aimed to bring the wage setting in the public sector closer to the private sector. The emphasis has been on the wage policies in the public sector, mainly with the reductions of basic salaries and benefits and the abolition of the 13th and 14th month of salary (see more, Table 1).

The minimum wage is also reformed in the private sector and moving away from multi-layered collective bargaining (Kosma et al. 2017; Lyberaki et al. 2017). Thus, Greek government has introduced is the reduction of gross national minimum wages by 22% (from 751€ to 586€ monthly rate). Moreover, has lowered the minimum wages for young people (below 25 years) by 32% (510€ monthly rate). At the end of 2011, the minimum wage was reduced by one third in nominal terms and a lower minimum; however, it increases with seniority, a unique case among OECD countries, which makes the effective minimum wage higher (OECD 2016). Christopoulou and Monastiriotis (2016) emphasize the wage differentials between public and private sector during the crisis. They found that although public-sector workers saw remarkable wage cuts, the private-sector employees were more deeply affected and found that wages in private-sector employees fell faster and deeper than in the public sector. Kollintzas et al. (2018) argue that Greece stands out among OECD countries having the highest public-sector wage premium[7]; thus, high values of the public-sector wage premium might be related to the influence exerted by public-sector employees organized in powerful unions. Iordanoglou and Matsaganis (2017) indicate that in spite of the recent labour market reforms public-sector employees still enjoy better benefits, easier working conditions, and far greater

[6]See more explanation on their analysis in Chapter 7: "Public sector adjustment amidst structural adjustment in Greece: Subordinate, spasmodic and sporadic". *Public Sector Shock: The Impact of Policy Retrenchment in Europe*, Edward Elgar by ILO, pp. 265–266.

[7]Defined as the ratio of the average wage in the public relative to the private sector.

job security. These wage reductions were also driven by the increase in enterprise agreements in the private sector (Koukiadaki and Kokkinou 2014) providing a more decentralized wage bargaining framework. All these changes produced a tremendous shift from sectoral/occupational agreements (which expired and were not renewed/renegotiated) to enterprise-level agreements (see more at Table 1). Consequently, in micro-enterprises, there has been a dramatic spread of individual agreements between the employer and single employees (Kapsalis 2012). Following the above, and with regard to collective bargaining, the Greek trade union movement is threatened and faces one of the most difficult periods since its foundation (Kousis and Karakiolaf 2013).

Describing the Greek Environment, Concluding Remarks

Labour market dualism has been one of the most discussing topics in recent European policy debates. We show that Southern European countries suffer from similar labour rigidities prior to the crisis period which fits the inside-outside model. Their labour segmentation has mainly taken the form of a divide between permanent and temporary jobs. It is accepted that labour duality has gained new momentum with the asymmetrical impact of recession on young people and the subsequent wave of labour market reforms implemented particularly in countries hit by the crisis (Eichhorst et al. 2017).

We focus on Greece's labour market which started to perform bad in terms of employment rates during the mid-/late 1980s and early 1990s and never succeeded a stable unemployment rate lower than the respective average of the European Union (EU) 15. Greece's general unemployment rate never fell below 7.8% the last 30 years. At the same time, employment rates in specific groups such as females and youths have been well below the EU-15, and well below the respective EU averages after 2010. Before the outbreak of the late global financial and economic crisis in the 2010s, reports from international organizations linked Greece poor labour market performance with strict labour market regulation (see, e.g., OECD 2004, 2007) and deemed that broader labour market reforms were essential for regaining lost competitiveness and reducing the unemployment rate (IMF 2007).

The prolonged period of the Greek economic crisis had a significant negative impact on the Greek labour market. It has led the country's economy into depression and skyrocketing unemployment figures. During the "deep recession era" (first phase of the Greek crisis 2009–2013), almost one million jobs had been lost and the unemployment rate increased over 25%. In order to promote employment amid fiscal consolidation, the Greek government adopted a plan of structural reforms which involved flexibility measures that deregulated the Greek labour market. Greece, with regard to the private sector, has managed to address partly one of its major labour market problems the strict EPL; thus, reduced severance payment and relaxed the protection against individual dismissals. Moreover, private-sector employment has experienced a shift from sectoral/occupational agreements to enterprise-level agreements that have resulted in deunionization and rising levels of atypical forms of employment.

During the second phase (2014–present), the Greek labour market is showing signs of recovery after the downward trend. Employment rates in the private sector increased by 5.3%, in other words 150,000 jobs created during the above period reversing 14% of the sizeable loss during the period 2009–2013 (NBG 2017). However, jobs mainly created under flexible working arrangements following the government reforms which also affect the firms' hiring decisions. The rate of part-time employment increased almost doubled, from about 6% of all employment in 2009 to nearly 11.5% in 2017. We also have to take into consideration that Greece indicates the higher rate of self-employed which seems that many Greeks turn to self-employment as an escape route from the dependent employment.

The overall plan of gradual deregulation of the Greek labour market adopted by the Greek government to enhance employment has failed to date to provide an exit from the crisis and concerned primarily the private-sector labour market. Employment in the public sector did not deteriorate due to job cuts and layoffs but due to hiring freezes, and public-sector employees suffered income losses due to fiscal consolidation. The unprecedented unemployment levels portray a dual labour market consisting of a public sector where entrance has been restricted, and a private sector where excess supply of labour favours the supply of atypical forms of employment (particularly in smaller firms). Under the consideration that the presence of this duality is due to the link between sectoral trade unions (which represent the public sector and are large vis-à-vis the smaller private sector firm unions) and clientelism.

To conclude, outsiders still suffer more compared to other working population groups (lower participation rates, lower employment rates, and higher unemployment rates). It is true that EU member states have started to take the issue of segmentation more seriously; there are plenty of policy initiatives with the goal of overcoming labour market divides, although the more pessimistic message is that they have achieved little success to date (Eichhorst et al. 2017). The overall view is not encouraging the Greek labour market recovery. The country implemented comprehensive reforms and recently exited from its memorandum programme; however, all labour reforms are still in force and progress is still unclear.

References

Amable, B. (2003). *The Diversity of Modern Capitalism.* New York: Oxford University Press. ISBN-13: 9780199261130.

Anagnostopoulos, A. (2011). *Labour Market Regulation in Greece—Assessing Impacts of Human Resource Management Practices and Outcomes Using a Workplace Survey.* PhD thesis, University of Birmingham.

Anagnostopoulos, A., & Siebert, W. S. (2015). The Impact of Greek Labour Market Regulation on Temporary Employment—Evidence from a Survey in Thessaly, Greece. *The International Journal of Human Resource Management, 26*(18), 2366–2393.

Bentolila, S., Dolado, J. J., & Jimeno, J. F. (2011). *Reforming an Insider-Outsider Labor Market: The Spanish Experience* (IZA DP No. 6186). ftp.iza.org/dp6186.pdf.

Bertola, G. (1999). *Cross-Sectional Wage and Employment Rigidities vs. Aggregate Employment ABCDE Europe 1999, Paris—New Thinking on Security in Labour Markets.* http://citeseerx.ist.psu.edu/viewdoc/summary?doi=10.1.1.39.6535.

Bitzenis, A., Vlachos, V. A., & Schneider, F. (2016). "An Exploration of the Greek Shadow Economy: Can Its Transfer into the Official Economy Provide Economic Relief Amid the Crisis? *Journal of Economic Issues, 50*(1), 165–196.

Boeri, T., Conde-Ruiz, I., & Galasso, V. (2012) The Political Economy of Flexicurity. *Journal of the European Economic Association*, 10(4), 684–715.

Botero, J., Djankov, S., La Porta, R., López de Silanes, F., & Shleifer, A. (2004). The Regulation of Labour. *Quarterly Journal of Economics, 119,* 1339–1382.

Christopoulou, R., & Monastiriotis, V. (2016). Public–Private Wage Duality During the Greek Crisis. *Oxford Economic Papers, 68*(1), 174–196.

Di Cintio, M., & Grassi, E. (2015). Wage Incentive Profiles in Dual Labour Markets. *Economica, 82,* 790–812.

Dolado, J. J. (2017). European Union Dual Labour Markets: Consequences and Potential Reforms. In L. Matyas, R. Blundell, E. Cantillon, B. Chizzolini, M. Ivaldi, W. Leininger et al. (Eds.), *Economics Without Borders: Economic Research for European Policy Challenges* (pp. 73–112). Cambridge: Cambridge University Press. https://doi.org/10.1017/9781316636404.004.

Eichhorst, W., Marx, P., & Wehner, C. (2017). Labor Market Reforms in Europe: Towards More Fexicure Labor Markets? *Journal of Labour Market Research, 51,* 3.

EIRO. (2004). *Industrial Relations in the EU, Japan and USA, 2002.* http://www.eurofound.europa.eu/eiro/2004/01/feature/tn0401101f.htm.

Elmeskov, M., Martin, J. P, & Scarpetta, S. (1998). 'Key Lessons for Labour Market Reforms: Evidence from OECD Countries' Experiences. *Swedish Economic Policy Review, 5,* 205–252.

Emerson, M. (1988). Regulation or Deregulation of the Labour Market: Policy Regimes for the Recruitment & Dismissal of Employees in the Industrialized Countries. *European Economic Review, 32,* 775–817.

Eurofound. (2016). *Greece: Reducing the Number of Public Servants—Latest Developments.* https://www.eurofound.europa.eu/printpdf/publications/article/2016/greece-reducing-the-number-of-public-servants-latest-developments.

Eurofound. (2017). *Portugal: Tripartite Commitment on Labour Market and Collective Bargaining Measures.* https://www.eurofound.europa.eu/publications/article/2017/portugal-tripartite-commitment-on-labour-market-and-collective-bargaining-measures.

European Commission (EC). (2014). *A Decade of Labour Market Reforms in the EU: Insights from the LABREF Database* (Economic Papers No. 522). ISSN 1725-3187. https://ec.europa.eu/social/BlobServlet?docId=13932&langId=en.

European Commission (EC). (2016). *Small Business Act.* https://ec.europa.eu/docsroom/documents/22382/attachments/15/translations/en/renditions/native.

European Employment Observatory Review (EEOR). (2010). *Self-Employment in Europe.* European Commission. http://ec.europa.eu/social/main.jsp?catId=738&langId=en&pubId=576.

Featherstone, K., Kazamias, G., & Papadimitriou, D. (2001). The Limits of External Empowerment: EMU and the Reform of the Greek Pension System. *Political Studies, 49*(3), 462–480.

Garibaldi, P., & Taddei, F. (2013). *Italy: A Dual Labour Market in Transition* (Employment Working Paper No. 144). Geneva: International Labor Organization.

Hepple, B. A. (Ed.). (1986). *The Making of Labour Law in Europe: A Comparative Study of Nine Countries Up to 1945.* London: Mansell.

International Monetary Fund (IMF). (2007). *Greece—2007 Article IV Consultation; Preliminary Conclusions of the Mission*. http://www.imf.org/external/np/ms/2007/121007a.htm.

Ioannides, Y. M., & Pissarides, C. A. (2015). "Is the Greek Crisis One of Supply or Demand?" *Brookings Papers on Economic Activity, 46*(2 (Fall)), 349–373.

Ioannou, C. (2000). Social Pacts in Hellenic Industrial Relations: Odysseys or Sisyphus. In G. Fajertag & P. Pochet (Eds.), *Social Pacts in Europe: New Dynamics*. Brussels: ETUI.

Iordanoglou, C. & Matsaganis, M. (2017). *Why Grexit Cannot Save Greece (But Staying in the Euro Area Might)* (LSE 'Europe in Question' Discussion Paper Series No. 123/2017).

Iosifidis, T. (2001). Working Conditions at Three Immigrant Groups. In A. Marvakis, D. Parsanoglou, & M. Paulou (Eds.), *Immigrants in Greece*. Athens: Ellinika Grammata Publishing (in Greek).

Kapsalis, A. (2012) *Greek Trade Unions in the Environment of Economic Recession-Crisis* (in Greek). http://rosalux.gr/sites/default/files/kapsalis_greekfinal_0.pdf.

Karantinos, D. (2013). *The Social and Employment Situation in Greece* (European Parliament Report), Directorate General for Internal Policies, IP/A/EMPL/NT/. http://www.europarl.europa.eu/RegData/etudes/note/join/2013/507491/IPOL-EMPL_NT(2013)507491_EN.pdf.

Katsios, K. (2006). The Shadow Economy and Corruption in Greece. *South-Eastern Europe Journal of Economics, 1*, 61–80.

Kollintzas, T., Papageorgiou, D., Tsionas, E., & Vassilatos, V. (2018). Market and Political Power Interactions in Greece: An Empirical Investigation. *IZA Journal of Labour Policy, 7*(1), 1–43.

Kosma, T., Papapetrou, E., Pavlou, G., Tsochatzi, C., & Zioutou, P. (2017). *Labour Market Adjustment and Labour Market Reforms in Greece During the Crisis: Microeconomic Evidence from the Third Wave of the Wage Dynamics Survey* (Working Paper). Bank of Greece.

Koukiadaki, A., & Kokkinou, C. (2014). *The Impact of the Labour Market Reforms on Collective Bargaining in Manufacturing: The Case of Greece*. http://www.research.mbs.ac.uk/ewerc/Portals/0/docs/SDDTEC/Greece%20national%20report%20%283%29.pdf.

Koukiadaki, A., & Kokkinou, C. (2016). Deconstructing the Greek System of Industrial Relations. *European Journal of Industrial Relations, 22*(3), 205–219.

Kousis, M., & Karakiolaf, C. (2013). *Labour Unions Confronting Unprecedented Austerity in Greece, 2010–2013*. ECPR General Conference Sciences, Bordeaux.

Kouzis, I. (2008). The Development of Labour Market and the Evolution of Distress. In N. Panagiotopoulos (Eds.), *H apomageysi tou kosmou*. Athens: Polytropo Publishing (in Greek).

Labrianidis, L., & Lyberaki, A. (2001). *Albanian Immigrants in Thessaloniki: Welfare Routes*. Thessaloniki: Paratiritis Publishing (in Greek).

Lavdas, K. (2005). Interest Groups in Disjointed Corporatism: Social Dialogue in Greece and European 'Competitive Corporatism'. *West European Politics, 28*(2), 297–316.

Lazaridis, G., & Koumandraki, M. (2003). Survival Ethnic Entrepreneurs in Greece: A Mosaic of Informal & Formal Business Activities. *Sociological Research Online, 8*(2), 1–12. http://www.socresonline.org.uk/8/2/lazaridis.html.

Lindbeck, A., & Snower, D. J. (2001). Insiders Versus Outsiders. *Journal of Economic Perspectives, 15*(1), 165–188.

Lindvall, J., & Rueda, D. (2014). The Insider-Outsider Dilemma. *British Journal of Political Science, 44*, 460–475.

Lyberaki, A. (2009). *Gender Equality Reforms in Post-1974 Greece*. Paper Presented at 2009 Yale Conference, The Challenge of Reform in Greece, 1974–2009: Assessment and Prospects.

Lyberaki, A., Meghir, C., & Nikolitsas, D. (2017). Labor Market Regulation and Reform in Greece. In C. Meghir, C. Pissarides, D. Vayanos, & N. Vettas (Eds.), *Beyond Austerity: Reforming the Greek Economy* (pp. 211–250). Cambridge, MA: The MIT Press.

Lyberaki, A., & Tsakalotos, E. (2002). Reforming the Economy Without Society: Social and Institutional Constraints to Reform in Post-1974 Greece. *New Political Economy, 7*(1), 93–114.

Matsaganis, M. (2007). Union Structures and Pension Outcomes in Greece. *British Journal of Industrial Relations, 45*(3), 537–555.

Mihail, D. (2004). Labour Flexibility in Greek SMEs. *Personnel Review Journal, 33*(5), 549–560.

Molina, O., & Rhodes, M. (2007). The Political Economy of Adjustment in Mixed Market Economies: A Study of Spain and Italy. In B. Hancké, M. Rhodes, & M. Thatcher (Eds.), *Beyond Varieties of Capitalism: Conflict, Contradictions, and Complementarities in the European Economy* (pp. 223–252). Oxford: Oxford University Press.

Monastiriotis, V., & Antoniadis, A. (2009). *Reform That! Greece's Failing Reform Technology: Beyond 'Vested Interests' and 'Political Exchange'* (GreeSE Paper No. 28). London School of Economics and Political Sciences, Hellenic Observatory. http://www.lse.ac.uk/collections/hellenicObservatory/pdf/GreeSE/GreeSE28.Pdf.

National Bank of Greece (NBG). (2017). *Greece: Macro View*. NBG Economic Analysis Department.

OECD. (2004). *Employment Outlook*. Paris: Organisation for Economic Cooperation and Development.

OECD. (2007). *Employment Outlook*. Paris: Organisation for Economic Cooperation and Development.

OECD. (2016). *OECD Economic Surveys: Greece*. Paris: Organisation for Economic Cooperation and Development.

OECD. (2017). *Employment Outlook*. Paris: Organisation for Economic Cooperation and Development.

Pagoulatos, G. (2003). *Greece's New Political Economy: State, Finance and Growth from Postwar to EMU*. London: Palgrave Macmillan.

Prosser, T. (2016). Dualization or Liberalization? Investigating Precarious Work in Eight European Countries. *Work, Employment and Society, 30*(6), 949–965. https://doi.org/10.1177/0950017015609036.

Psychogios, A. G., & Wood, G. (2010). Human Resource Management in Greece in Comparative Perspective: Alternative Institutionalist Perspectives and Empirical Realities. *The International Journal of Human Resource Management, 21*(14), 2614–2630.

Robinson, J. A., & Verdier, T. (2013). The Political Economy of Clientelism. *The Scandinavian Journal of Economics, 115*(2), 260–291.

Saint-Paul, G. (1996). Exploring the Political Economy of Labour Market Institutions. *Economic Policy, 11*(23), 263–315.

Saint-Paul, G. (2004). Why Are European Countries Diverging in Their Unemployment Experience? *The Journal of Economic Perspectives, 18*(4), 49–68.

Schmidt, V. A. (2002). *The Futures of European Capitalism*. Oxford: Oxford University Press. ISBN: 9780199253685.

Sotiropoulos, D. (2004). The EU's Impact on the Greek Welfare State: Europeanisation on Paper? *Journal of European Social Policy, 14*(3), 267–284.

Spanou, C. (2008). State Reform in Greece: Responding to Old and New Challenges. *International Journal of Public Sector Management, 21*(2), 150–173.

Tatsios, N. (2001). *Shadow Economy and Tax Evasion in Greece*. Athens: Foundation of Economic and Industrial Research (IOBE) and Papazizi Publications (in Greek).

The Economist. (2010, July 8). The Future of Europe: Staring into the Abyss. http://www.economist.com/node/16536898.

The Economist. (2012). And the Winner Is.... https://www.economist.com/special-report/2012/01/21/and-the-winner-is.

The New York Times. (2010, October 14). Push to End Job Barriers Rattles Greece and Economy. http://www.nytimes.com/2010/10/15/world/europe/15greece.html.

Tsakloglou, P., & Cholezas, I. (2005). *Education and Inequality in Greece* (IZA DP No. 1582). ftp.iza.org/dp1582.pdf.

Tzannatos, Z., & Monogios, Y. (2013). "Public Sector Adjustment Amidst Structural Adjustment in Greece: Subordinate, Spasmodic and Sporadic." In

D. Vaughan-Whitehead (Ed.), *Public Sector Shock*, chapter 7 (pp 259–299). Edward Elgar Publishing.

Visser, J. (2000). From Keynesianism to the Third Way: Labour Relations and Social Policy in Postwar Western Europe. *Economic and Industrial Democracy, 21*, 421–456.

Vlachos, V. A. (2013). Not Business as Usual. In A. Bitzenis, I. Papadopoulos, & V. A. Vlachos (Eds.), *Reflections on the Greek Sovereign Debt Crisis*. Newcastle upon Tyne: Cambridge Scholars.

Zambarloukou, S. (2006). Collective Bargaining and Social Pacts: Greece in Comparative Perspective. *European Journal of Industrial Relations, 12*(2), 211–229.

Zambarloukou, S. (2015). "Greece After the Crisis: Still a South European Welfare Model?" *European Societies, 17*(5), 653–673.

How the Economics Profession Got It Wrong on Brexit

Ken Coutts, Graham Gudgin and Jordan Buchanan

Introduction

Economic Forecasters in the UK have a poor record over the last decade. The failure to foresee the 2008 economic crisis has become infamous, even involving the Queen's famous question: "*Why did nobody notice it?*" That failure showed up how little work had been done in understanding the importance of credit markets in the UK. One aspect of this was the strange lack of a banking sector in the Bank of England model, a lacuna now being rectified. The failure to predict the crisis was followed by a large overestimate of the speed of recovery of the UK from the 2009 recession. The tendency of the Office for Budget Responsibility to overestimate the speed of recovery (see Fig. 1) is now recognised by the OBR itself. The OBR has since dropped its assumption that growth in UK productivity will return to a pre-recession norm. However, the OBR will continue to base its forecasts on *assumptions* for productivity and

K. Coutts (✉) · G. Gudgin
University of Cambridge, Cambridge, UK
e-mail: kjc1@cam.ac.uk

J. Buchanan
Ulster University Economic Policy Centre,
Newtownabbey, Northern Ireland, UK

V. Vlachos and A. Bitzenis (eds.), *European Union*,
https://doi.org/10.1007/978-3-030-18103-1_13

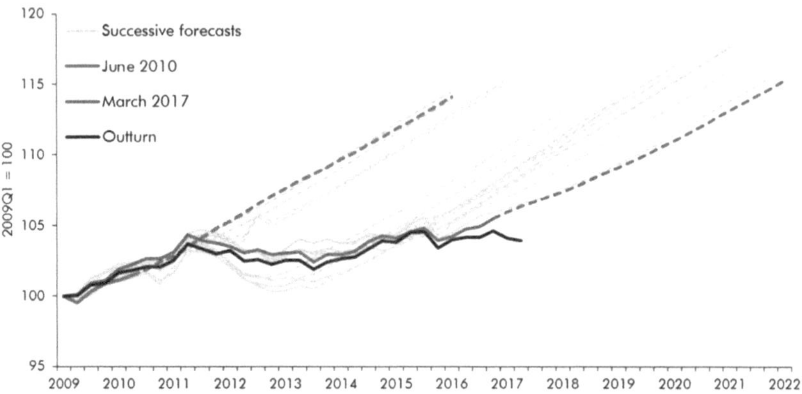

Fig. 1 Successive OBR productivity forecasts (output per hour) (*Source* Office for Budget Responsibility [2017]. Available at https://obr.uk/download/forecast-evaluation-report-charts-tables-october-2017/. Accessed 17 March 2019. *Note* Solid lines represent the outturn data that underpinned the forecasts at the time [the dashed lines])

population rather than attempting to forecast these things econometrically. The common tendency to describe OBR projections as forecasts rather than assumptions has compounded the importance of its over-optimism. The term "productivity puzzle" sums up the profession's difficulties in understanding the slow growth of productivity in the UK, and the related lack of growth in real wages.

In the light of these shortcomings, it might have been expected that the profession would take extra care to make its assessment of the potential impact of Brexit as fair and accurate as possible. A further failure would add substantially to the questioning of the underlying soundness of economic theory and practice related to forecasting. We argue that this did not happen and that much of the economic assessment of the impact of Brexit has been flawed, leading to a conclusion that the profession does indeed need to reassess its methods.

Short-Term Impact of the Brexit Referendum

Several reports published during the referendum campaign included separate estimates for both the short-term impact of uncertainty and the long-term impact of changed trading arrangements. The short-term impacts reflected assumptions that the uncertainty surrounding Brexit would undermine the confidence of companies and consumers leading to lower consumption and investment. The estimates, made in 2016, generally refer to a period before the UK leaves the EU, but some stretch into the early years outside the EU.

A summary of short-term impacts from non-government sources is shown in Table 1. The UK Government's own estimates are shown in Table 2. The estimates vary depending on what is assumed about the nature of the likely eventual relationship sought with the EU.

Table 1 HMT summary of studies of short-term impact of Brexit on GDP

Effect on level of GDP (%)	
PwC/CBI	−3.1 to −5.5 (over 5 years)
Citi	−4.0 (over 3 years)
Credit Suisse	−1.0 to −2.0 (over 2 years)
Deutsche Bank	−3.0 (over 3 years)
HSBC	−1.0 to −1.5 (over 1 year)
JP Morgan	−1.0 (over 1 year)
Morgan Stanley	−1.5 to −2.5 (over 2 years)
Nomura	−4.0 (over 1 year)
Société Générale	−4.0 to −8.0 (over 5 years)

Source HM Treasury (2016a). *HM Analysis: The Long-term Economic Impact of EU Membership and the Alternatives*. April 2016. Cmnd. 9250. Box 3.D

Table 2 HM Treasury estimates of the short-term impact of Brexit

	Shock scenario[a]	*Severe shock scenario*[b]
GDP	−3.6%	−6.0%
CPI inflation rate (percentage points)	+2.3	+2.7
Unemployment rate (percentage points)	+1.6	+2.4
Unemployment (level)	+520,000	+820,000
Average real wages	−2.8%	−4.0%
House prices	−10%	−18%
Sterling exchange rate index	−12%	−15%
Public sector net borrowing (£ billion)[b]	+£24 billion	+£39 billion

Note Immediate impact of a vote to leave the EU on the UK (% difference from base level unless specified otherwise)

Source HM Treasury (2016b). *HM Treasury Analysis: The Immediate Economic Impact of Leaving the EU*. May 2017 Cmnd. 9292, p. 8

[a]Peak impact over two years. Unemployment level rounded to the nearest 10,000

[b]Fiscal year 2017–2018

The largest estimates of losses of GDP stem from an expectation that the UK will leave the single market and customs union and will fall back on WTO rules. Something of a consensus emerges from these studies with an expectation that uncertainty will reduce GDP (relative to a pre-referendum baseline) by around 1% after one year, 2–4% after 2 years, 3–4% after three years and 4–6% after 5 years. The Treasury's estimates are at the high end of this spectrum of views with a view that GDP would be reduced by between 3.5 and 6%.

The Treasury's Short-Term Assessment

The Treasury summarised its own view in the following words, "The analysis shows that the economy would fall into recession with *four quarters of negative growth*. After two years, *GDP would be around 3.6% lower*.... the fall in the value of the pound would be around 12%, and *unemployment would increase by around 500,000*, with all regions experiencing a rise in the number of people out of work. The exchange-rate-driven increase in the price of imports would lead to a material increase in prices, with the CPI *inflation rate higher by 2.3 percentage points after a year*" (our emphasis added). The Bank of England and IMF agreed that recession was possible.[1]

The mechanism underlying the Treasury assessment is that:

- Firms and households would begin adjusting to the expected new relationship with the EU, and
- Household consumption and business investment would be damaged by uncertainty.
- Financial markets would react immediately with a 10–14% fall in the sterling exchange rate. Credit conditions would tighten and equity prices would fall, leading to a 10–18% reduction in house prices relative to the baseline.

Two-and-a-half years after the referendum result, only one of the Treasury's expectations has been clearly realised. This is the fall in the value of sterling, and the consequential rise in inflation. A 10–15% fall in the effective exchange rate matches the HMT "shock" scenario, but is

[1]Mark Carney, Governor of the Bank of England, *Inflation Report Press Conference* (May 2016). Christine Lagarde, IMF Managing Director, *Press Conference for the IMF UK Article IV Concluding Statement* (May 2016).

also close to its "severe shock" scenario. No recession materialised over the 12 months following the referendum. Nor has unemployment risen. Since the referendum, unemployment had fallen to its lowest level for 34 years. The UK Treasury expectation that equity risk premia would rise, leading to lower equity prices, has proved wrong. The sterling depreciation instead led to higher UK equity prices as corporate earnings from abroad became worth more in sterling.

Long-Term Impact of the Brexit Referendum

Once again, a substantial number of reports were written during the referendum campaign on the long-term impact of Brexit. Some of these have been subsequently updated. A range of results was generated, nearly all of them suggesting a negative long-term impact. Most reports considered a range of potential Brexit scenarios including a free trade agreement and no deal on trade leading to a reliance on WTO tariffs and non-tariff barriers. A range of predictions is shown in Table 3 and Fig. 2. In this section, we focus on the WTO scenarios as a worst case.

The Long-Term Forecasts of HM Treasury

The Treasury approach involved using gravity models to calculate how much extra UK trade was undertaken with the EU as a result of the UK's membership. It was then assumed that most of this additional trade would be lost to the UK on leaving the UK and adopting WTO rules. A similar exercise was undertaken for foreign direct investment (FDI). An additional knock-on impact on productivity was added to reflect a belief that productivity is positively related to trade openness and lower FDI. Finally, the results of these exercises were entered into the NiGEM macroeconomic model to generate forecasts for GDP, unemployment, etc. In this section, we briefly report our previous work which replicated the Treasury's gravity model analyses to estimate the potential trade losses from Brexit. This work reproduced the Treasury gravity model analysis for trade in goods, involving a huge database of trade and other variables including almost a million pieces of data. As far as we know, we are the only research group to have done so, and hence are the only group fully capable of identifying the key shortcomings in the Treasury analysis. The productivity links are dealt with in a later section.

The gravity model-based methods used by the Treasury are described in HM Treasury April (2016a) and in Gudgin et al. (2017a, b).

Table 3 Long-term (2030) impact of Brexit on GDP in the UK

Organisation	*Scenario*	*Estimate (% GDP)*	*Range*	*Impacts modelled*
CEP (2016a)	Dynamic EEA/FTA	−7.9	(−6.3 to −9.5)	Budget, trade, productivity
	Static EEA	−1.3	N/A	Trade only
	Static WTO	−2.6	N/A	Trade only
HM Treasury	EEA	−3.8	(−3.4 to −4.3)	Budget, trade, FDI, productivity
	FTA	−6.2	(−4.6 to −7.8)	
	WTO	−7.5	(−5.4 to −9.5)	
OECD	WTO/FTA	−5.1	(−2.7 to −7.7)	Budget, trade, FDI, productivity, migration, regulation
NIESR	EEA	−1.8	(−1.5 to −2.1)	Budget, trade, FDI
	FTA	−2.1	(−1.9 to −2.3)	
	WTO	−3.2	(−2.7 to −3.7)	
	WTO+	−7.8	N/A	Adds productivity
PwC/CBI	FTA	−1.2	N/A	Budget, trade, FDI, regulation
	WTO	−3.5	N/A	
Oxford Economics	FTA[a]	−2.0	(−0.1 to −3.9)	Budget, trade, FDI, migration, regulation
Open Europe	FTA	−0.8 to +0.6	(−2.2 to 1.6)	Budget, trade, migration, regulation
Economists for Brexit	WTO	+4.0	N/A	Budget, trade[b]

Note Estimates are for impact on GDP in 2030
Source Institute of Fiscal Studies (2016). For references in the Table check the source
[a] FTA with moderate policy scenario used as central estimate; range includes "liberal customs union" (−0.1) to "populist MFN scenario" (−3.9)
[b] Regulation impacts assessed separately

The approach involves analysing trade flows between around 120 countries over a 65-year period and estimating an equation relating bilateral trade to the size of the two economies in each trade pair, their distance apart and other factors such as a common language. This basic gravity equation is then used to estimate how much more trade is conducted between countries that are both members of the EU than between other trade-pairs. There are several important shortcomings in the Treasury's use of the gravity model approach to measuring the impact of EU membership on trade:

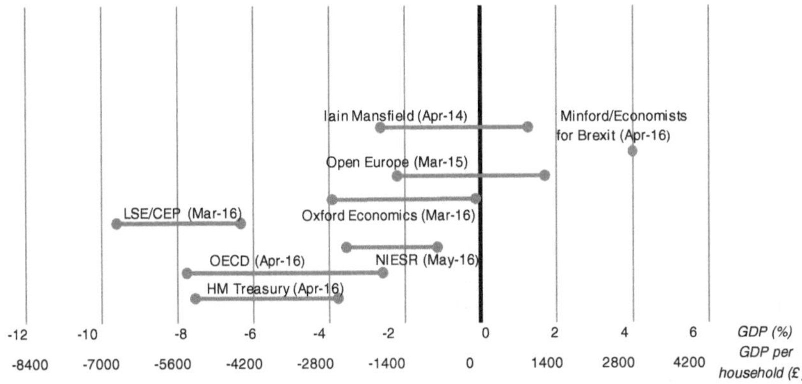

Fig. 2 Estimates of long-term impact of Brexit on UK GDP (*Source* House of Commons [2016, p. 19]. *Note* The ranges shown in this chart cover all of the possible forms of Brexit. The most negative [LHS] end of each range represents no deal on trade)

- The number of country pairs is very large, many of which are small developing nations undertaking minimal trade with the UK. The inclusion of such countries affects the underlying gravity equation and hence the size of the average deviation from the underlying equation. In technical terms, the variance of trade is much higher for small countries than large countries and hence the measured errors are heteroscedastic.
- The Treasury measures the average impact of EU membership across all EU members and does not investigate whether this calculated impact is relevant to the UK alone. When we replicate the Treasury analysis, we find that there is a large and significant *negative* residual for the UK. Indeed, the Treasury Report provides virtually no information directly about UK trade with the EU. We will return to this issue below.
- Although the Treasury does not in all cases assume that the benefits to trade of EU membership are fully reversed on leaving, in their upper (worst-case) scenario they do assume a full reversal of benefits, despite the fact that UK firms must currently be compliant with EU regulations and are likely to maintain compliance to continue trading.

Table 4 HM Treasury Table A.5 external and HM Treasury estimate of EU and FTA membership effects

	EU membership effect	*FTA membership effect*
HM Treasury	68%/76%/85%	14%/17%/21%
OECD (2015)	60%	N/A
Baier, Bergstrand et al. (2008)	92%	58%
Hufbauer and Schott (2007)	31%	27%
Carrere (2006)	104%	N/A
Eicher and Henn (2011)	37%	Insignificant
Eicher et al. (2012)	51%	N/A

Note The range of impacts for the HM Treasury is based on a +/−1 standard error range
Source HM Treasury. (2016a). *HM Treasury Analysis: the Long-Term Economic Impact of UK Membership and the Alternatives*. CM 9250, April. For references in the Table check the source

The Treasury analysis contains further weaknesses.

- The Treasury makes no allowance for changes in migration as a consequence of Brexit. It thus assumes that any change in GDP is mirrored by a change in per capita GDP.

Despite predicting a depreciation of sterling in its "Immediate Impact" report, the Treasury makes no allowance for a long-term lower level of the sterling exchange rate which might offset higher costs imposed by EU tariffs. If the large post-referendum depreciation in sterling proves to be permanent, this will offset much, or all, of the increases in costs due to higher tariffs in most sectors.

In the academic literature on trade, gravity models generate estimates of the impact of EU membership on exports which vary in size but for all EU members are always positive and significant. The Treasury's review of the gravity model literature also found a wide variety of estimates for the average impact of EU membership on trade in both goods and services. Their Table A.5 is reproduced in Table 4.

This shows that the gravity model technique can generate different results dependent on the data sources, periods used and other aspects of the precise methodology. Gudgin et al. (2017a) apply a range of different ways of applying the gravity approach. All of these alternative estimates for the average EU effect across all member states are lower than that of the Treasury with the range of estimates still approximating to a doubling of export goods trade inside the EU. However, the most important point is that this *average* impact does not relate directly to UK trade. The UK is the only EU state, other than Malta, which exports more to non-EU countries than to other EU member states. UK exports of goods to the EU have usually been well below the levels predicted by these gravity model equations. Instead of the Treasury's *average* impact *across all 28 EU member states* of around 115% extra trade, the increase in the UK alone appears to be much lower, in the range 20–25%. There is evidence that the impact on UK exports was somewhat higher than this before 2000, which accords with the evidence from time series trends showing that the share of UK exports (of goods and services) rose rapidly from accession in 1973 to 1990. Since 1990, the share first stalled and in recent years has been falling rapidly as non-EU markets have grown much faster than those within the EU and within the Eurozone. An analysis at company level finds that many British companies have been diversifying their trade away from the EU (Mayer et al. 2017).

The Treasury's estimated uplift in goods exports due to EU membership is 115%. A similar exercise for services trade gives an uplift of 24%. The weighted average for both goods and services is 76%. If fully reversed, this overall uplift of 76% gives a loss for EU trade in goods and services of 43%. This is equivalent to a loss in total trade (both EU and non-EU) of 24%. However, not all of the gains are likely to be reversed, and especially not immediately. While tariffs on goods may be imposed overnight if the UK reverts to WTO rules, these tariffs are much smaller than when the UK joined the EEC in 1973. For many non-agricultural commodities, the tariffs are now very low. Even if there is a new free trade agreement, evidence suggests that many firms may prefer to pay the (low) tariffs to avoid paperwork (Keck and Lendle 2012). With the UK outside the customs union, there will also be additional administrative costs but the WTO Trade Facilitation Agreement of February 2017, recently signed by the EU, will help to minimise these. Other non-tariff barriers should be initially low since UK firms are mostly already compliant with EU regulations. The Treasury takes this latter point into account in its low and medium impact projections but not for its high (no-trade deal) projection.

Our estimate for the impact of no deal on UK exports is much lower. The total loss of EU exports of goods due to tariff and non-tariff barriers is 20–25%. In Gudgin et al. (2017a), we did not calculate trade losses for services and implicitly accepted the Treasury estimate of a 20% loss for services, even though we had little detail on the Treasury analysis for services. We have subsequently become aware of a study of service trade (Walsh 2006). This finds that services trade is influenced by size of economy and common language but not by distance. The growth of Internet and social media usage since 2006 is likely to have strengthened this conclusion on distance. Walsh found no significant trade uplift due to EU membership, although we do not know whether this conclusion applied specifically to the UK.

If we were to accept Walsh's conclusion of no EU membership impact on services trade with the EU, then our estimate of the total loss of EU trade following no deal on trade would be 12%. This equates to a 5% loss of total (EU plus non-EU) trade. This is much smaller than the Treasury's estimate of 24% for the loss of trade in the event of no deal on trade. In our view, not all of the trade gains would be lost. UK firms would face a trade-weighted tariff of around 4%, but outside food, drink, clothing and vehicles the tariffs are lower at around 1–2%. If firms were to increase their prices by the amount of the tariff and face an average price elasticity of −2 on their sales, then the loss of exports might be 4–8%. Regulatory issues should initially be minor due to the existing compliance of UK firms with EU rules, although there may be regulatory divergence over time. Kee and Nicita (2017) suggest that the loss of UK goods exports might be as low as 2% since commodities facing higher tariffs tend to have low price elasticities.

We have been unable to get a meeting with the Treasury to discuss these differences, nor were HMT willing to release any further details of their methods or equations. We do know however that there is an internal Treasury paper from 2005 which generates much smaller estimates of the impact of EU membership on intra-EU trade (HM Treasury 2005). Importantly, this paper recognises that the impact of EU membership was much smaller for the UK than for other EU members. We had assumed that HMT's failure to recognise this key point in their 2016 report was due to an oversight, but the existence of the 2005 Treasury paper suggests that it was more deliberate. The omission could, of course, be due to a lack of institutional memory in an organisation with high staff turnover, but it is important to note that the official responsible for the 2016 report, Treasury Chief Economist, Sir Dave Ramsden (now Deputy Governor at the Bank of England), was employed at the Treasury in 2005.

Foreign Direct Investment

The Treasury Report's analysis of the impact of Brexit on FDI also uses a gravity model applied to OECD and UNCTAD data and estimated across 40 countries for the period 2000–2012. The data are financial, i.e. the value in money terms of the change in the stock of foreign-owned businesses within a country. HMT find that EU membership increases FDI flows within the EU by 35%, but there is no significant increase in FDI flows into EU members from outside the EU. The latter finding, of no increase from outside the EU is ignored by HMT. The analysis instead assumed that the scale of flows from outside the EU should be the same as for intra-EU flows. If we follow the Treasury and take the estimate of a 22% mid-range fall in the flow of FDI from all sources due to no deal on trade (i.e. a reversion to WTO rules), our calculations suggest that this scale of reduction in the *inflow* would be associated with about a 1% p.a. decline in the *stock* of FDI. The Treasury uses a sectoral production-function approach to calculate that each 1% reduction in the stock of FDI in the UK would, in turn, reduce productivity in the UK by 0.04%. Hence a decade after leaving the EU, it would reduce the level of productivity by 0.4%, which is a small effect. In fact, since the HMT gravity model analysis only suggests that intra-EU investment would be affected by Brexit, the potential fall in FDI flows and hence the stock would be a little over half of the HMT estimate, and give an even smaller reduction in productivity.

These calculations for FDI are complicated by the fact that FDI is measured as financial flows, and that these are dominated by mergers and acquisitions and by financing flows rather than by new physical investment. The OECD estimates that on average only one-third of FDI flows consists of physical investment. Our estimate for the UK is around one quarter. While FDI in new productive activities is likely to raise productivity, mergers and acquisitions may or may not do so. Mergers like the Kraft take over of Cadbury which result in plant closures and the removal of the HQ to a tax haven, have a less obvious positive impact on productivity. In such cases, productivity may be raised at the cost of lower levels of activity. For these reasons, we feel that the potential impact of leaving the EU on productivity via the FDI channel is particularly uncertain. However, since survey evidence suggests that multinational companies value the UK's membership of the EU in making decisions to invest in the UK, we assume that leaving the EU single market will have some detrimental impact on physical FDI.

The Link Between (Goods) Trade and Productivity

Around half of the total negative impact of Brexit calculated by the Treasury comes from a link between trade and productivity. The belief is that greater openness to trade leads to higher productivity. HMT use a relationship in which a 1% increase in the UK's trade openness (i.e. the ratio of trade to GDP), leads to a 0.2–0.3% increase in UK productivity. This estimate is derived from a number of studies, chiefly Feyrer (2009a, b), which conduct gravity model analyses across a wide number of countries. These countries are dominated by small emerging economies and appear not to apply to relatively small trade changes in an advanced economy. Even if we adopt the Treasury assumption, the impact would, in our view, be small. However, we believe that no aggregate link exists between trade and productivity for advanced open economies, unlike emerging economies where a relaxation of constraints on trade allow multinational companies to enter, and to raise both exports and productivity.

In Fig. 3, we indicate the relationship between trade and per capita GDP over the 27-year period 1981–2017. In Fig. 3, we "reproduce" chart 5 from Feyrer showing the relationship between trade and per capita GDP across 76 countries over the 35-year period 1960–1995. This indicates that an increase in growth in trade of ten percentage points was associated with a five-percentage-point higher level of growth in per capita GDP. Feyer was concerned with the possibility that the causal link might flow from productivity to trade rather than vice versa but concluded that there was a direct relationship between trade and productivity with an elasticity of 0.5. In a second paper (Feyrer 2009b), the same author used the 1967–1975 closure of the Suez Canal as a natural experiment to estimate the relationship between trade and per capita GDP. He concluded that the link was weaker, estimating an elasticity in the range 0.15–0.25. This result is dominated by four countries from the Indian subcontinent, since these were most affected by the closure of the Suez Canal. Most European countries were little affected. The Treasury adopted an elasticity between the two Feyrer estimates, but closer to the latter. The Centre for Economic Performance (Dhingra et al. 2016)

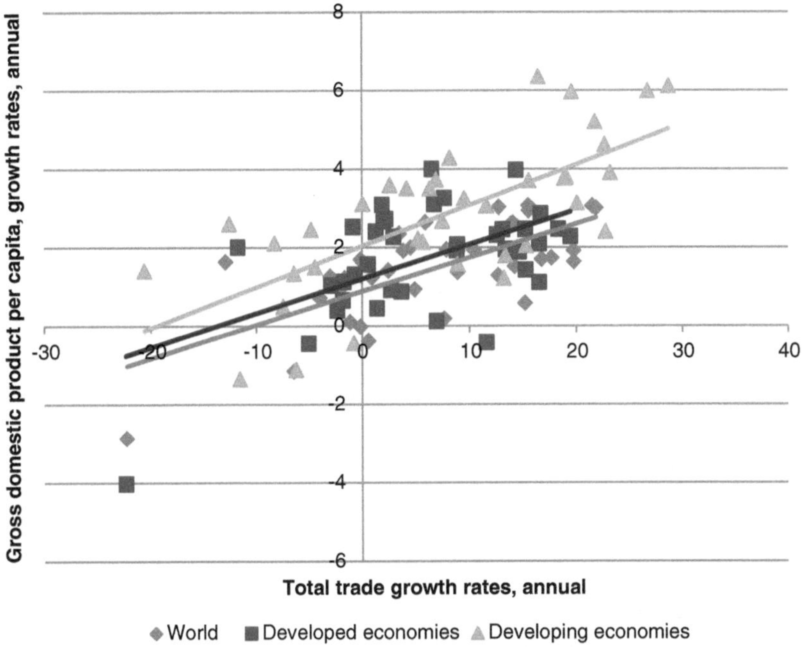

Fig. 3 The link between trade and productivity (1981–2017) (*Source* UNCTADstat [United Nations Conference on Trade and Development]. Available at https://unctadstat.unctad.org/wds/ReportFolders/reportFolders.aspx?sCS_ChosenLang=en. Accessed 19 March 2019)

criticised the Treasury for being too cautious and took the view that HMT should have used the higher estimate from Feyrer (2009a).

The important point here is that all of Feyrer's estimates are dominated by emerging economies, as well as being based on data largely from the 1960s and 1970s. Neither HMT nor the CEP asked whether such results were relevant to an advanced economy leaving the EU in the twenty-first century. In fact, the evidence is that they are not relevant. We have updated the figure shown above from Feyrer (2009a). We have preserved the 35-year period, but taken this from 1980–2015. Crucially, we have focussed on OECD countries and hence excluded most emerging economies, although the OECD includes Chile, Turkey and Poland. The results shown in Fig. 4 exclude South Korea and Ireland as large

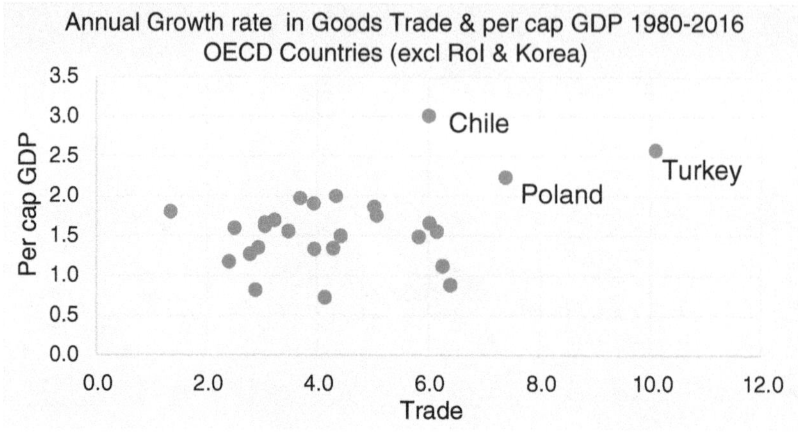

Fig. 4 The link between trade goods and productivity for OECD countries (*Source of data*: WTO and Conference Board Total Economy Database, Authors' calculations)

positive outliers. In the Irish case, both the trade and GDP data are distorted by Ireland's tax haven status. For the remaining OECD countries, there is a weak and barely significant relationship between (goods) trade and productivity. A 10 percentage-point higher annual rate of growth in trade is associated with a 1% higher rate of growth in per capita GDP. However, as the figure shows, even this relationship is dependent on the OECD's three poorer members. For the richer countries, those in Western Europe, North America and Japan, there is no relationship whatsoever. In these advanced economies, faster growing goods trade is not associated with faster growth in productivity. The UK had one of the slowest rates of goods trade over this period, but this was offset by rapid growth in exports of services supported its important, high productivity financial services sector, among others.

The CEP's Computable General Equilibrium and Dynamic Analyses

In this section, we examine a discussion paper from members of the Centre for Economic Performance, London School of Economics. It reports the technical analysis underlying the group's assessment of the consequences for economic welfare, resulting from the trade losses that might occur when the UK leaves the EU.[2] It is worth studying in some detail because it is one of the most comprehensive and sophisticated analyses of this issue by academic economists to date. The group's work is widely cited in the media and in policy circles as representing an authoritative quantitative assessment of the impact on economic welfare of the decision to leave the EU.

Their approach is firmly rooted in a large literature on trade theory and its empirical implementation. The paper has two objectives. The first is to employ a static analysis which uses counter-factual scenarios to evaluate the change in welfare from the UK decision to leave the EU. The second is to attempt to evaluate the "dynamic" losses not captured by the static analysis by using what the paper calls reduced form estimates. We will examine each in turn.

The Static Analysis

At the core of the analysis is a static computable general equilibrium (CGE) model of trade. They describe it as one of a class of "new quantitative trade models" (NQTMs). The underlying claim is that trade liberalisation "tends to increase welfare because it allows countries to specialise in their areas of comparative advantage and reduces the costs of goods, services and intermediate inputs" (p. 3). The paper outlines a simple version of the CGE model, based on the Armington (1969) model, although the authors focus on a variant—the Eaton-Kortum (2002) model. The supporting papers by Ottaviano (2014) and Costinot and Rodríguez-Clare (2014) use a version of Armington as a simple illustrative model.

The common feature of the trade models is that they cover all world trade (both inter- and intra-country trade), are general equilibrium in their scope and have micro-foundations that can generate a form of gravity model in which the principal variables are proportionally related. This class of NQTMs is based on highly restrictive assumptions as listed by Ottaviano (2014). These micro-foundations are: (a) Dixit-Stiglitz consumer preferences; (b) one factor of production; (c) linear cost functions;

[2] The Costs and Benefits of Leaving the EU: The Trade Effects. CEP Discussion Paper No. 1478 April 2017. For brevity, we refer to the authors: Dhingra, Huang, Ottaviano, Pessoa, Sampson and van Reenan as Dhingra et al.

(d) perfect or monopolistic competition. There are also three macro-level restrictions: (e) trade is balanced; (f) aggregate profits are a constant share of aggregate revenues; and (g) the import demand system exhibits constant elasticity of substitution (CES). Being a CGE model, it has the property that all prices adjust to clear all the markets for goods and services.

These models are common in the international trade literature despite their highly unrealistic assumptions. The methodology appears to follow the instrumentalist approach of Milton Friedman, in which the unreality of the assumptions is irrelevant if the resulting model can make testable predictions about the real world. In the present case, this would require that the model's parameters are estimated from the data and the model is used to make predictions of further data. It is not clear from the paper that the authors have done more than calibrate the static model to the data. The unrealistic nature of the assumptions is therefore an important criticism of their analysis. Besides, the authors are not principally interested in the nature of the static model. Their interest in this class of NQTM is in its comparative static properties for the purpose of policy evaluation.

It is a property of this class of models that if one is only interested in comparisons of one alternative scenario with a given state, the amount of information about the underlying static model needed to compute the comparison is significantly reduced. The welfare gains from trade, compared for example with autarky, can be calculated using two key values, the observed share of domestic expenditure and an estimate of the trade elasticity. The former is defined as the share of expenditure of country *j* on imports from country *i*, where expenditure is the value of the consumption of country *j* on all goods. The latter is the elasticity of the relative change in trade resulting from a change in trade barriers (trade friction, trade resistance, etc.). In this class of models, the elasticity is a common constant because of the assumption of CES preferences. This framework can be extended to compare two alternative counter-factual scenarios. The data needed are the initial expenditure shares, the initial income levels and an estimate of the trade elasticity. Further information is required on the alternative level of tariffs and trade obstacles that would arise when the UK leaves the EU compared with the current status quo.

It is important to note that although there is a saving on the information needed to compute comparative static scenario changes compared with the general equilibrium level results, the scenarios are still dependent on all the highly unrealistic assumptions of the CGE model. The reason is that the simplification obtained in comparing changes depends on the structural specification of the underlying general equilibrium model. Since this model's predictions do not appear to have been tested in the Friedman manner, the scenario estimates depend on the full set of assumptions of the general equilibrium model. This is a serious limitation on the applicability of the model to policy changes such as Brexit.

A further level of detail is introduced because the model disaggregates each country's trade into industrial sectors. For agriculture, mining and the manufacturing sector they use a set of trade elasticity estimates, covering each sector of production, taken from Table 1 of Caliendo and Parro (2015), which are quoted in Table A3 of the CEP paper. For the service sectors, they assume an elasticity of 5. It is worth noting that the Caliendo and Parro estimates show considerable heterogeneity,[3] depending on whether the full sample or a 97.5% sample is used. The estimated elasticities appear to be sensitive to the inclusion of countries which have a low share of trade in the relevant sectors. The CEP analysis depends on the full sample.

Armed with estimates from this technically sophisticated model and results taken from other studies, the key scenario results for the static analysis are presented in Tables 3 and 4 of the CEP paper. Note that while the tariff rates as given in Table 1 of the CEP paper are relatively modest, the calculation of the tariff-equivalent non-tariff barriers is 8.31% in the case of returning to WTO rules. The tariff-equivalent exclusion from future trade cost reductions given by Dhingra et al. on page 17 is 12.65%.

In Table 3, the pessimistic scenario is where the UK leaves the EU and each imposes most favoured nation WTO tariffs on each other's trade in goods. The calculated loss in the present value of consumption is 2.66% of consumption, or a fall of £1773 in income per household. It is not directly possible to compare with HM Treasury estimates, but the Treasury Report (HMT April 2016) estimated a permanent loss of 7.5%

[3]The CGE model is divided into 35 world regions; each region is disaggregated into 31 industrial sectors for goods and services. The data consist of bilateral trade relationships between each region and sector, using the United Nations COMTRADE database. The inter-sectoral relationships use the WIOD input-output tables from the European Commission (see Timmer et al. 2015).

Table 5 Contribution to total welfare loss, pessimistic scenario

Rise in EU-UK tariffs	−0.13%
Rise in EU-UK non-tariff barriers	−1.31%
Exclusion from future cost reductions	−1.61%

Source Dhingra et al. (2017)

of GDP or £5200 per household.[4] The CEP calculations of the welfare loss are considerably smaller than the Treasury's estimates in 2016, published just before the referendum. Dhingra et al. (2016), commenting on the Treasury's estimates, stated that if anything, the welfare losses were likely to be greater than those given by the Treasury. This is not supported, at least for the static estimates, by the work of Dhingra et al. (2017).

Table 5 aims to decompose the welfare losses into the three components: imposition of tariffs; the increase in non-tariff barriers; exclusion from future cost reductions as members of the single market.

The totals do not add to −2.66% because each is a separate scenario. It is interesting to note that the losses arising from the imposition of tariffs are quite small. Most WTO tariffs on manufactures are already low. There are higher tariffs on motor vehicles and on agricultural products. Similarly, the non-tariff costs are low. This is consistent with the UK already being compliant with EU regulation. Some of the non-tariff costs will depend on the cost of administering the movement of goods across borders after Brexit. It is the third component which has the largest effect, although the evidence for this cost-benefit from further integration of intra-EU markets is open to question. In search of additional losses from leaving the EU, Dhingra et al. turn to the dynamic effects.

Dynamic Effects

The paper argues that by increasing competition, trade integration raises R&D and facilitates the diffusion of knowledge across the intra-trade

[4]Dhingra et al. quote their results from the working paper by Méjean and Schwellnus (2009). In the published version, Table 1, column (3) gives a convergence rate for OECD countries of 0.584 (=1−0.416) for OECD countries and 0.394 for EU countries.

countries. This appears to be additional to the gains from cost reductions counted above as static.

The authors claim that dynamic productivity and welfare losses from leaving the EU, not captured by the static analysis include:

- Reductions in the variety of goods and services;
- Weaker competition;
- The erosion of vertical production chains;
- Falls in foreign direct investment;
- Slower technology diffusion;
- Less learning from exports;
- Lower research and development.

The authors concede that these gains "are less well understood than the static gains captured by our model". One of the authors claims in a separate paper (Sampson 2016) that "lower trade costs increase the long-run growth rate generating dynamic welfare gains that roughly triple the gains from trade compared to conventional static estimates" (p. 22). This is a very strong claim—a rise in the long-run growth rate from a step reduction in costs. Although these arguments are about dynamic effects of trade on productivity, the calculations that follow are static in nature.

This second part of the paper on dynamic impacts uses a more familiar methodology. The first stage is to use gravity equations to estimate the loss of UK trade with EU countries from leaving the EU. For this, they rely on Baier et al. (2008) who estimate the loss of UK trade with the EU, due to leaving the EU and joining EFTA, as 25.2%. The estimates appear considerably lower than the Treasury estimates (HM Treasury 2016a). In a commentary paper on the Treasury report (Dhingra et al. 2016) stated: "*In fact, our view is that the Treasury have been too conservative in many of their assumptions and should have generated larger effects*".

The second stage is to consider trade diversion effects. After reviewing a variety of literature they conclude that there is no convincing evidence of trade diversion effects. They assume, as did the Treasury, that the UK would not gain trade from outside the EU after leaving. The third stage is to take account of a potential link between trade and productivity and relies on the estimates of Feyrer (2009a) discussed above. The estimate used by the CEP is that a 10% loss of trade is associated with a 5 to 7.5% loss of income per head.

Using Baier's and Feyrer's estimates for trade and income per head respectively, CEP calculates the loss of UK income per head of leaving the EU and joining EFTA as 6.3 to 9.4%. They say that this is similar to results in Crafts (2016). On page 25, they compare these estimates with Mulabdic et al. (2017) who estimate the trade loss of the UK in leaving and trading under WTO rules as 53.3%. Dhingra et al. appear not to want to place too much weight on these estimates. "*While we have based our calculations on estimates obtained using best practice empirical methodologies, sampling error and identification challenges inevitably mean that some degree of uncertainty must be attached to these estimates*". They say that the estimates could just as well underestimate the losses in income per head as overstate them. Despite these caveats, they say that these estimates support the conclusion from the static analysis that there would be a "*sizeable negative impact on UK welfare*".

In our view, outlined above, there is no evidence for advanced economies that growth in goods trade over recent decades is associated with higher productivity. If this relationship is omitted from the CEP analysis, then all that remains is the direct trade effect with a 25% loss of UK trade with the EU (12.6% loss of total trade). Again, as outlined above while we do not disagree with the gravity model estimates for changes in trade made by Baier et al. and used by the CEP analysis, we argue that the estimates are inappropriate for estimating the impact of Brexit. This is because the estimates are an average for all EU member states and do not allow for the fact that the UK does more trade outside the EU than any other member state. Hence our view is that the dynamic estimates of Dhingra et al. are greatly exaggerated.

Direct Estimates of the Impact of Tariff and Non-tariff Barriers on Exports

Several reports have calculated an impact of Brexit on trade without further full equilibrium impacts on the GDP and the wider economy. Two of these are from the Economic and Social Research Institute (ESRI) in Dublin and one from World Bank/UNCTAD economists. We refer to these as direct estimates since they are based on observed trade outcomes as in gravity model studies. Instead, they directly calculate the additions to production costs from tariff and non-tariff barriers and use sector or commodity-specific elasticities to estimate the impact on demand for exports and imports. We describe in greater detail the approach taken by these reports in Coutts et al. (2018). Here, we summarise the main findings.

ESRI, Dublin

Lawless and Morgenroth (2016) at the ESRI examined the potential impact on EU trade of the UK adopting WTO tariffs after Brexit. The study examined detailed trade flows between the UK and all other EU members, matching over 5200 products to the WTO tariff applicable to external EU trade. The study assumes that tariffs are fully reflected in higher prices and uses broad sector-level elasticity estimates as calculated by Imbs and Méjean (2017).[5]

The results for the UK were a fall in EU to UK trade by 30% and a 22% reduction in the UK to EU trade if median elasticity estimates are used. Mean elasticities give slightly higher impacts and would generate falls of 37% in EU-UK trade and 27% in UK-EU trade. The upper and lower bounds of the estimates are given by the maximum elasticity estimates which would generate trade falls of 56 and 45% in EU-UK and UK-EU trade respectively and the minimum estimates would result in trade declines of 17 and 12%, respectively.

A second ESRI study (Lawless and Studnicka 2017) was undertaken for InterTradeIreland, an organisation in Northern Ireland which promotes cross-border trade on the island of Ireland. The study focusses on trade between Ireland and Northern Ireland and Ireland and Great Britain. It uses a similar method as in Lawless and Morgenroth in calculating the impact of tariffs, using a different database, but also takes into account non-tariff barriers and exchange rates.

Whereas Lawless and Morgenroth calculate that WTO tariffs would reduce UK exports to Ireland by 28%, the calculation in Lawless and Studnicka is a much smaller reduction of 3%. Comparison of the two papers thus shows that quite different estimates can be made for the impact of tariffs on trade, dependent on such things as the source of trade data and the precise form of elasticities.

World Bank/UNCTAD

Kee and Nicita (2017) assess the short-term impact of Brexit on goods exports is using their Overall Trade Restrictiveness Index of the UK's major trading partners.

[5] Imbs and Méjean (2017) define their sectors at the ISIC 2-digit level.

The results show that in the short run, leaving the European Union without a trade deal may cause the UK's exports to the European Union to decrease by 2%, and the prospect of a major trade collapse post-Brexit is unlikely. The impact is small because the European Union's demand for imports from the UK is fairly inelastic, especially for products that face the higher tariffs. High EU tariffs tend to be on less elastic products including transport equipment, food, apparel and plastics. Low tariffs are generally on more elastic products including pulp and paper and scientific instruments.

The Kee and Nicita analysis is analogous to the ESRI studies and the results appear much closer to Lawless and Studnicka (2017) than to Lawless and Morgenroth (2016).

CBR Forecasts for Brexit

To complete the story, we add our own forecasts for Brexit using the CBR macroeconomic model of the UK. This is an econometric model based on past-relationships between macroeconomic aggregates and hence similar in approach to the models used by Cambridge Econometrics or Oxford Economics. The purpose of including these forecasts is not to judge their accuracy. The short-term forecasts are generated in the knowledge of the post-referendum outturn data for 2016 and 2017. Indeed, these data have been used in the model to estimate what degree of Brexit-related uncertainty is likely to have been in evidence. Neither is there any claim about the accuracy of the long-term forecasts. It will be many years before it will be possible to make a judgement on this. Rather, the purpose is to set out our predictions, based on a set of clear assumptions, to place alongside those discussed above.

Our assumptions on Brexit, input into the model are:

- Small (0.25%) "uncertainty" reduction in business and household investment and in household consumption for 2017, diminishing through 2018–2019.
- Assumes a 2-year transition period until 2021 followed by a free trade agreement from 2022.
- Loss of EU trade from 2022 building up within 3 years to 10%, with slow replacement in non-EU markets.
- Reduction in imports from EU but half replaced by imports from non-EU countries.

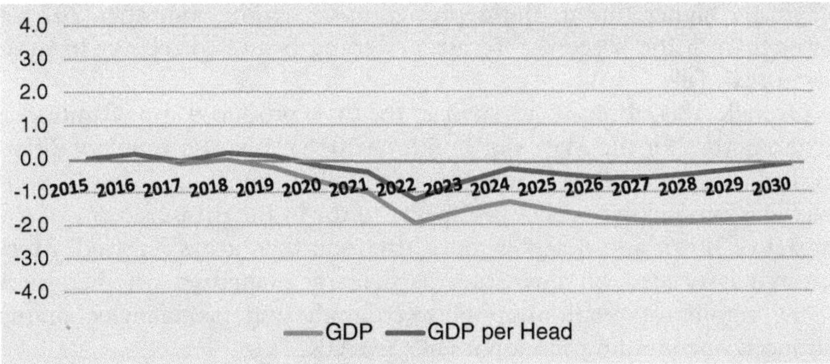

Fig. 5 Impact of Brexit (% difference from baseline forecast) (*Source* Authors' February 2018 data updates for CBR macro-economic model of the UK [UKMOD] from Gudgin et al. [2015])

- Interest rates remain very low and public spending a little higher than would have been the case without Brexit.
- Brexit effect on net migration is a fall of 35K, but sterling depreciation adds further declines (initially 55K).

The results of these forecasts are shown in Fig. 5. The short-term forecast is for little change compared with a non-Brexit baseline. The small negative confidence effect is offset by the positive impact of a lower sterling exchange rate. The temporarily lower bank interest rate has little effect.

After 2021, the loss of trade leads to GDP being 2% below the baseline, and this degree of loss is maintained through the rest of the period. Part of this loss is due to a lower level of net migration, which itself is partly due to a lower exchange rate and partly due to a Brexit "chill effect". Lower migration implies a smaller workforce and hence lower output as firms find themselves unable to expand, or in some cases have to close their UK operations. Part of the loss of output does not have a direct impact on the indigenous workforce, and hence per capita GDP falls less than GDP itself. EU trade losses are assumed to be slowly replaced after 2021 by FTAs with other countries, leading to a small recovery. By 2030, per capita GDP is predicted to be at the same level it would have been in the absence of Brexit. Unemployment is a little lower in the Brexit scenario due to reduced migration. Price inflation is initially higher due to the depreciation in sterling, but after 2023 is lower than in the baseline forecast as sterling begins to recover from its post-Brexit fall.

Overall, this forecast is similar to that produced by Cambridge Econometrics for the Mayor of London (2018). It is also not very different from that of CEP, as long as the productivity knock-on effect is omitted. This productivity effect is a major factor in the measurement of the impact of Brexit and deserves more attention than it has received. More research is needed on this issue, particularly examining whether there is any significant relationship between trade and productivity among advanced open trading economies like the UK.

Concluding Comments

In this paper, we have reviewed economists' assessments of the economic performance of the UK within the EU, and the short-term and long-term economic effects of the referendum decision to leave the EU. Many of these assessments have been by government departments and international agencies. In estimating the economic effects of Brexit on living standards, these rely on a range of analytic approaches, including the use of gravity models, computable general equilibrium models and macroeconomic forecasting models. Our conclusion is that much of this work contains flaws of analysis, and a treatment of evidence that leads to exaggerated costs of Brexit.

Gravity models are well established as a technique for estimating the impact of trade associations or currency unions but require more care than has been shown, when being applied to a specific issue like Brexit. The Treasury has been particularly cavalier in its approach, both in its application of gravity analysis and in applying a "knock-on" impact from trade to productivity. Other organisations have been a little more circumspect about the productivity link, which we doubt exists to any significant degree for advanced economies, but several have used it without much questioning.

The short-term forecasts which have turned out to be wrong have further damaged confidence in economists' contributions to public debate. Partly as a result, very little attention has been given by politicians or the public on either side of the debate to the impact assessments published at the time of the referendum.

The consequences of these shortcomings go well beyond Brexit itself. We believe that the credibility of the economic forecasting profession and some of the major parts of the economic press have been damaged again. It will take more than a decade to be sure of this, but the failure of the short-term forecasts indicates what could happen. The fact that the flaws we identify all point in the direction of pessimism on Brexit, and hence in the direction that most academics and economists tend to lean ideologically, will increase the scepticism of many. The refusal of the Treasury to discuss their approach, at least until the issue was aired in Parliament, is in our view unacceptable in an open democracy.

Our conclusion is that in order to restore public confidence in economic forecasting for major policy issues like Brexit, economists need to use more relevant analyses, based on a wider range of evidence. We expect that econometric models used by commercial forecasters like Cambridge Econometrics will prove to be most accurate in the long-run. If so, the academic profession needs to reconsider both the relevance of its current attachment to theory based on unrealistic assumptions, and to the general quality of policy-relevant applied work. Whatever techniques are used need to be applied with more balance and scepticism. The CEP in discussing the Treasury reports could only think of changes which would have made the HMT predictions even more pessimistic on Brexit. In the words of Oliver Cromwell to the General Assembly of the Church of Scotland, the economic forecasting profession needs to "*think it possible ye may be mistaken*".

Acknowledgements We are grateful for insights gained in discussion with Adam Slater of Oxford Economics. He is not responsible for the views expressed in this paper. We are also grateful to Rachel Wagstaff of the Centre for Business Research for considerable help in the final preparation of this papers on which this chapter is based.

References

Armington, P. S. (1969). A Theory of Demand for Products Distinguished by Place of Production. *Staff Papers, International Monetary Fund, 16*(1), 159–178.

Baier, S. L., Bergstrand, J. H., Egger, P., & McLaughlin, P. H. (2008). Do Economic Integration Agreements Actually Work? *Issues in Understanding the Causes and Consequences of the Growth of Regionalism, The World Economy, 31*(4), 461–497.

Berden, K., François, J., Taminen, S., Thelle, M., & Wymenga, P. (2013). *Non-tariff Measures in EU-US Trade and Investment: An Economic Analysis* (IIDE Discussion Papers, 20090806). Institute for International and Development Economics.

Caliendo, L., & Parro, F. (2015). Estimates of the Trade and Welfare Effects of NAFTA. *Review of Economic Studies, 82*(1), 1–44.

Cambridge Econometrics. (2018, January). *Preparing for Brexit, Report for Greater London Authority.*

Costinot, A., & Rodríguez-Clare, A. (2014). Trade Theory with Numbers: Quantifying the Consequences of Globalisation. In *Handbook of International Economics* (Vol. 4). Elsevier.

Coutts, K., Gudgin, G., & Buchanan, J. (2018). *How the Economics Profession Got It Wrong on Brexit* (Working Paper 493). Centre for Business Research, University of Cambridge. http://www.cbr.cam.ac.uk/fileadmin/user_upload/centre-for-business-research/downloads/working-papers/wp493.pdf.

Crafts, N. (2016). *The Growth Effects of EU Membership for the UK: A Review of the Evidence* (Social Market Foundation Global Perspectives Series Paper 7).

Dhingra, S., Huang, H., Ottaviano, G., Pessoa, J. P., Sampson, T., & van Reenan, J. (2017, April). *The Costs and Benefits of Leaving the EU: The Trade Effects* (CEP Discussion Paper No. 1478).

Dhingra, S., Ottaviano, G., Sampson, T., & van Reenan, J. (2016). *The UK Treasury Analysis of 'The Long-Term Economic Impact of UK Membership and the Alternatives': CEP Commentary* (Brexit Paper 04).

Eaton, J., & Kortum, S. (2002). Technology, Geography and Trade. *Econometrica, 70*(5), 1741–1779.

Feyrer, J. (2009a). *Trade and Income—Exploiting Time Series in Geography* (NBER Working Papers, 14910). National Bureau of Economic Research, Inc.

Feyrer, J. (2009b, December). *Distance, Trade and Income—The 1968–75 Closing of the Suez Canal as a Natural Experiment* (NBER Working Paper 15557).

Gudgin, G., Coutts, K., & Gibson, N. (2015). *The CBR Macro-Economic Model of the UK Economy* (Working Paper No. 472). Centre for Business Research, University of Cambridge.

Gudgin, G., Coutts, K., Gibson, N., & Buchanan, J. (2017a). *The Role of Gravity Models in Estimating the Economic Impact of Brexit* (Working Paper No. 490). Centre for Business Research, University of Cambridge. https://www.cbr.cam.ac.uk/fileadmin/user_upload/centre-for-business-research/downloads/working-papers/wp490.pdf/.

Gudgin, G., Coutts, K., Gibson, N., & Buchanan, J. (2017b). Defying *Gravity. A Critique of Estimates of the Economic Impact of Brexit.* London: Policy Exchange. https://policyexchange.org.uk/wp-content/uploads/2017/06/

Defying-Gravity-A-critique-of-estimates-of-the-economic-impact-of-Brexit.pdf/.

HM Treasury. (2005). *EU Membership and Trade. Internal Paper Unclassified.* (Authors unknown) https://www.gov.uk/government/uploads/system/uploads/attachment_data/file/220968/foi_eumembership_trade.pdf/.

HM Treasury. (2016a, April). *HM Treasury Analysis: The Long-Term Economic Impact of UK Membership and the Alternatives.* CM 9250. https://www.gov.uk/government/uploads/system/uploads/attachment_data/file/517415/treasury_analysis_economic_impact_of_eu_membership_web.pdf/.

HM Treasury. (2016b, May). *The Immediate Economic Impact of Leaving the EU.* Cmnd 9292. https://www.gov.uk/government/uploads/system/uploads/attachment_data/file/524967/hm_treasury_analysis_the_immediate_economic_impact_of_leaving_the_eu_web.pdf/.

House of Commons. (2016, May). Treasury Committee, The Economic and Financial Costs and Benefits of the UK's EU Membership, First Report of Session 2016–2017.

Imbs, J., & Méjean, I. (2017, May). Trade Elasticities. *Review of International Economics, 25*(2), 383–402.

Keck, A., & Lendle, A. (2012). *New Evidence on Preference Utilisation* (Staff Working Paper, ERSD 2012–12). World Trade Organisation.

Kee, H. L., & Nicita, A. (2017). *Short Term Impact of Brexit on the UK's Exports of Goods.* Vox Blog, World Bank and UNCTAD.

Lawless, M., & Morgenroth, E. (2016, November). *The Product and Sector Level Impact of a Hard Brexit Across the EU* (ESRSI Working Paper No. 550).

Lawless, M., & Studnicka, Z. (2017, June). *Potential Impact of WTO Tariffs on Cross-Border Trade.* InterTradeIreland.

Mayer, M., Hautz, J., Stadler, C., & Whittington, R. (2017). *While Corporate UK was for Remain, Their Business Strategies Tell a Different Story.* LSE, Politics and Policy. http://blogs.lse.ac.uk/politicsandpolicy/a-close-look-at-british-business-was-it-destined-to-leave-the-eu/#Author/.

Méjean, I., & Schwellnus, C. (2009). *Price Convergence in the European Union: Within Firms or Composition of Firms?* (Working Papers, hal-00354190, HAL).

Mulabdic, A., Osnago, A., & Ruta, M. (2017). *Deep Integration and UK-EU Trade Relations* (Policy Research Working Paper Series 7947). The World Bank.

Office for Budget Responsibility. (2017, October). *Forecast Evaluation Report October 2017—Executive Summary.*

Ottaviano, G. (2014, September). *European Integration and the Gains from Trade* (Working Paper 470). Centre for Financial Studies.

Sampson, T. (2016). Dynamic Selection: An Idea Flows Theory of Entry, Trade and Growth. *The Quarterly Journal of Economics, 131*(1), 315.

Timmer, M. P., Dietzenbacher, E., Los, B., Stehrer, R., & de Vries, G. J. (2015). An Illustrated User Guide to the World Input-Output Database: The Case of Global Automotive Production. *Review of International Economics, 23*, 575–605.

Walsh, K. (2006). *Trade in Services: Does Gravity Hold? A Gravity Model Approach to Estimating Barriers to Services, Trade* (Discussion Paper Series, No. 183). Dublin: Revenue Commissioners.

Index

V. Vlachos and A. Bitzenis (eds.), *European Union*,
https://doi.org/10.1007/978-3-030-18103-1

FSC
www.fsc.org
MIX
Papier | Fördert
gute Waldnutzung
FSC® C083411

Kolibri 360 GmbH
Ferdinand-Jühlke-Straße 7
99095 Erfurt, Deutschland
produktsicherheit@kolibri360.de